TOEFL® MAP

MAP Listening

New TOEFL® Edition

Intermediate

DARAKWON

TOEFL® MAP New TOEFL® Edition
Listening Intermediate

Publisher Chung Kyudo
Editor Cho Sangik
Authors Michael A. Putlack, Stephen Poirier, Angela Maas, Maximilian Tolochko
Proofreader Talib Din
Designers Park Narae, Jung Kyuok

First published in November 2022
By Darakwon, Inc.
Darakwon Bldg., 211, Munbal-ro, Paju-si, Gyeonggi-do 10881
Republic of Korea
Tel: 82-2-736-2031 (Ext. 250)
Fax: 82-2-732-2037

ISBN 978-89-277-8031-1 14740
         978-89-277-8025-0 14740 (set)

www.darakwon.co.kr

Photo Credits
Shutterstock.com

Components Main Book / Answers, Explanations, and Scripts
9 8 7 6 5 4 3   24 25 26 27 28

Introduction

Studying for the TOEFL® iBT is no easy task and is not one that is to be undertaken lightly. It requires a great deal of effort as well as dedication on the part of the student. It is our hope that by using *TOEFL® Map Listening Intermediate* as either a textbook or a study guide, the task of studying for the TOEFL® iBT will become somewhat easier for the student and less of a burden.

Students who wish to excel on the TOEFL® iBT must attain a solid grasp of the four important skills in the English language: reading, listening, speaking, and writing. The Darakwon *TOEFL® Map* series covers all four of these skills in separate books. There are also three different levels in all four topics. This book, *TOEFL® Map Listening Intermediate*, covers the listening aspect of the test at the intermediate level. Students who want to listen to lectures and conversations, learn vocabulary terms, and study topics that appear on the TOEFL® iBT will have their wishes granted by using this book.

TOEFL® Map Listening Intermediate has been designed for use both in a classroom setting and as a study guide for individual learners. For this reason, it offers a comprehensive overview of the TOEFL® iBT Listening section. In Part A, the different types of questions that are found on the TOEFL® iBT Listening section are explained, and hints on how to answer these questions properly are also provided. In Part B, learners have the opportunity to build their background knowledge of the topics that appear on the TOEFL® iBT by listening to the lectures and conversations of varying lengths that are found in each chapter. Each lecture and conversation are followed by the types of questions that appear on the TOEFL® iBT. Each chapter also has a vocabulary section, which enables learners to test their knowledge of vocabulary that is specific to the particular topics covered in each chapter. Finally, in Part C, students can take two TOEFL® iBT practice tests. These are lectures and conversations that have the same numbers and types of questions that appear on actual TOEFL® iBT Listening section passages. Combined, all of these should be able to help learners prepare themselves to take and, more importantly, to excel on the TOEFL® iBT.

TOEFL® Map Listening Intermediate has a great amount of information and should prove to be invaluable as a study guide for learners who are preparing for the TOEFL® iBT. However, while this book is comprehensive, it is up to each person to do the actual work. In order for *TOEFL® Map Listening Intermediate* to be of any use, the individual learner must dedicate him or herself to studying the information found within its pages. While we have strived to make this book as user friendly and as full of crucial information as possible, ultimately, it is up to each person to make the best of the material in the book. We wish you luck in your study of both English and the TOEFL® iBT, and we hope that you are able to use *TOEFL® Map Listening Intermediate* to improve your abilities in both of them.

Michael A. Putlack
Stephen Poirier
Angela Maas
Maximilian Tolochko

TABLE OF CONTENTS

How Is This Book Different?   6
How to Use This Book   7

Part A | Understanding Listening Question Types

Question Type 01   Gist-Content   10
Question Type 02   Gist-Purpose   12
Question Type 03   Detail   14
Question Type 04   Understanding the Function of What Is Said   17
Question Type 05   Understanding the Speaker's Attitude   20
Question Type 06   Understanding Organization   23
Question Type 07   Connecting Content   26
Question Type 08   Making Inferences   29

Part B | Building Background Knowledge of TOEFL Topics

Chapter 01

Life Sciences 1 & Conversations

Mastering Question Types with Lectures & Conversations A1   32
Mastering Question Types with Lectures & Conversations A2   34
Mastering Topics with Lectures B1, B2, B3   36
Mastering Topics with Conversations B4   39
TOEFL Practice Tests C1   40
TOEFL Practice Tests C2   42
Star Performer Word Files   44
Vocabulary Review   45

Chapter 02

Life Sciences 2 & Conversations

Mastering Question Types with Lectures & Conversations A1   48
Mastering Question Types with Lectures & Conversations A2   50
Mastering Topics with Lectures B1, B2, B3   52
Mastering Topics with Conversations B4   55
TOEFL Practice Tests C1   56
TOEFL Practice Tests C2   58
Star Performer Word Files   60
Vocabulary Review   61

Chapter 03

Social Sciences 1 & Conversations

Mastering Question Types with Lectures & Conversations A1   64
Mastering Question Types with Lectures & Conversations A2   66
Mastering Topics with Lectures B1, B2, B3   68
Mastering Topics with Conversations B4   71
TOEFL Practice Tests C1   72
TOEFL Practice Tests C2   74
Star Performer Word Files   76
Vocabulary Review   77

Chapter 04
Social Sciences 2
& Conversations

Mastering Question Types with Lectures & Conversations A1 — 80
Mastering Question Types with Lectures & Conversations A2 — 82
Mastering Topics with Lectures B1, B2, B3 — 84
Mastering Topics with Conversations B4 — 87
TOEFL Practice Tests C1 — 88
TOEFL Practice Tests C2 — 90
Star Performer Word Files — 92
Vocabulary Review — 93

Chapter 05
Physical Sciences 1
& Conversations

Mastering Question Types with Lectures & Conversations A1 — 96
Mastering Question Types with Lectures & Conversations A2 — 98
Mastering Topics with Lectures B1, B2, B3 — 100
Mastering Topics with Conversations B4 — 103
TOEFL Practice Tests C1 — 104
TOEFL Practice Tests C2 — 106
Star Performer Word Files — 108
Vocabulary Review — 109

Chapter 06
Physical Sciences 2
& Conversations

Mastering Question Types with Lectures & Conversations A1 — 112
Mastering Question Types with Lectures & Conversations A2 — 114
Mastering Topics with Lectures B1, B2, B3 — 116
Mastering Topics with Conversations B4 — 119
TOEFL Practice Tests C1 — 120
TOEFL Practice Tests C2 — 122
Star Performer Word Files — 124
Vocabulary Review — 125

Chapter 07
Arts 1
& Conversations

Mastering Question Types with Lectures & Conversations A1 — 128
Mastering Question Types with Lectures & Conversations A2 — 130
Mastering Topics with Lectures B1, B2, B3 — 132
Mastering Topics with Conversations B4 — 135
TOEFL Practice Tests C1 — 136
TOEFL Practice Tests C2 — 138
Star Performer Word Files — 140
Vocabulary Review — 141

Chapter 08
Arts 2
& Conversations

Mastering Question Types with Lectures & Conversations A1 — 144
Mastering Question Types with Lectures & Conversations A2 — 146
Mastering Topics with Lectures B1, B2, B3 — 148
Mastering Topics with Conversations B4 — 151
TOEFL Practice Tests C1 — 152
TOEFL Practice Tests C2 — 154
Star Performer Word Files — 156
Vocabulary Review — 157

Part C | Experiencing the TOEFL iBT Actual Tests

Actual Test 01 — 160
Actual Test 02 — 180

How Is This Book Different?

When searching for the ideal book to use to study for the TOEFL® iBT, it is often difficult to differentiate between the numerous books available on a bookstore's shelves. However, *TOEFL® Map Listening Intermediate* differs from many other TOEFL® iBT books and study guides in several important ways.

Many TOEFL® iBT books arrange the material according to the types of questions on the test. This often results in learners listening to a lecture on astronomy, followed by a lecture on history, followed by a conversation between a student and a professor, and so on. Simply put, there is little cohesion except for the questions. However, *TOEFL® Map Listening Intermediate* is arranged by subject. This book has eight chapters, all of which cover subjects that appear on the TOEFL® iBT. For instance, there are two chapters on life sciences, two chapters on social sciences, two chapters on physical sciences, and two chapters on the arts. By arranging the chapters according to subjects, learners can listen to lectures related to one another all throughout each chapter. This enables them to build upon their knowledge as they progress through each chapter. Additionally, since many vocabulary terms are used in certain subjects, learners can more easily recognize these specialized terms, understand how they are used, and retain the knowledge of what these terms mean. Finally, by arranging the chapters according to subjects, learners can cover and become familiar with every TOEFL® iBT question type in each chapter rather than just focus on a single type of question.

TOEFL® Map Listening Intermediate, unlike many other TOEFL® iBT books and study guides, does not have any translations into foreign languages within its pages. All too often, learners rely on translations in their native language. They use these translations to help them get through the material. However, the actual TOEFL® iBT has no translations, so neither does this book. This will better prepare learners to take the test the test by encouraging them to learn difficult terms and expressions through context, just as native speakers of English do when they encounter unfamiliar terms and expressions. Additionally, learners will find that their fluency in English will improve more rapidly when they use *TOEFL® Map Listening Intermediate* without relying on any translations.

Finally, the lectures and conversations in *TOEFL® Map Listening Intermediate* are based on topics that have appeared on the actual TOEFL® iBT in the past. Therefore, learners can see what kinds of topics appear on the TOEFL® iBT. This will enable them to recognize the difficulty level, the style of TOEFL® iBT lectures and conversations, and the difficulty of the vocabulary on the test. Second, learners can enhance their knowledge of topics that have appeared on the TOEFL® iBT. By knowing more about these topics when they take the actual test, test takers will be sure to improve their scores. Third, learners will also gain knowledge of the specialized vocabulary in particular topics, which will help them more easily understand lectures and conversations on the actual test. Finally, many topics appear multiple times on the TOEFL® iBT. Thus, students who study some of these topics may be pleasantly surprised to find the same topic when they take the actual TOEFL® iBT. That will no doubt help them improve their test scores.

How to Use
This Book

TOEFL® Map Listening Intermediate is designed for use either as a textbook in a classroom in a TOEFL® iBT preparation course or as a study guide for individuals who are studying for the TOEFL® iBT on their own. *TOEFL® Map Listening Intermediate* has been divided into three sections: Part A, Part B, and Part C. All three sections offer information which is important to learners preparing for the TOEFL® iBT. Part A is divided into 8 sections, each of which explains one of the question types that appear on the TOEFL® iBT Listening section. Part B is divided into 8 chapters. There are two chapters that cover each of the four subjects that appear on the TOEFL® iBT. Part C has 2 complete practice tests that resemble those which appear on the TOEFL® iBT.

Part A Understanding Listening Question Types

This section is designed to acquaint learners with each question type on the TOEFL® iBT Listening section. Therefore there are 8 sections in this chapter—one for each question type. Each section is divided into 5 parts. The first part offers a short explanation of the question type. The second part shows the ways in which questions of that particular type often appear on the test. The third part provides helpful hints on how to answer these questions correctly. The fourth part has either a lecture or a conversation followed by one or two questions.

Part B Building Background Knowledge of TOEFL Topics

The purpose of this section is to introduce the various subjects that most frequently appear on the TOEFL® iBT. There are 8 chapters in Part B. Each chapter covers a single subject and contains 7 Listening lectures and 3 Listening conversations of various lengths as well as vocabulary words and exercises. Each chapter is divided into several parts.

Mastering Question Types with Lectures & Conversations

This section contains 3 Listening lectures that are between 300 and 350 words in length and 1 Listening conversation that is 200 to 250 words long. Following each lecture, there are 4 Listening questions. Each question is identified by type. The first and third Listening lectures always ask the same types of questions while the second lecture asks different types of questions. This ensures that all 8 question types are covered in this section. In addition, there are four true/false questions about the lectures for learners to answer. Following each conversation, there are 4 Listening questions. Each question is identified by type. The most common types of questions that appear after TOEFL® iBT Listening conversations are asked here. In addition, there is a short summary of each lecture or conversation after the questions with four blanks for learners to fill in.

Mastering Topics with Lectures

This section contains 3 Listening lectures that are between 500 and 550 words in length. There is a graphic organizer for learners to fill out as they listen to each lecture. This will help learners improve their organizational skills. Following each lecture, there are 3 Listening questions. These questions may be from any of the 8 types of Listening questions. In addition, there is a short summary of each lecture after the questions with four blanks for learners to fill in.

Mastering Topics with Conversations

This section contains 1 Listening conversation that is between 300 and 350 words in length. There is a graphic organizer for learners to fill out as they listen to each conversation. This will help learners improve their organizational skills. Following each conversation, there are 3 Listening questions. These questions may be from any of the 8 types of Listening questions. In addition, there is a short summary of each lecture after the questions with four blanks for learners to fill in.

TOEFL Practice Tests

This section contains 1 Listening lecture that is between 700 and 750 words in length and 1 Listening conversation that is 400 to 450 words in length. The lecture has 6 Listening questions of any type while the conversation has 5 Listening questions of any type. The purpose of this section is to acquaint learners with the types of lectures and conversations they will encounter when they take the TOEFL® iBT.

Star Performer Word Files and Vocabulary Review

This section contains around 80 vocabulary words that are used in the lectures in each chapter. The words include nouns, verbs, adjectives, and adverbs. Definitions are provided for each word. There are also 15 questions that review the vocabulary words that learners cover in each chapter. The purpose of this section is to teach learners specific words that often appear in lectures on certain subjects and to make sure that learners know the meanings of these words and how to use them properly.

Part C Experiencing the TOEFL Actual Tests

This section contains 6 long TOEFL® iBT Listening lectures and questions and 3 long TOEFL® iBT Listening conversations and questions. The purpose of this section is to let learners experience long Listening lectures and conversations and to see if they can apply the knowledge they have learned in the course of studying *TOEFL® Map Listening Intermediate.*

Part **A**

Understanding Listening Question Types

01 Gist-Content

Gist-Content questions cover the test taker's basic understanding of the listening passage. They are usually asked after lectures. But they are also asked after conversations. These questions require the test taker to understand the gist of the passage. They focus on the entire passage. So the test taker should listen for the main point of the lecture or note what the two people in the conversation are talking about. The test taker needs to know the theme of the lecture or conversation to answer this question correctly.

Gist-Content questions often appear as follows:

→ What problem does the man have?

→ What are the speakers mainly discussing?

→ What is the main topic of the lecture?

→ What is the lecture mainly about?

→ What aspect of X does the professor mainly discuss?

Follow these tips to answer the questions:

◆ Listen for the overall idea of the passage. Gist-Content questions do not ask about minor parts of the passage. They focus on the entire passage. Avoid answers that cover minor themes.

◆ Recognize the key words that will let you identify the main idea. The speakers often use certain phrases that indicate what they intend to speak about. Listen for these key words and ignore answer choices that are unconnected with the passage or are too general.

◆ Identify the main idea by noting the examples, explanations, and summaries said about it. For example, focus on what problem and solution the speakers are referring to.

◆ Pay close attention to the beginning of the passage. At the beginning of a lecture, the professor often indicates what the topic is. But make sure that the professor is describing the lecture and is not talking about a previously discussed topic or giving background information. At the beginning of a conversation, the student, professor, or employee often states the problem or the reason for having the conversation.

Example

Listen to part of a lecture in a virology class.

M Professor: Viruses are incredibly tiny organisms—microorganisms really—that infect living hosts. Oh, and I'm referring to biological viruses, not computer viruses. Okay? All viruses must have a living host in order to survive and to replicate. Viruses can also pass from one host to another. Because of this ability, they are responsible for many of the world's contagious diseases. Some, such as the common cold, are usually not too serious. Others, however, have killed millions. Among these are malaria, which even today kills more than a million people each year, and the bubonic plague, which was responsible for the infamous Black Death during the late Middle Ages. It killed, uh, nearly half of Europe's population.

01-01

Now, let's look at how viruses infect humans. They can be passed from a mother to her unborn child. That's vertical transfer. You've probably heard of babies being born with AIDS, right . . . ? Well, uh, that's an example of vertical transfer.

Viruses may also be transferred from person to person. In this case, their ages and relationships do not matter at all. We call this horizontal transfer. It, by the way, is the most common way that viruses get transferred. Horizontal transfer can occur in several ways. A virus can be passed through the air. For instance, when someone coughs or sneezes, the common cold and influenza viruses can get transferred. Viruses can spread through food and water. Other viruses are carried by insects, which sometimes bite humans and thus spread infections. Mosquitoes and fleas are known to be carriers of several types of deadly viruses. Viruses can also spread through the transfer of blood from one person to another. This can happen through sexual contact and blood transfusions, among other ways. Finally, some viruses can actually survive outside a host for short periods of time. In some instances, a virus can be picked up by a new host, which gets infected, while the virus is airborne.

Q What aspect of viruses does the professor mainly discuss?

Ⓐ The animals that may transfer them to humans
Ⓑ The number of people they kill each year
Ⓒ The ways in which they may infect humans
Ⓓ Their physical characteristics and appearances

✪ Explanation of the above question and answer:

Choice Ⓒ is the aspect of viruses that the professor mainly discusses. The professor notes that viruses spread through both horizontal and vertical transfer. Then, he explains some specific ways that they are transferred through both methods. Choices Ⓐ, Ⓑ, and Ⓓ are all incorrect because they cover minor parts of the lecture.

02 Gist-Purpose

Gist-Purpose questions cover the theme of the passage. They are usually asked after conversations. But they are also asked after lectures. These questions focus on the purpose or theme of the conversation or lecture. So they always begin with "why." These questions focus on the entire conversation or lecture, not on details. They are concerned about why a student is speaking with a professor or employee or why a professor is discussing a certain topic.

Gist-Purpose questions often appear as follows:

→ Why does the student visit the professor?

→ Why does the student visit the Registrar's office?

→ Why did the professor ask to see the student?

→ Why does the professor explain X?

Follow these tips to answer the questions:

◆ Determine the reason for the conversation or lecture. For example, a student may visit a professor to get some help on an upcoming test on reptiles. They might talk about some different reptiles. However, the reason the student visits the professor is to get some assistance on a test. So avoid answer choices that claim the reason the student visits the professor is to learn about reptiles.

◆ Recognize the purpose of the conversation by understanding how the student's problem can be solved. In a service encounter, the student often has a specific problem. Knowing what the problem is will let you answer the question properly.

◆ Pay attention to the beginning of the passage. The student usually explains why he or she is visiting the professor. The professor also almost always states why he or she requested to speak with the student. The same thing often occurs during service encounters.

◆ Pay attention to the end of the passage, too. The speakers often sum up the conversation. The professor may also explain the purpose of the lecture at that time.

◆ Some answer choices only cover a small part of the conversation. Other answer choices contain incorrect information. Incorrect answer choices sometimes use words that appear in the conversation but are not connected with the student's problem as well. Avoid these answer choices.

Example

Listen to part of a conversation between a student and a Registrar's office employee.

01-02

M Student: Good afternoon. I'm here to pick up some copies of my transcript. I filled out the form on the Internet and submitted it two days ago.

W Registrar's Office Employee: Of course. May I see your student ID, please? I need that before I can give you the copies. We do that to make sure that no one else gets a hold of your transcript.

M: That makes sense to me. Just let me get my ID out of my wallet . . . Uh, here you are.

W: Thank you very much . . . John Wilson. Okay, I need to type your information into the computer, and . . . hmm . . . That's interesting.

M: Uh, what does that mean? Is there some kind of a problem?

W: Well, there's no problem really, but . . . uh, when did you say you submitted the transcript request form?

M: Two days ago. I have a copy of the online receipt I got right here. See . . . I filled out the form.

W: Ah, okay. We had a problem with the computers two days ago, so that's probably why I can't find your information. But you definitely filled out the form. I can clearly see that.

M: So, uh, does this mean I'm not going to get my transcripts today?

W: Not at all. It's our mistake, so I'm going to print them for you right now. It's going to take me about ten minutes though. Why don't you have a seat over there? I'll call you when your transcripts are ready.

Q Why does the student visit the Registrar's office?

- Ⓐ To pay for his school transcripts
- Ⓑ To receive something he requested
- Ⓒ To show the woman the receipt he printed
- Ⓓ To complain about a computer problem

✪ Explanation of the above question and answer:

Choice Ⓑ is the reason why the student visits the Registrar's office. At the beginning of the conversation, the student states that he is there to pick up some copies of his transcript. While the student shows the woman the receipt he printed (Choice Ⓒ), it is not the reason he goes to the office. Choices Ⓐ and Ⓓ are both untrue statements.

03 ⌣ Detail

Detail questions cover the test taker's ability to understand the facts and the data in the listening passage. These questions most commonly appear after lectures. But they also come after conversations. Detail questions require the test taker to listen for and remember details from the passage. Most of these questions concern the main topic of the lecture or conversation rather than minor issues. But sometimes there may be a long digression not related to the main topic. In this case, there may be a detail question about the digression.

Detail questions have two basic formats:

① Most Detail questions are multiple-choice questions with four answer choices and one correct answer. One-answer questions usually appear like this:

→ According to the professor, what is one way that X can affect Y?

→ What is X?

→ What resulted from the invention of the X?

→ According to the professor, what is the main problem with the X theory?

② Some detail questions have two or more correct answers. These questions either require you to click on two answers or to indicate whether a number of statements are true or not. Two-answer questions usually appear like this:

→ According to the professor, what information should the student include in her statement of purpose? [Click on 2 answers.]

→ In the lecture, the professor describes a number of facts about extinction level events. Indicate whether each of the following is a fact about extinction level events. [Click in the correct box for each sentence.]

Follow these tips to answer the questions:

◆ Recognize the main topic of the passage. Then, listen carefully for any facts or details related to it. Ignore the facts and the details about minor topics or ideas.

◆ Take good notes and record as many details about the main topic as you can. The correct answers to detail questions do not always use the same words that are spoken in the passage. Check your notes to see if the correct answers have been paraphrased.

◆ When you are not sure about the answer, select the answer choice most closely related to the main topic. In addition, pay attention to words or concepts that are repeated throughout the passage since this indicates that they are important.

Examples

Listen to part of a lecture in an archaeology class.

M Professor: Mound-building cultures were some of the earliest Native American civilizations. As the name suggests, these people built mounds of earth. Some mounds have been found in the states of Illinois, Louisiana, Mississippi, Ohio, and, uh . . . a few other locations. The Mississippi River area had a large number of mound-building cultures. The mounds vary in size and shape. Some are just a meter or two high while others rise more than thirty meters in height. The longest one is Serpent Mound in Ohio. It's over 300 meters long and is—as its name implies—shaped like a snake. Here on the screen you can see a picture of it . . . Fascinating, isn't it? Notice how low it is as well as its snake-like shape. Here's another mound . . . Take a look . . . It's the highest Native American mound in the U.S. It's more than thirty meters high and is located in Illinois.

01-03

The oldest mounds date back to around 3500 B.C. Native tribes were still building them when the Spanish arrived in the mid, uh, the mid-1600s. But by the time others, such as the French and the English, reached these areas, the mound building had ceased. Interestingly, the local natives didn't always know who had built the mounds. The reason for this was that the mound builders had likely been killed by European diseases such as smallpox.

W Student: Why did they build these mounds? I mean, uh, what purpose did they serve?

M: It varied from place to place. In some cases, they had religious purposes. For instance, the Natchez people . . . they lived in what's Mississippi today . . . they built mounds to worship the sun. Here on the screen is an artist's representation of what a small mound with a temple on it may have looked like. See . . . ? And other tribes buried their leaders in the mounds. Some excavations have found human remains and artifacts inside mounds, too. There is also speculation that some mounds were astronomical observatories, but no one is certain about that.

Q1 Which area had many mound-building cultures?

- Ⓐ The region around the Mississippi River
- Ⓑ The land near the Atlantic Ocean
- Ⓒ The states beside the Pacific Ocean
- Ⓓ The area close to the Great Lakes

✪ Explanation of the above question and answer:

Choice Ⓐ is the area that had many mound-building cultures. The professor states, "The Mississippi River area had a large number of mound-building cultures." Choices Ⓑ, Ⓒ, and Ⓓ are not mentioned in the lecture.

Q2 According to the professor, why did Native Americans build mounds?

Click on 2 answers.

Ⓐ To serve as defensive walls against enemy attacks

Ⓑ To bury important members of their tribes in them

Ⓒ To have places where they could worship

Ⓓ To store weapons and artifacts within them

✪ Explanation of the above question and answer:

Choices Ⓑ and Ⓒ best answer the question about why Native Americans built mounds. For Choice Ⓑ, the professor says, "And other tribes buried their leaders in the mounds." For Choice Ⓒ, while talking about mounds, the professor mentions, "In some cases, they had religious purposes." Choice Ⓐ is incorrect because the professor says nothing about warfare. Choice Ⓓ is also not mentioned in the lecture.

04 | Understanding the Function of What Is Said

Understanding the Function of What Is Said questions cover the test taker's ability to determine the meaning of what is said in the passage. These questions often involve replaying a part of the listening passage. There are two types of these questions. Some ask the test taker to infer the meaning of a phrase or sentence. So the test taker must understand what is being implied. Other questions ask the test taker to infer the purpose of a statement. These questions ask about the intended effect of a particular statement on the listener.

Understanding the Function of What Is Said questions have two basic formats:

① Some Understanding Function questions ask about what the speaker is inferring. These are usually replay questions. They may appear like this:

→ What does the professor imply when he says this: (replay)

→ What can be inferred from the professor's response to the student? (replay)

② Other Understanding Function questions ask about the purpose of a statement or a topic in the lecture or conversation. These can be regular questions or replay questions. They may appear like this:

→ What is the purpose of the woman's response? (replay)

→ Why does the student say this: (replay)

→ Why does the professor ask the student about his grades?

→ Why does the man tell the student about the library?

Follow these tips to answer the questions:

◆ Remember that people do not always speak literally. Learn to read between the lines of what the speakers are saying. Understanding what people are implying will help you answer these questions correctly.

◆ Listen to the speaker's tone of voice. This can help you understand what people are implying.

◆ Listen carefully when there is dialogue between a professor and a student in a lecture. In those instances, the student usually either asks or answers a question. These parts of the passage are often used in replay questions.

◆ Listen carefully to the entire part of the conversation or lecture that is replayed. Listening to everything will help you understand what the speaker means or is implying.

Examples

Listen to part of a conversation between a student and a professor.

M1 Professor: Ah, hello there, Larry. Thank you for taking the time to drop by. I see that you got my email.

M2 Student: Yes, sir, I did. I came here just as soon as I read it. Uh, you were a little cryptic though. Is this something about the test we just took? I thought I did pretty well on it, but, uh, maybe I didn't since you've called me in here.

01-04

M1: Test? Oh, no. I haven't even looked at the tests yet. In fact, I'm still trying to grade papers from another one of my classes.

M2: Well, that's a relief. So, uh, what do you want to speak with me about?

M1: Ah, yes. Here . . . Take a look at this brochure, please . . .

M2: Uh . . . It's a brochure for a study abroad program in Italy. You know, that sounds totally wonderful, sir. But I'm afraid my family can't afford to send me abroad. Thanks for letting me know about it though.

M1: Oh, you don't have to worry about paying for it. You see, Larry, the department just selected you to receive the Mary Stewart Scholarship.

M2: The Mary Stewart Scholarship? What's that?

M1: It's a scholarship given to the best student in the department each year. It pays for one semester of studying abroad, and it even includes airfare, room and board, and a small monthly stipend. Congratulations.

M2: My goodness. I'm . . . I'm stunned. Thank you so much, sir. Uh, I guess I need to look more carefully at that brochure, don't I?

Q1 Listen again to a part of the conversation. Then answer the question.

M1: It's a scholarship given to the best student in the department each year. It pays for one semester of studying abroad, and it even includes airfare, room and board, and a small monthly stipend. Congratulations.

M2: My goodness. I'm . . . I'm stunned.

What can be inferred from the student's response to the professor?

M2: My goodness. I'm . . . I'm stunned.

   Ⓐ He is going to reject the scholarship offer.
   Ⓑ He has never traveled abroad before.
   Ⓒ He was not expecting to win the scholarship.
   Ⓓ He thinks the scholarship pays too much money.

✪ Explanation of the above question and answer:

Choice ⓒ best describes what the student is implying. When the student says, "I'm stunned," he is indicating his surprise. He was clearly not expecting to win the scholarship. Choices Ⓐ, Ⓑ, and Ⓓ are not suggested in the conversation.

Q2 Listen again to a part of the conversation. Then answer the question.

M1: I see that you got my email.

M2: Yes, sir, I did. I came here just as soon as I read it. Uh, you were a little cryptic though.

Why does the student say this: 🎧

M2: Uh, you were a little cryptic though.

Ⓐ To request that the professor speak more directly to him
Ⓑ To complain about having to visit the professor's office
Ⓒ To tell the professor that he does not have much time
Ⓓ To indicate he is unsure why the professor wants to see him

✪ Explanation of the above question and answer:

Choice Ⓓ best describes why the student makes that statement. The professor emailed the student and asked the student to visit him. However, the student indicates that the professor was "a little cryptic." The student means that he does not know why the professor wants to see him. Choice Ⓐ is incorrect because the student makes no request like that. Choice Ⓑ is incorrect since the student makes no complaints either. And Choice Ⓒ is incorrect because the student says nothing about having a limited amount of time.

05 Understanding the Speaker's Attitude

Understanding Attitude questions cover the speaker's attitude or opinion toward something. These questions appear after both lectures and conversations. They often involve replaying a part of the listening passage. There are two types of these questions. Some questions ask how the speaker feels about something, if the speaker likes or dislikes something, or why the speaker feels a certain emotion. Other questions ask about the speaker's opinion. They may ask about the speaker's degree of certainty. Or they may ask what the speaker thinks or implies about a topic, person, thing, or idea.

Understanding the Speaker's Attitude questions have two basic formats:

① Some Understanding Attitude questions ask about the speaker's feelings. These can be regular questions or replay questions. They may appear like this:

→ What is the professor's attitude toward X?

→ What is the professor's opinion of X?

→ What does the woman mean when she says this: (replay)

② Other Understanding the Speaker's Attitude questions ask about the speaker's opinions. These can be regular questions or replay questions. They may appear like this:

→ What can be inferred about the student?

→ What can be inferred about the student when she says this: (replay)

→ What does the professor imply about the student's paper?

Follow these tips to answer the questions:

◆ Listen to the speaker's tone of voice. This will help you determine the speaker's opinion about a topic. The speaker's intonation and the words that are stressed are also important.

◆ Listen carefully when the speaker gives an opinion about a topic. Distinguish between opinions and facts. In addition, focus on the speaker's attitudes and opinions regarding the main theme of the lecture or conversation. Ignore opinions and attitudes about minor topics.

◆ Learn to read between the lines of what the speakers are saying. Do not take every statement literally. Statements often convey messages different from their literal meanings.

◆ Listen carefully to the entire part of the conversation or lecture that is played in the replay question. Listening to everything will help you understand what the speaker means or is implying.

Examples

Listen to part of a conversation between a student and a professor.

01-05

M Student: Professor Reid, may I have a word with you, please?

W Professor: Of course, David. What would you like to speak to me about?

M: I'm here about the paper you just handed back today. I, uh, I'm not too happy about my grade. So I was wondering what I could do to improve my work.

W: Okay. First of all, a B isn't a bad grade at all.

M: Yes, I know, but I'm used to getting all A's. And, well . . . I'm not the kind of person to settle just for good grades. I want to get the best grades possible.

W: That's the kind of attitude I like to see in my students. Okay . . . As I recall, the main problem with your paper was that there were too many small mistakes. You had several grammatical mistakes and a few misspellings. You just shouldn't make those kinds of errors.

M: But this is an economics class, not an English class. Why should grammar and spelling be important in economics?

W: David, you need to be able to present your ideas in clear and proper English. If you don't, no one will take you seriously. That's why grammar and spelling are crucial for every topic. Oh, you also need to add footnotes.

M: Footnotes? Oh, you mean that I should cite my sources?

W: Precisely. I need to know where you're getting your facts from. If you do those things, I'm positive that your next paper will be an A.

Q1 What is the professor's opinion of the student's paper?

   Ⓐ It could have been better.

   Ⓑ It was poorly researched.

   Ⓒ It was the best in the class.

   Ⓓ It had too many serious mistakes.

✪ Explanation of the above question and answer:

Choice Ⓐ best describes the professor's opinion of the student's paper. She says, "Okay, first of all, a B isn't a bad grade at all." Then, she states, "As I recall, the main problem with your paper was that there were too many small mistakes." So the student's paper was not bad but could have been better. Choices Ⓑ, Ⓒ, and Ⓓ do not reflect the professor's opinion.

Q2 Listen again to a part of the conversation. Then answer the question.

W: You just shouldn't make those kinds of errors.

M: But this is an economics class, not an English class. Why should grammar and spelling be important in economics?

What can be inferred about the student when he says this: 🎧

M: Why should grammar and spelling be important in economics?

(A) He has very poor grammar skills.

(B) He is majoring in economics.

(C) He is confused by what the professor is saying.

(D) He thinks he deserved to get a perfect grade.

✪ Explanation of the above question and answer:

Choice (C) is what can be inferred about the student. He indicates that he does not understand why the professor feels that grammar and spelling are important since he is writing an economics paper. This shows his confusion about what the professor tells him. Choice (A) may be a true statement, but the student does not imply that. Choice (B) is not implied either. And Choice (D) is incorrect because the student may feel that he deserves a higher grade, but he does not imply that he deserves a perfect one.

06 Understanding Organization

Understanding Organization questions cover the test taker's ability to determine the organization of the passage. These questions almost always appear after lectures. They rarely appear after conversations. For these questions, the test taker should pay attention to two factors. The first is how the professor organizes the lecture and presents the information to the class. The second is how the individual information given relates to the lecture as a whole. Test takers should focus on the presentation of the facts and the professor's purpose in stating these facts rather than the facts themselves.

Understanding Organization questions have two basic formats:

① Some Understanding Organization questions ask about the organization of the material in the professor's lecture. They may appear like this:

→ How does the professor organize the information about X that he presents to the class?

→ How is the discussion organized?

② Other Understanding Organization questions ask about specific information in the lecture. They ask about why the professor discusses or mentions certain pieces of information. They may appear like this:

→ Why does the professor discuss X?

→ Why does the professor mention X?

Follow these tips to answer the questions:

◆ Pay attention to how the lecture is organized. Lectures are often organized in the following ways: by chronology, by complexity, by comparing or contrasting, by giving examples, by classifying, by categorizing, by describing a problem and a solution, and by describing a cause and an effect.

◆ Pay attention to the beginning and end of the lecture. The professor may explain why he or she is going to present some information or say why the information was presented in a certain way.

◆ Pay attention to how the different pieces of information the professor mentions or explains relate to the overall lecture. If the professor mentions something that seems unrelated to the topic, think about why the professor is covering that information.

◆ Listen for words and phrases that the professors use to indicate how they are organizing their ideas. Professors often start their lectures by explaining how they are going to present the information. For example, a professor may say, "I'd like to discuss two different types of trees," or, "Today, we're going to cover the life of Alexander the Great."

Examples

Listen to part of a lecture in an astronomy class.

W Professor: Let's move on to lunar and solar eclipses. An eclipse occurs when Earth, the sun, and the moon are aligned with one another. This alignment can happen in two ways. Sometimes the moon is between Earth and the sun. We call this a solar eclipse. In other instances, Earth is between the sun and the moon. As you can probably guess, we call this a lunar eclipse.

01-06

Now, I want to talk about solar eclipses in more detail. From the point of view of a person on Earth, the moon and sun appear to be the same size. Therefore, when the moon passes between Earth and the sun, the moon, uh, completely blocks the sun. This can prevent the sun's light from reaching Earth. The result is that it appears to be night on the sunny side of the planet.

M Student: Does a solar eclipse cover the entire planet or just a part of it?

W: Just a small part. It's usually a very narrow area. In addition, some places get a total eclipse of the sun. This means there's complete blockage. Others only get a partial eclipse, so just a, uh, a part of the sun is blocked. In fact, solar eclipses are rare. There has to be a perfect alignment between Earth, the moon, and the sun. And that's pretty, uh, well, it's pretty unusual. When it happens, the eclipse is short lived. It might just last for a few minutes or so.

On the other hand, lunar eclipses are more common. They happen when the moon falls into Earth's shadow. Lunar eclipses always occur during a full moon phase and take place at night. They may be observed over the entire night side of Earth, not just in one small area. And lunar eclipses last for several hours, not merely minutes. But there's nothing, um . . . spectacular about them. In general, the moon merely appears more orange in color than white. That's about it.

Q1 Why does the professor discuss the effects of a lunar eclipse?

- Ⓐ To contrast them with the effects of a solar eclipse
- Ⓑ To encourage the students to watch a lunar eclipse when one occurs
- Ⓒ To note that they can be somewhat spectacular
- Ⓓ To make sure that the students understand the material

✪ Explanation of the above question and answer:

Choice Ⓐ best describes why the professor mentions the effects of a lunar eclipse. The professor notes how much of Earth is affected when there is a lunar eclipse and how the moon appears during one. She does this to make a contrast with the effects of a solar eclipse. Choices Ⓑ and Ⓓ are incorrect because there is nothing mentioned about them in the lecture. Choice Ⓒ is incorrect. In fact, the exact opposite is true.

Q2 How does the professor organize the information about eclipses that she presents to the class?

- (A) By showing video of the effects of each type
- (B) By individually describing both types
- (C) By discussing them in order of their regularity
- (D) By asking the students questions about each

✪ Explanation of the above question and answer:

Choice (B) best describes how the professor organizes the information about eclipses. First, she describes solar eclipses, and then she covers lunar eclipses. Choice (A) is incorrect because she shows no videos. Choice (C) is incorrect because she does the opposite. And Choice (D) is incorrect because she asks the students no questions about eclipses.

07 Connecting Content

Connecting Content questions cover the test taker's ability to understand how the ideas in the passage relate to one another. They almost always appear after lectures, but they can occasionally appear after conversations. Sometimes the relationships are explicitly stated. Other times, the relationships must be inferred. Most of these questions concern major relationships in the passage. These questions usually appear when the professor discusses several different themes, ideas, objects, or individuals.

Connecting Content questions have two basic formats:

① Many Connecting Content questions appear as charts or tables. There are four sentences or phrases. The test taker must match them with a theme, idea, cause, effect, object, or individual. They may appear like this:

→ Based on the information in the lecture, do the following sentences refer to X or Y? [Click in the correct box for each sentence.]

	X	Y
① [a statement]		
② [a statement]		
③ [a statement]		
④ [a statement]		

② Other Connecting Content questions ask the test taker to make inferences from the relationships that are mentioned in the passage. They may appear like this:

→ What is the likely outcome of doing procedure X before procedure Y?

→ What can be inferred about X?

→ What does the professor imply about X?

→ What comparison does the professor make between X and Y?

Follow these tips to answer the questions:

◆ These questions are often charts or tables. They may also require you to put sentences or phrases in the correct order. When the professor mentions various steps in a procedure, take notes to make sure you know the correct order.

◆ Pay attention to the relationships between any facts, concepts, or ideas that the professor mentions. For example, note whether the professor is mentioning similarities and differences between various topics he or she is discussing.

- These questions often require you to make comparisons, recognize cause and effect, follow a sequence, or identify a contradiction or agreement. You may have to identify these relationships and classify items and ideas into various categories.

- Try to infer information about the relationships the professor describes. In addition, pay attention to the possible results of future actions. You may have to predict an outcome, draw a conclusion, extrapolate some additional information, or infer a cause-effect relationship.

Examples

Listen to part of a lecture in a zoology class.

M Professor: The second-biggest species of penguins is the king penguin. The largest, of course, is the emperor penguin. We'll get to that animal next. Anyway, king penguins live and breed on the numerous small islands in the South Atlantic Ocean north of Antarctica. In autumn, they come ashore and form massive colonies. Then, they prepare to breed. The first stage of the breeding process is called molting. Basically, the penguins shed their excess feathers and grow a new set. Until this happens, they can't swim well or hunt for food. Once their new feathers grow, the penguins can begin their search for a mate.

01-07

Both male and female king penguins try to attract their mates. They do this by, uh, performing. For instance, they raise their heads, puff out their chests, and call out to attract mates. Then, they begin the selection process. Each penguin stays with its mate throughout the mating season. But penguins may change mates from season to season.

The female lays one egg per season. Both parents take turns protecting it and, later, the newborn chick. While one is off feeding and hunting, the other stays to guard against predators. Oh, king penguins are unlike many other penguins in one way: They don't build nests of rocks or other things. Instead, they use their bodies to protect their eggs and chicks from the weather. And they breed in the summer months. Remember that they live in the Southern Hemisphere, so December is summer down there. This improves the survival chances of their chicks.

King penguins don't all breed at the same time. Early breeders pick mates in September and lay their eggs in November. But late breeders pick their mates in November and lay their eggs in January. Early breeders' chicks have better chances of surviving. Often, when a late-breeding pair loses a chick, the penguins become early breeders the next year.

Q1 Based on the information in the lecture, indicate which statements refer to the behavior of king penguins during or after the mating season.

Click in the correct box for each sentence.

	During the Mating Season	After the Mating Season
1 Call out to others		
2 May change mates		
3 May puff out their chests a lot		
4 Watch out for predators		

✪ Explanation of the above question and answer:

Choices [1] and [3] are actions that king penguins do during the mating season. They are both ways that penguins try to attract their mates. Choices [2] and [4] are actions that king penguins do after the mating season. They do not always keep the same mates every year. In addition, after their babies are born, they stand guard and look for predators to protect their babies.

Q2 What can be inferred about king penguins that are molting?

- Ⓐ They find their mates during this period.
- Ⓑ They may be killed or injured by the weather.
- Ⓒ They do not spend much time in the water.
- Ⓓ They spend more time with their chicks.

✪ Explanation of the above question and answer:

Choice Ⓒ is the correct answer. About molting, the professor says, "Basically, the penguins shed their excess feathers and grow a new set. Until this happens, they can't swim well or hunt for food." It can therefore be inferred that they do not spend much time in the water while they are molting. Choice Ⓐ is incorrect because penguins find their mates after they molt. Choice Ⓑ is incorrect because the professor mentions nothing about penguins dying or getting hurt. And Choice Ⓓ is incorrect because penguins do not have chicks while they are molting.

08 | Making Inferences

Making Inferences questions cover the test taker's ability to recognize implications made in the passage and to understand what they mean. These questions appear after both conversations and lectures. For these questions, the test taker must hear the information and then make conclusions about what it means or what is going to happen as a result.

Making Inferences questions often appear as follows:

→ What does the professor imply about X?

→ What will the student probably do next?

→ What can be inferred about X?

→ What does the professor imply when he says this: (replay)

Follow these tips to answer the questions:

◆ Listen carefully to the end of the lecture or conversation. The information spoken at the end often indicates what the student, professor, or employee is going to do next.

◆ Learn to read between the lines. The literal meaning is not always the only meaning of a statement. Speakers often make implications that give their words a secondary meaning.

◆ The words in the correct answer choice are typically not used in the lecture or conversation. Instead, the words may be different but have similar meanings.

◆ Listen carefully to the entire part of the conversation or lecture that is replayed. This will help you determine what the speaker means or is implying.

Example

Listen to part of a lecture in a music class.

W1 Professor: Another aspect of twentieth century American jazz was something called scat singing. I'm sure that you've all heard it before. It's, um, it's an improvisational form of singing in which the singer strings together a series of nonsensical words in the form of a melody. Simply put, it's singing, and it uses words, but the words, uh . . . the words don't always make sense. Think about words like, uh, bibbity bobbity do dap. And the, uh, words might not even be clear to the audience. In scat, it's almost as if the singer is using his or her mouth like it's a musical instrument.

01-08

W2 Student: I heard that scat originated in Africa. Is that true, or did it come from somewhere else?

W1: Hmm . . . Good question, Susan. To be honest, scat's origins are in dispute. First, it's definitely an American creation and not an African one. Some musicologists believe scat singing comes from slave songs from the nineteenth century. These were sung by people who came from Africa. That could be the African connection you're thinking of. Yet others claim that scat has its roots in the early twentieth century in the jazz era. Jazz musicians often sounded out melodies with their voices before attempting to play them on their instruments. In fact, Louis Armstrong is occasionally credited with inventing scat singing. Whatever its origins may be, scat was well established in the U.S. by the 1920s. Yet you won't find any sheet music or lyrics for it. The words were improvised, and they often changed from performance to performance.

One of the most famous scat singers was Ella Fitzgerald. She debuted at the world-famous Apollo Theater in Harlem, New York. During the 1940s, she began using scat singing. Today, that's what most people remember her for. So I suppose that now is as good a time as any to listen to her perform.

Q What will the professor probably do next?

- Ⓐ Further discuss the origins of scat
- Ⓑ Talk more about Louis Armstrong's life
- Ⓒ Listen to some music by Ella Fitzgerald
- Ⓓ Give the students their homework assignment

✪ Explanation of the above question and answer:

Choice Ⓒ best describes what the professor will do next. She tells the students, "So I suppose that now is as good a time as any to listen to her perform." Thus, it can be inferred that the class is going to listen to some music by Ella Fitzgerald. Choices Ⓐ and Ⓑ are incorrect because the professor has already covered both topics. Choice Ⓓ is incorrect because the professor mentions nothing in her lecture about homework.

Part **B**

Building Background Knowledge of TOEFL Topics

Chapter 01 Life Sciences 1 | Conversations

zoology • biology • marine biology • medicine • virology • ecology • biochemistry • botany • public health

Mastering **Question Types**
with Lectures & Conversations

TYPE • 1 Gist-Content   TYPE • 2 Understanding Organization   TYPE • 3 Connecting Content   TYPE • 4 Speaker's Attitude

02-01

Listen to part of a lecture in a zoology class.

TYPE 1 What is the lecture mainly about?
- (A) How ants act socially
- (B) The sizes and shapes of ant colonies
- (C) The physical characteristics of ants
- (D) The use of pheromones by ants

TYPE 2 How does the professor organize the information about the types of ants that he presents to the class?
- (A) By naming each type and then explaining its duties
- (B) By describing the physical characteristics of each type
- (C) By discussing them in order of importance to the colony
- (D) By describing them all but then focusing on one type in detail

TYPE 3 Based on the information in the lecture, indicate which statements refer to male or female ants. Click in the correct box for each sentence.

	Male Ants	Female Ants
1 Care for the queen's eggs		
2 Are sent out to search for food		
3 Have a single task to do		
4 Are known as drones		

TYPE 4 What is the professor's opinion of ants' abilities to do specific chores?
- (A) He finds it unbelievable.
- (B) He believes it is instinctual.
- (C) He thinks it is impressive.
- (D) He claims they are taught to do it.

Summarizing   Complete the summary by using the words in the box.

using pheromones   shapes and sizes   mate with the queen   back to the colony

The professor first describes ant colonies and says they may have different _____ . He then mentions that all colonies have a queen, males, and females. The queen lays eggs. Males _____ . And females do work such as guarding the colony, foraging for food, and taking care of the eggs. Ants communicate what work needs to be done by _____ . These help ants work together to do tasks such as gathering food and bringing it _____ .

02-02

Listen to part of a lecture in a physiology class.

TYPE 5 What aspect of mitochondria does the professor mainly discuss?

- (A) Which cells have the greatest number of them
- (B) How they benefit the human body
- (C) What their relationship with ATP molecules is
- (D) How their two membranes differ

TYPE 6 According to the professor, which parts of the body have a large amount of mitochondria?

- (A) Hair
- (B) Fat cells
- (C) Skin
- (D) The heart

TYPE 7 What does the professor imply about skin?

- (A) It has an outer membrane.
- (B) It contains ATP molecules.
- (C) It does not create energy.
- (D) It is the body's protective covering.

TYPE 8 Listen again to part of the lecture. Then answer the question.
What does the professor imply when she says this: 🎧

- (A) ATP molecules are not important to the body.
- (B) She wants the students to research ATP molecules.
- (C) She will ask about ATP molecules on the final exam.
- (D) She will not tell the students what ATP stands for.

Summarizing   Complete the summary by using the words in the box.

asks what they are   create ATP molecules   inner and outer membrane   such as hair and skin

The professor starts discussing mitochondria and mentions how small they are. A student interrupts and
_____ . The professor explains that mitochondria are like energy factories in cells. They have
an _____ , which convert nutrients to energy for the cells. The mitochondria use oxygen to
_____ , which contain energy. All cells in the body have mitochondria. Some—such as fat
cells—have many, but others— _____ —have few mitochondria.

Mastering **Question Types**
with Lectures & Conversations

TYPE • **1** Gist-Content   TYPE • **2** Understanding Organization   TYPE • **3** Connecting Content   TYPE • **4** Speaker's Attitude

02-03

Listen to part of a lecture in a botany class.

TYPE ① What is the main topic of the lecture?

- (A) The factors needed for photosynthesis to occur
- (B) The way that oxygen built up on the Earth
- (C) The importance of the process of photosynthesis
- (D) The role of chlorophyll in photosynthesis

TYPE ② Why does the professor mention chloroplast?

- (A) To say which part of the plant absorbs sunlight
- (B) To compare its role in photosynthesis with that of chlorophyll
- (C) To state in which parts of plants it is commonly found
- (D) To explain its role in inhaling carbon dioxide

TYPE ③ What can be inferred about chlorophyll?

- (A) It is found in the leaves of plants.
- (B) It is crucial to the production of oxygen by plants.
- (C) It is absent from certain plant species.
- (D) It helps plants absorb water from the ground.

TYPE ④ Listen again to part of the lecture. Then answer the question.
What does the professor mean when he says this: 🎧

- (A) The Earth will change if all of its plants die.
- (B) Photosynthesis can physically change the Earth.
- (C) Some life forms have no need to undergo photosynthesis.
- (D) Life on the Earth would die without photosynthesis occurring.

Summarizing **Complete the summary by using the words in the box.**

more complex life forms   billions of years ago   carbon dioxide, water, and sunlight   leaves and stems

The professor explains that plants undergo photosynthesis. This happens when they use _____
to make sugar and oxygen. The professor mentions that chlorophyll gives plants' _____
their green color. And plants have chloroplasts, which allow them to absorb sunlight. The professor then states
why photosynthesis is so important. _____, the Earth had no free oxygen until plants
started producing it. As more oxygen was created, _____ were able to evolve.

34

02-04

Listen to part of a conversation between a student and a professor.

 TYPE 5   Why did the professor ask to see the student?

- (A) To return an assignment to him
- (B) To discuss an upcoming project
- (C) To ask about his summer plans
- (D) To answer his question about an exam

TYPE 6   What does the professor say about the student's thesis proposal?

- (A) It is not acceptable.
- (B) It is too narrow.
- (C) It is the best she has ever seen.
- (D) It is original.

TYPE 7   What will the professor probably do next?

- (A) Respond to the student's question
- (B) Give the student some research material
- (C) Go over the student's proposal again
- (D) Tell the student about a different assignment

TYPE 8   Listen again to part of the conversation. Then answer the question.
What does the professor imply when she says this: 🎧

- (A) The student is qualified to write a senior thesis.
- (B) She is willing to help the student with his thesis.
- (C) A senior thesis does not require too much research.
- (D) The student's topic is sufficient for a senior thesis.

Summarizing   Complete the summary by using the words in the box.

| rewrite the proposal | should produce a quality thesis | the effects of the environment | the proposal he turned in |

The professor asks to see the student to discuss _____ for a senior thesis. She says that the idea is original and _____ . However, she says that the topic is too broad and needs to be narrowed down. Instead of studying _____ on the reproductive habits of seven butterfly species, she wants him to research two or three species. The student agrees and says he will _____ and submit it the next day.

Listen to part of a lecture in a marine biology class.

02-05

Giant Kelp

Characteristics:		Spores:
	➡	
		Kelp Harvesting:

---

1 What is the main topic of the lecture?

Ⓐ The reproduction methods of giant kelps

Ⓑ The physical characteristics of giant kelp growth

Ⓒ The places where giant kelps are harvested

Ⓓ The growing conditions that giant kelps require

2 Why does the professor discuss giant kelps' large bladders?

Ⓐ To state where they keep their spores before releasing them

Ⓑ To describe why they only grow in shallow water

Ⓒ To explain how they can stand upright in the water

Ⓓ To mention what lets them grow so rapidly

3 Listen again to part of the lecture. Then answer the question.
What does the professor mean when she says this: 🎧

Ⓐ The kelps need to produce more spores.

Ⓑ The number of spores is extremely high.

Ⓒ Most of the spores produced are useless.

Ⓓ She does not have a good imagination.

Summarizing Fill in the blanks to complete the summary.

Giant kelps are a _____ found in the eastern Pacific Ocean. They can be up to 200 feet long and grow in kelp forests that resemble _____. The top parts of kelps often float on the ocean's surface. The kelps can release _____ a year, but most spores do not develop for various reasons. Some people harvest kelps to use as additives for _____. Because kelps are becoming endangered, kelp harvesting is now regulated in some places.

Mastering **Topics** with Lectures

Listen to part of a lecture in a zoology class.

02-06

┌─────────────────────────────── **Color Blindness in Monkeys** ───────────────────────────────┐
│ Color Blindness in Humans: Color Blindness in Monkeys: │
│   │
│   ➡   │
└──┘

1 Why does the professor explain the results of the experiment with male squirrel monkeys?

    (A) To identify the species of monkey that was experimented on

    (B) To mention what kind of color blindness the monkeys had

    (C) To describe the reason why the monkeys were color blind

    (D) To prove that the monkeys' color blindness is genetic

2 Based on the information in the lecture, indicate which statements refer to color blindness in humans and color blindness in monkeys.
Click in the correct box for each sentence.

	Color Blindness in Humans	Color Blindness in Monkeys
1 Can occur because of an injury to the head		
2 Has been corrected through an experiment		
3 May be the complete inability to see any colors at all		
4 May be caused by the lack of a certain protein in the body		

3 Listen again to part of the lecture. Then answer the question.
Why does the professor say this: 🎧

    (A) To let the students know he will talk about that in another class

    (B) To inform the students that they need to read ahead in their books

    (C) To imply that he has no interest in discussing that topic

    (D) To remind the students that he has already covered that subject

Summarizing Fill in the blanks to complete the summary.

Many humans are color blind, but the professor says that animals _____ may be color blind, too. For humans, genetic factors and injuries to their _____ can cause color blindness. Some monkey species are color blind while others are not. The foods monkeys eat often determine whether they will be harmed by being color blind or not. In an experiment with _____, they were cured of their color blindness after receiving _____. But scientists do not know exactly why they were cured.

Listen to part of a lecture in a marine biology class.

02-07

The Caudal Fins of Fish

Characteristics:

Differences in Fins:

Eels:

Seahorses:

---

1 According to the professor, what does a fish use its caudal fin to do?

- Ⓐ Move itself through the water
- Ⓑ Change directions while swimming
- Ⓒ Dive deeper in the water
- Ⓓ Help it with undulation

2 How does the professor organize the information about the different types of caudal fins that she presents to the class?

- Ⓐ By comparing and contrasting the most common types of caudal fins
- Ⓑ By discussing the material that is covered in the students' textbooks
- Ⓒ By mentioning some fish and then stating what kind of caudal fin each has
- Ⓓ By showing pictures to help the students visualize what she is explaining

3 Listen again to part of the lecture. Then answer the question.
What does the professor imply when she says this: 🎧

- Ⓐ Sharks only have one type of caudal fin.
- Ⓑ Many sharks are powerful swimmers.
- Ⓒ Sharks do not often use their caudal fin.
- Ⓓ The caudal fin of most sharks is fairly large.

Summarizing   Fill in the blanks to complete the summary.

Fish propel themselves through the water by _____, which is called the caudal fin. They move their caudal fin back and forth quickly to create movement. The caudal fins of fish are always vertical. There are _____ of caudal fins. These fins mostly differ in their shapes. For example, some caudal fins are forked while _____. Some fish do not need a caudal fin to move. In addition, eels have no caudal fin but move _____.

Listen to part of a conversation between a student and a printing office employee.

02-08

--- **Service Encounter** ---

Reason for Visiting:

→

Result:

Student's Decision:

↖
→

Man's Response:

1 Why does the student visit the printing office?

(A) To pick up some copies that she had made

(B) To complain about the prices of copies elsewhere

(C) To inquire about having some flyers made

(D) To tell the man how many copies she wants to make

2 What will the student probably do next?

(A) Wait for the man to make her copies

(B) Go to the cafeteria for lunch

(C) Leave the printing office

(D) Print the flyer she wants to have copied

3 Listen again to part of the conversation. Then answer the question.
Why does the man say this: 🎧

(A) To convince the woman to make copies at the printing office

(B) To compare the prices of copies there with another place

(C) To make sure the woman knows color copies are more expensive

(D) To ask the woman if she can afford the price he quoted her

Summarizing   Fill in the blanks to complete the summary.

The woman _____ because she wants to _____ . She asks the man if
he can make color copies, and he responds positively. Then, she asks for the rates, and he tells her the prices of
printing _____ . The woman is surprised by how cheap color copies are. The man says that
if she prints _____ , she can get an even cheaper price. The woman agrees and gives the
man her flyer.

02-09

Listen to part of a lecture in a biology class.

1 What aspect of alligators does the professor mainly discuss?

    (A) The similarities between American and Chinese alligators

    (B) Their physical characteristics and feeding habits

    (C) The danger that they pose to humans on occasion

    (D) Their reproductive methods and how they raise their young

2 In the lecture, the professor describes a number of facts about American alligators. Indicate whether each of the following is a fact about American alligators.
Click in the correct box for each sentence.

	Fact	Not a Fact
[1] Has a diet that consists solely of animals		
[2] Guards its eggs by remaining seated on them		
[3] Are roughly one million living in the wild		
[4] Has a U-shaped snout that is wide		

3 Why does the professor mention the size of the alligator's prey?

    (A) To say that alligators have trouble capturing larger prey animals

    (B) To describe the different ways alligators kill and eat their prey

    (C) To explain why alligators prefer to hunt smaller prey animals

    (D) To give the reason why alligators do not hunt or eat very often

4 What comparison does the professor make between alligators and crocodiles?

    (A) The shape of a part of their bodies

    (B) The size that they can grow to be

    (C) The number of people they kill each year

    (D) The number of eggs they lay at a time

5 What will the professor probably do next?

    (A) Show a film on the American alligator

    (B) Discuss some crocodile species

    (C) Explain why American alligators must be protected

    (D) Talk about the Chinese alligator

6 Listen again to part of the lecture. Then answer the question.
What can be inferred from the professor's response to the student?

    (A) Alligators are safe to be around when they are in the wild.

    (B) Several people are killed by crocodiles in the wild every year.

    (C) Crocodiles are more likely to attack people than alligators.

    (D) No one has been killed by an alligator attack in several years.

Listen to part of a conversation between a student and a professor.

1 What problem does the man have?

   Ⓐ There is a conflict between two classes he wants to take.

   Ⓑ He cannot decide which subject he should major in.

   Ⓒ He wants to change his major from marketing to journalism.

   Ⓓ A class he wants to take is not being offered next semester.

2 Why does the professor ask the student about the level of the marketing class?

   Ⓐ To imply that it is too difficult for him

   Ⓑ To note that it is a graduate-level class

   Ⓒ To find out how many students can enroll in it

   Ⓓ To encourage him to take that class

3 Why does the professor mention her graduate-level class?

   Ⓐ To tell the student about her day's schedule

   Ⓑ To complain about an upcoming class

   Ⓒ To explain why she appears to be busy

   Ⓓ To apologize for the mess in her office

4 What can be inferred about the professor?

   Ⓐ She is the student's academic advisor.

   Ⓑ She is a professor in the Astronomy Department.

   Ⓒ She will teach a class in a few minutes.

   Ⓓ She wants the student to enroll in her class.

5 Listen again to part of the conversation. Then answer the question.
What does the professor mean when she says this: 🎧

   Ⓐ The student should set up an appointment with Professor Madsen.

   Ⓑ The student has a promising future in journalism.

   Ⓒ Following her suggestion will solve the student's problem.

   Ⓓ She has arranged for the student to enroll in the class.

- **avoid** (v) to soak up something
- **accomplish** (v) to do; to complete; to finish
- **achieve** (v) to attain
- **aggressive** (adj) tending to attack; bold
- **anchor** (v) to attach something to another thing
- **aquatic** (adj) related to the water
- **aspect** (n) a nature; a characteristic; a quality
- **behavior** (n) the way someone or something acts
- **breed** (v) to reproduce
- **byproduct** (n) a secondary result
- **captive** (adj) captured
- **cartilage** (n) firm connective tissue in the body
- **color blindness** (n) the inability to see certain colors
- **complex** (adj) complicated
- **composition** (n) a makeup
- **consume** (v) to eat; to take in
- **convert** (v) to change; to alter
- **cooperate** (v) to work together
- **crucial** (adj) very important; critical
- **distinctive** (adj) having a special feature or characteristic
- **distinguish** (v) to tell the difference between two or more people or things
- **drown** (v) to kill by submerging someone or something in water
- **duplication** (n) the act of copying or duplicating something
- **emerge** (v) to arise; to form
- **endangered** (adj) rare; scarce; dying out
- **erect** (adj) standing; upright
- **evolve** (v) to change over time; to adapt
- **examine** (v) to look at very closely
- **exhale** (v) to breathe out
- **extract** (v) to remove; to take out
- **feature** (n) a characteristic; an aspect
- **fertile** (adj) productive
- **forage** (v) to hunt for; to look for
- **grip** (v) to grab; to grasp
- **habitat** (n) the place where an organism lives
- **harvest** (v) to reap; to collect, as in grain from a field
- **hatch** (v) to emerge from an egg
- **horizontal** (adj) flat; level; straight
- **impressive** (adj) remarkable; imposing; amazing
- **inhale** (v) to breathe in
- **inject** (v) to introduce something into another body or tissue

- **interconnected** (adj) unified; interrelated
- **latter** (n) the second of two things
- **layer** (n) a tier; a stratum
- **mark** (v) to indicate; to designate; to point out
- **mature** (v) to become an adult; to grow older
- **maximum** (adj) the most; the greatest; the highest
- **membrane** (n) a thin sheet of tissue; a thin covering of a cell
- **muscle** (n) a tissue in the body that can produce movement
- **mysterious** (adj) strange; unexplained; curious
- **nutrient** (n) a substance that provides a benefit to the body
- **ocean** (n) a large body of saltwater
- **overcome** (v) to defeat
- **perform** (v) to do; to carry out; to act
- **perennial** (n) a plant that lives for several years
- **predator** (n) a hunter; an animal that hunts others
- **pronounced** (adj) obvious; apparent; clear
- **propulsion** (n) movement; forward motion
- **rainforest** (n) a thick forest of trees and other vegetation that is often hot and humid
- **raised** (adj) elevated
- **release** (v) to let go
- **remain** (v) to stay; to be unchanged
- **renewable** (adj) able to be used again
- **reproduce** (v) to have children or offspring
- **respiration** (n) breathing
- **snout** (n) an animal's nose
- **sole** (adj) only
- **species** (n) a type of organism
- **specific** (adj) exact; precise
- **specimen** (n) a sample, often of an organism
- **store** (v) to save; to conserve
- **strike** (v) to attack, often suddenly
- **survive** (v) to live; to avoid dying or being killed
- **task** (n) a duty; a job
- **therapy** (n) rehabilitation; treatment
- **twig** (n) a small stick from a tree or bush
- **unimaginable** (adj) inconceivable; unbelievable
- **undulation** (n) a wavelike motion
- **vertical** (adj) upright; straight up or down
- **vegetation** (n) plant life
- **venture** (v) to travel; to move
- **wonder** (v) to be curious about; to think about

⛯ Choose the word with the closest meaning to each highlighted word or phrase.

1   The rabbits became scared when the predator approached them.

   Ⓐ animal
   Ⓑ hunter
   Ⓒ mammal
   Ⓓ lizard

2   The problem was so complex that the engineers could not solve it.

   Ⓐ mysterious
   Ⓑ complicated
   Ⓒ unique
   Ⓓ simple

3   The pigs consumed their meal as soon as the farmer fed them.

   Ⓐ examined
   Ⓑ prepared
   Ⓒ ate
   Ⓓ saved

4   The invading army overcame the defenders and won the battle.

   Ⓐ attacked
   Ⓑ challenged
   Ⓒ spied on
   Ⓓ defeated

5   Could you please give me a specific example of what is wrong?

   Ⓐ precise
   Ⓑ extreme
   Ⓒ bothersome
   Ⓓ talented

6   The employees have many tasks to do before their day is complete.

   Ⓐ experiments
   Ⓑ chores
   Ⓒ applications
   Ⓓ researches

7   Jets attain propulsion thanks to their huge engines.

   Ⓐ takeoff
   Ⓑ flight
   Ⓒ departure
   Ⓓ movement

8   Some animals reproduce rapidly while others do that much more slowly.

   Ⓐ breed
   Ⓑ mature
   Ⓒ migrate
   Ⓓ hibernate

9   There was just a sole survivor from the airplane crash.

   Ⓐ injured
   Ⓑ frightened
   Ⓒ possible
   Ⓓ single

10 I prefer the latter of the two choices that you gave me.

   Ⓐ first
   Ⓑ second
   Ⓒ third
   Ⓓ last

⛯ Match each word with the correct definition.

11 concern   •   • Ⓐ to separate into different groups

12 abbreviation   •   • Ⓑ to be about

13 apparently   •   • Ⓒ a shortened form of a word or phrase

14 shape   •   • Ⓓ a form; the way that something looks

15 classify   •   • Ⓔ seemingly; from the look of things

Part **B**

Chapter 02 **Life Sciences 2** | **Conversations**

zoology • biology • marine biology • medicine • virology • ecology • biochemistry •
botany • public health

TYPE • **1** Gist-Content   TYPE • **2** Understanding Organization   TYPE • **3** Connecting Content   TYPE • **4** Speaker's Attitude

02-11

Listen to part of a lecture in an ecology class.

TYPE ❶ What aspect of eutrophication does the professor mainly discuss?

- Ⓐ Where it usually occurs
- Ⓑ What its causes and effects are
- Ⓒ How people can stop it from happening
- Ⓓ Why it creates algae blooms

TYPE ❷ How is the discussion organized?

- Ⓐ The professor shows slides and then explains what they are looking at.
- Ⓑ The professor asks questions and then answers them herself.
- Ⓒ The professor conducts a class discussion in which the students participate.
- Ⓓ The professor describes the results of a scientific experiment.

TYPE ❸ Based on the information in the lecture, do the following sentences refer to the causes or effects of eutrophication?
Click in the correct box for each sentence.

	Cause	Effect
1 Nitrates enter the water.		
2 The water loses its oxygen supply.		
3 An algae bloom is created.		
4 The water becomes fertilized.		

TYPE ❹ What is the professor's attitude toward the student?

- Ⓐ She feels he is her best student.
- Ⓑ She is disappointed in him.
- Ⓒ She is condescending.
- Ⓓ She is complimentary.

Summarizing Complete the summary by using the words in the box.

increased production   an algae bloom   the oxygen   nitrates and phosphates

The professor asks the class about eutrophication. A student gives her a partial definition. The teacher explains that eutrophication is the _____ of algae in water such as lakes. _____ enter the water. This fertilizes it, so algae grow quickly. This forms _____. When the algae die, bacteria begin eating them. But there are so many algae that the bacteria increase tremendously and remove _____ from the lake. This kills all of the fish in the water.

02-12

Listen to part of a lecture in a marine biology class.

TYPE 5   What is the lecture mainly about?

 (A) Sea fish and their feeding habits

 (B) Fish that can survive in different types of water

 (C) The reproductive habits of some fish

 (D) The lifestyles of salmon and sharks

TYPE 6   According to the professor, what is true about euryhaline sea fish?

 (A) They include some species of eels.

 (B) They migrate to the sea in order to spawn.

 (C) They have habits like those of bull sharks.

 (D) They live in salt water for most of their lives.

TYPE 7   What does the professor imply about salmon?

 (A) They are the most common euryhaline fish.

 (B) They only reproduce one time in their lives.

 (C) They live in fresh water more than in salt water.

 (D) They are larger in size than mackerel and sea bass.

TYPE 8   Why does the professor tell the students about bull sharks?

 (A) To encourage the students to avoid these sharks

 (B) To compare them with great white sharks

 (C) To mention that they swim into fresh water to reproduce

 (D) To demonstrate how far upriver they can swim

Summarizing   Complete the summary by using the words in the box.

| great white sharks | the bull shark | in the ocean | freshwater and saltwater |

The professor discusses euryhaline fish, which can survive in _____ environments.
There are euryhaline sea fish and river fish. The salmon hatches in fresh water but lives most of its life
_____. Later, it returns to the river or stream where it was born, reproduces, and
dies. _____ is another euryhaline fish. It is dangerous and attacks more people than
_____. Bull sharks have been found swimming more than 1,000 miles from the ocean in the
Mississippi River and the Amazon River.

Mastering **Question Types**
with Lectures & Conversations

A2

TYPE • 1 Gist-Content   **TYPE • 2** Understanding Organization   **TYPE • 3** Connecting Content   **TYPE • 4** Speaker's Attitude

02-13

Listen to part of a lecture in a physiology class.

TYPE 1 What is the main topic of the lecture?

- (A) The roles of enzymes in the body
- (B) The main types of enzymes
- (C) The way in which enzymes are produced
- (D) The types of foods that contain enzymes

TYPE 2 Why does the professor mention metabolic enzymes?

- (A) To say that the human body does not produce these enzymes
- (B) To note that they are found in some uncooked foods
- (C) To explain that they are the most important type of enzymes
- (D) To include them in his discussion on the types of enzymes

TYPE 3 What comparison does the professor make between enzymes and proteins?

- (A) He states that enzymes help break down proteins.
- (B) He identifies enzymes as a type of protein.
- (C) He claims that enzymes can develop proteins.
- (D) He says that enzymes have more nutrients than proteins.

TYPE 4 What does the professor imply about the homework assignment on enzymes?

- (A) It took the students a long time to complete.
- (B) It may have been too advanced for the students.
- (C) It will be due within the next week.
- (D) It will only be worth a few points on their final grades.

Summarizing Complete the summary by using the words in the box.

food enzymes	the chemical reactions	process and digest	reading assignment

The professor comments on the difficulty of the students' _____. So he says he will go over what enzymes are. He identifies them as proteins and states that a body cannot live without them because of _____ that they help accelerate. There are three types of enzymes: metabolic, digestive, and _____. All three of these enzymes have unique roles. Mostly, enzymes help the body _____ food. They also release nutrients such as vitamins and minerals that the body can use.

02-14

Listen to part of a conversation between a student and a housing office employee.

TYPE 5 Why does the student visit the housing office?

    Ⓐ To apply for a room in a dormitory

    Ⓑ To complain about a missing item

    Ⓒ To ask that his room be repaired

    Ⓓ To fill out some forms for the man

TYPE 6 When will the housing office make a delivery to the student?

    Ⓐ By tomorrow

    Ⓑ Two days from now

    Ⓒ On the weekend

    Ⓓ In one week

TYPE 7 What will the student probably do next?

    Ⓐ Return to his dormitory

    Ⓑ Leave the housing office

    Ⓒ Complete a form

    Ⓓ Pay his bill

TYPE 8 Listen again to part of the conversation. Then answer the question.
What can be inferred from the student's response to the employee?

    Ⓐ He is disappointed by what the employee said.

    Ⓑ He doubts that the employee understands his problem.

    Ⓒ He is surprised by the employee's comment.

    Ⓓ He wants the employee to give him some advice.

Summarizing Complete the summary by using the words in the box.

how quickly he will get	missing a desk	to complain about	fill out a form

The student visits the housing office _____ a problem in his dormitory room. His room is
_____ . The student says that he does not want to go the entire semester without a desk.
The employee remarks that there is a procedure for the student to follow. He tells the student that a desk will be
delivered. The student is surprised by _____ his desk. The employee then asks the student
to _____ .

Listen to part of a lecture in a zoology class.

02-15

Coyotes

Coyote Characteristics:	*Mating Habits:*
	Communication:

---

1 What is the main topic of the lecture?

(A) The mating habits of coyotes

(B) A comparison of coyotes and wolves

(C) An overview of coyotes

(D) Forms of animal communication

2 What is the professor's attitude toward coyotes?

(A) He has positive feelings toward them.

(B) He considers them to be pests.

(C) He thinks their numbers should be limited.

(D) He offers no opinions on them.

3 What does the professor imply about coyotes?

(A) They can grow to be bigger than wolves.

(B) They prefer to hunt animals much larger than they are.

(C) They sometimes use camouflage when hunting.

(D) They can survive in all kinds of temperatures.

Summarizing Fill in the blanks to complete the summary.

Coyotes are dog-like animals that live in _____. They have grayish-brown or grayish-yellow fur and grow to be about _____. They are adaptable animals that can live in many different habitats. They live together in packs but often _____. They may sometimes hunt in packs when chasing large animals. When they breed, the average litter has six pups. Only about half of all coyotes live to adulthood. They also use different sounds _____ one another.

Mastering **Topics** with Lectures

Listen to part of a lecture in an ecology class.

02-16

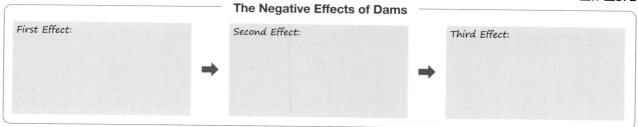

The Negative Effects of Dams

First Effect:

Second Effect:

Third Effect:

1 Why does the professor explain the effects of the construction of the Three Gorges Dam?

- Ⓐ To comment on how dams can force people and animals to move
- Ⓑ To praise the Chinese for completing a massive engineering project
- Ⓒ To note that the dam produces electricity for millions of people
- Ⓓ To emphasize that the dam is preventing silt from going downriver

2 What are fish ladders?

- Ⓐ Special places near dams that people may go fishing in
- Ⓑ Manmade stairs that both fish and boats are able to use
- Ⓒ Artificial steps that let fish swim upstream past dams
- Ⓓ Types of ladders that people use to climb up and down dams

3 Why does the professor mention the Nile River?

- Ⓐ To note its geographical location
- Ⓑ To comment on its relationship with silt
- Ⓒ To say that it is the most important river in Egypt
- Ⓓ To describe the Aswan Dam built across it

Summarizing Fill in the blanks to complete the summary.

The professor describes the _____ of dams. First is that they can adversely impact fish, such as salmon, that travel upriver to _____. He points out there are fish ladders, however, that fish use to get by dams. Second is that dams prevent _____ from going downriver. He notes that the dam across the Nile River is disrupting the flow of silt. Third is that dams flood the land upstream. So _____ often get displaced and have to move or may even die.

Listen to part of a lecture in a marine biology class.

02-17

Dolphin Communication and Navigation

Dolphin Communication:

➡

Dolphin Navigation:

---

1 How does the professor organize the information about dolphin navigation that she presents to the class?

- Ⓐ By explaining the scientific process involved
- Ⓑ By comparing it with the manner in which bats fly
- Ⓒ By describing how echolocation works
- Ⓓ By defining several key terms in detail

2 Based on the information in the lecture, do the following statements refer to vocalization or echolocation in dolphins?
Click in the correct box for each sentence.

	Vocalization	Echolocation
① Is interpreted by the melon in a dolphin's head		
② Is caused by the contracting of muscles		
③ Is similar to the way sonar works		
④ Relies upon a dolphin's blowhole		

3 Listen again to part of the lecture. Then answer the question.
Why does the professor say this: 🎧

- Ⓐ To add some humor to her lecture
- Ⓑ To respond to a student's question
- Ⓒ To make a comparison
- Ⓓ To expand upon her main point

Summarizing Fill in the blanks to complete the summary.

The professor says that dolphins are intelligent, so they can communicate with each other. They can vocalize by using _____. By forcing air out of its blowhole, a dolphin can make some _____. This lets it make different sounds. Dolphins also make whistling sounds and use _____ to communicate with each other. As for navigating, dolphins emit _____. These are a form of echolocation. Dolphins use a kind of sonar to see underwater and to identify whatever they are pursuing.

Mastering **Topics** with Conversations

Listen to part of a conversation between a student and a professor.

02-18

┌─────────────────────── **Office Hours** ───────────────────────┐

Reason for Visiting:

Result:

Student's Complaint:

Professor's Response:

└──┘

1 Why does the student visit the professor?

(A) To confirm which chapter she should read

(B) To ask him about an assignment

(C) To have him review her movie script

(D) To get some advice on her final project

2 According to the professor, what does the student need to do?

(A) Complete her final project on time

(B) Read two chapters from the textbook

(C) Submit a synopsis of a recently released film

(D) Write an original script that has one scene

3 Listen again to part of the conversation. Then answer the question. What does the student mean when she says this: 🎧

(A) She is pleased with the professor.

(B) She is glad the professor has praised her.

(C) She feels she is doing her work properly.

(D) She wants to know more about the professor's thoughts.

Summarizing   Fill in the blanks to complete the summary.

The student visits the professor to ask _____. The professor tells her to read chapter four. The student says she is there about a different assignment. She wants to confirm that she should write one scene _____. He says she is right. The student complains that it is difficult to do this assignment. The professor says to make the scene _____ since that will be easier. He then mentions that she can use that scene as a part of _____.

02-19

Listen to part of a lecture in a biology class.

Biology

1   What aspect of flowers does the professor mainly discuss?

      (A) Why they appear in many colors

      (B) What they need in order to grow

      (C) How they manage to reproduce

      (D) Where most flowering plants live

2   Why does the professor explain the nectar that flowers produce?

      (A) To describe how it helps flowers bloom

      (B) To explain some of its health benefits for animals

      (C) To say that it has a role in determining flowers' colors

      (D) To note how some animals are attracted by it

3   According to the professor, why can orchids bloom anytime during the year?

      (A) They are able to survive in all seasons.

      (B) They grow in very hot climates.

      (C) They have short life cycles.

      (D) They require only small amounts of sunlight.

4   Based on the information in the lecture, do the statements refer to flowers or to fruits and berries? Click in the correct box for each sentence.

	Flowers	Fruits and Berries
[1] May get dropped on the ground and then germinate		
[2] Typically bloom during the spring		
[3] Produce nectar that bees and other animals suck		
[4] Attract animals due to their various colors		

5   What can be inferred about bees?

      (A) They are crucial to many flowering plants getting pollinated.

      (B) They tend to live only in places with warm climates.

      (C) They are only attracted to flowers with certain colors.

      (D) They pollinate more flowers than birds or other animals do.

6   Listen again to part of the lecture. Then answer the question. Why does the professor say this: 🎧

      (A) To tell the students that they are not paying close attention

      (B) To ask the students to take better notes in class

      (C) To indicate that she is going to say something important

      (D) To mention that she is making a complicated point

TOEFL **Practice Tests**

Listen to part of a conversation between a student and a bookstore employee.

1 What are the speakers discussing?

- (A) A book that the speaker would like to purchase
- (B) A recent change in the bookstore's policies
- (C) The courses that the student is currently enrolled in
- (D) A purchase for which the student wants his money back

2 Why does the bookstore manager explain the store's policies?

- (A) To tell the student why she can only give him a half-refund
- (B) To insist that the student needs to leave the bookstore
- (C) To say why she is not allowed to make a decision
- (D) To indicate why she cannot grant the student's request

3 What is the student's attitude toward the bookstore's policy?

- (A) He finds it reasonable.
- (B) He agrees that it is necessary.
- (C) He believes it is unfair.
- (D) He thinks it is discriminatory.

4 Why does the student mention that he dropped a class?

- (A) To comment on how hard the course was
- (B) To request that the manager order a new book
- (C) To say why he no longer needs the book
- (D) To talk about his current course load

5 Listen again to part of the conversation. Then answer the question.
What is the purpose of the student's response?

- (A) To accept the woman's offer
- (B) To continue making his demands
- (C) To ask to see the woman's supervisor
- (D) To reject what the woman has to say

- **abandon** (v) to desert; to leave one all alone; to give up on
- **accelerate** (v) to increase in speed
- **adaptable** (adj) able to change or adapt
- **aggressive** (adj) tending to make unprovoked attacks; having a violent nature
- **avoid** (v) to keep away from
- **blowhole** (n) a hole in some aquatic mammals' heads that lets them breathe
- **bounce** (v) to reflect; to deflect
- **burrow** (n) an underground lair or den in which an animal lives
- **carnivorous** (adj) meat-eating
- **catalyst** (n) something that causes an event to occur
- **clarify** (v) to make clear
- **convert** (v) to change from one form to another
- **cover** (v) to go over; to discuss
- **crevice** (n) a crack or opening in a mountain or rocky area
- **cub** (n) a baby animal, such as a wolf or bear
- **decompose** (v) to break down
- **dense** (adj) thick
- **desert** (n) an area that receives a very small amount of annual rainfall
- **digest** (v) to break down food in one's body
- **dislocate** (v) to cause someone or something to move from one place to another
- **downriver** (n) the part of a river near its end
- **emit** (v) to send out
- **ensure** (v) to guarantee
- **essentially** (adv) basically; fundamentally
- **estuary** (n) the part of a river that meets the sea or ocean
- **exclusively** (adv) solely; completely; wholly
- **fascinating** (adj) very interesting; amazing; incredible
- **floodgate** (n) a gate in a dam that controls the flow of water
- **freshwater** (adj) referring to water with no salt, like the water in rivers, streams, and lakes
- **frost** (n) ice; a time when it is cold enough for water to freeze
- **germinate** (v) to begin to develop
- **gill** (n) the part of a fish that enables it to breathe underwater
- **guarantee** (n) a promise; a vow; a certainty
- **harsh** (adj) difficult; hard; dangerous
- **howl** (n) a cry made by an animal, often one such as a dog or wolf
- **intelligence** (n) cleverness; brains

- **interpret** (v) to determine the meaning of something
- **key** (adj) important; crucial
- **livestock** (n) animals such as cows, pigs, and sheep that are often raised on farms
- **locate** (v) to detect where someone or something is
- **massive** (adj) huge; enormous; very large
- **maturity** (n) adulthood
- **migrate** (v) to move from one place to another
- **monogamous** (adj) having only one mate
- **multiply** (v) to increase in number at a rapid rate
- **navigate** (v) to steer, as in a ship or airplane
- **nectar** (n) a sweet substance secreted by plants
- **nocturnal** (adj) active at night
- **nonexistent** (adj) missing; fictional; not in existence
- **nutritionist** (n) a person who is knowledgeable about nutrition
- **organism** (n) a living creature
- **petal** (n) one of the colored parts of a flower
- **plain** (n) a flat area with few trees but many grasses
- **pluck** (v) to pick
- **process** (v) to transform something into another form
- **production** (n) the manufacture of goods
- **proximity** (n) nearness; closeness
- **puzzled** (adj) confused
- **recognize** (v) to distinguish; to identify; to know
- **reproduction** (n) the act of creating offspring
- **run** (v) to operate; to manage
- **saltwater** (adj) referring to ocean or sea water with a high salt content
- **shallow** (adj) lacking depth, as in water; not deep
- **silt** (n) sediment; dirt and other particles that are carried downriver by flowing water
- **slap** (v) to smack; to hit
- **snap** (n) a sudden event
- **spawn** (v) to deposit sperm or eggs into the water like fish
- **supplement** (v) to add; to enhance
- **swift** (adj) very fast; rapid
- **tasty** (adj) delicious; good-tasting
- **trait** (n) a characteristic
- **tremendous** (adj) very large; enormous
- **tundra** (n) a treeless plain in a very cold region
- **upriver** (n) the part of a river near its source
- **vie** (v) to compete for
- **visible** (adj) able to be seen
- **vocalization** (n) the act of making a sound or noise
- **wildlife** (n) wild animals; undomesticated animals

Vocabulary Review

👆 Choose the word with the closest meaning to each highlighted word or phrase.

1 The fallen tree is beginning to decompose in the forest.
- (A) disappear
- (B) germinate
- (C) grow
- (D) rot

2 Let me discuss fish that can handle living in both fresh and salt water.
- (A) satisfy
- (B) manage
- (C) resist
- (D) approve

3 Scientists are not sure about the amount of intelligence some animals have.
- (A) thoughts
- (B) ideas
- (C) talent
- (D) cleverness

4 In case you don't know, that's approximately 1,100 miles away from the saltwater Gulf of Mexico.
- (A) easily
- (B) apparently
- (C) roughly
- (D) commonly

5 The bank robber avoided being captured by the police.
- (A) escaped
- (B) stopped
- (C) helped
- (D) remembered

6 Lisa has many good traits, but being on time is not one of them.
- (A) intentions
- (B) theories
- (C) characteristics
- (D) appearances

7 I've described features of fish living in fresh water.
- (A) names
- (B) lifestyles
- (C) studies
- (D) characteristics

8 The engineers were puzzled about why the equipment would not work.
- (A) upset
- (B) amazed
- (C) surprised
- (D) confused

9 Various enzymes help the body digest the food a person eats.
- (A) break down
- (B) break away
- (C) break out
- (D) break for

10 The blue whale is a massive creature that weighs more than 100 tons.
- (A) warm-blooded
- (B) enormous
- (C) aquatic
- (D) peaceful

👆 Match each word with the correct definition.

11 disappear •
12 litter •
13 prevent •
14 deplete •
15 visibility •

• (A) to decrease the amount of something; to run low on
• (B) to vanish; to go away
• (C) to stop something from happening
• (D) the ability to see or be seen
• (E) a group of young born to an animal

Part B

Chapter 03 | Social Sciences 1 | Conversations

history • archaeology • anthropology • economics • sociology • psychology • education • geography • political science • linguistics

Mastering **Question Types**
with Lectures & Conversations

A1

TYPE • **1** Gist-Content   TYPE • **2** Understanding Organization   TYPE • **3** Connecting Content   TYPE • **4** Speaker's Attitude

Listen to part of a lecture in a history of science class.

02-21

TYPE 1   What is the lecture mainly about?

- Ⓐ The scientific works of Aristotle
- Ⓑ The sixteenth century revolution in scientific thought
- Ⓒ The heliocentric theory of the universe
- Ⓓ Two different models of the solar system

TYPE 2   How is the discussion organized?

- Ⓐ By describing how people tried to prove each theory
- Ⓑ By starting with the correct theory and then moving to the incorrect one
- Ⓒ By naming the two main theories and discussing them
- Ⓓ By listing the achievements of the scientists who believed in each theory

TYPE 3   Based on the information in the lecture, do the following statements refer to geocentricism or heliocentricism?
Click in the correct box for each sentence.

	Geocentricism	Heliocentricism
1 Was believed by Aristotle		
2 Was the dominant theory for two thousand years		
3 Was believed by Nicolaus Copernicus		
4 Was confirmed by the use of the telescope		

TYPE 4   Listen again to part of the lecture. Then answer the question.
What does the professor mean when she says this: 🎧

- Ⓐ The student gave an incomplete answer.
- Ⓑ The student must have done the reading.
- Ⓒ The student should be more careful when answering.
- Ⓓ The student's answer was well stated.

Summarizing   Complete the summary by using the words in the box.

> center of the solar system   Galileo Galilei   most ancient Greeks   for 2,000 years

The professor asks the students what geocentricism and heliocentricism are. A student answers that geocentricism places Earth at the _____ while heliocentricism puts the sun at the center of the solar system. The professor explains that _____ believed in the heliocentric model. This included Aristotle and Ptolemy. So this model dominated _____. Then, Nicolaus Copernicus proposed the heliocentric model. Johannes Kepler expanded on the idea. And _____ used a telescope to prove it was correct.

64

02-22

Listen to part of a lecture in a history class.

TYPE 5 Why does the professor explain the Greeks' and Romans' biases against the Celts?

- (A) To mention that the Greeks and the Romans fought wars against the Celts
- (B) To imply that they may not be accurate as sources of Celtic history
- (C) To show that many people in ancient times disliked one another
- (D) To show why Greek and Roman art pictures the Celts as wild animals

TYPE 6 What resulted from the excavation at Hallstatt, Austria?

- (A) A Greek account of the Celts was unearthed.
- (B) More than 1,200 Celtic artifacts were found.
- (C) Ancient archaeological evidence was discovered.
- (D) The Celts' former capital city was dug up.

TYPE 7 What will the professor probably do next?

- (A) Take a short break
- (B) Go over the midterm exam
- (C) Discuss another aspect of the Celts
- (D) Answer some questions

TYPE 8 Listen again to part of the lecture. Then answer the question.
Why does the professor say this: 🎧

- (A) To remind the students they will take a test soon
- (B) To indicate that he feels the students need to study more
- (C) To ask the students if they have any questions about their exam
- (D) To stress the importance of what he is going to say

Summarizing   Complete the summary by using the words in the box.

use iron	like wild beasts	no written tradition	Celtic languages

The professor declares that he wants to give a short overview of the Celts. He says that the Celts comprised many groups of people. They all spoke _____ such as Irish, Cornish, Welsh, and Breton. The Celts lived all over Central and Western Europe. They were among the first people in Europe to _____ . The Greeks and the Romans wrote about the Celts but disliked them. They thought the Celts fought _____ and were uncivilized. The Celts had _____ , so they left no records of themselves.

Mastering **Question Types**
with Lectures & Conversations

TYPE • 1 Gist-Content   **TYPE • 2** Understanding Organization   **TYPE • 3** Connecting Content   **TYPE • 4** Speaker's Attitude

02-23

Listen to part of a lecture in a sociology class.

TYPE 1 What is the main topic of the lecture?

- Ⓐ Technology and its effects on food
- Ⓑ Food blogs on the Internet
- Ⓒ Cooking in modern times
- Ⓓ Healthy eating habits

TYPE 2 Why does the professor mention computer games and TV shows?

- Ⓐ To point out some of the most popular ones these days
- Ⓑ To credit them with improving the health of some people
- Ⓒ To say they have a negative effect on people's food choices
- Ⓓ To cite them as examples of how technology has improved

TYPE 3 Based on the information in the lecture, do the following statements refer to advantages or disadvantages of modern technology?
Click in the correct box for each sentence.

	Advantage	Disadvantage
① Lets people learn about nutritional information		
② Allows people access to food blogs		
③ Results in young people eating frozen food		
④ Lets people avoid criticism for certain choices		

TYPE 4 What is the professor's opinion of social media?

- Ⓐ It intrudes on people's privacy to a great extent.
- Ⓑ It has made people more aware of the food they eat.
- Ⓒ It is one of the biggest timewasters in modern times.
- Ⓓ It helps people get in touch with others with similar interests.

Summarizing   **Complete the summary by using the words in the box.**

| social media   on social media   computer games   being overweight |

The professor states that modern technology has changed how people eat. He says that _____
has made people more conscious about their food choices since others will comment about them
_____ . He then notes that the Internet has changed eating habits. People can get many
more recipes today than they could in the past. He also blames people _____ on modern
technology. He remarks that people play _____ and watch TV programs, so they do not
cook. Instead, they eat food with poor nutritional value.

66

Listen to part of a conversation between a student and a professor.

02-24

TYPE 5 Why does the student visit the professor?

- Ⓐ To seek approval for a topic she has chosen
- Ⓑ To get some information on shellfish
- Ⓒ To find out when her homework is due
- Ⓓ To ask the professor to look at her lab report

TYPE 6 What is the student's assignment?

- Ⓐ To go to the laboratory to conduct an experiment
- Ⓑ To read the next chapter and to answer some questions
- Ⓒ To write a paper on a topic they covered in a lab
- Ⓓ To prepare for a class discussion on worms

TYPE 7 What can be inferred about the professor?

- Ⓐ He gives very few high grades in his class.
- Ⓑ He does not mind assisting his students.
- Ⓒ He insists that his students attend every class.
- Ⓓ He wants the student to leave his office soon.

TYPE 8 Listen again to part of the conversation. Then answer the question.
What is the purpose of the student's response?

- Ⓐ To propose a new topic
- Ⓑ To reject the professor's idea
- Ⓒ To say that she will consider his proposal
- Ⓓ To express her dislike of eating shellfish

Summarizing   Complete the summary by using the words in the box.

on butterflies   a lab assignment   ask a question   rejects his idea

The student visits the professor to _____ . She wants to know about the short
paper due next week. The professor asks what she would like to know about it. She responds that her
topic is _____ , but the professor says that is a bad choice. Her paper should be
about something connected to _____ . He suggests writing about shellfish, but she
_____ . Then, he mentions worms. The student states that she loved the lab on worms, so
she will write about them.

Listen to part of a lecture in a history class.

02-25

The Northern European Renaissance

Causes of the Spread of Ideas:		Effects of the Spread of Ideas:

1 Why does the professor explain humanism?

- (A) To prove its connection with the modern world
- (B) To compare it with the ideas of the Reformation
- (C) To say that many Protestants focused on humanism
- (D) To note that it became influential in the Renaissance

2 What comparison does the professor make between French kings and Italian architects?

- (A) They both tried to improve the quality of architecture in Italy.
- (B) They both were the main factors involved in the Renaissance.
- (C) They both promoted the advance of literacy in Europe.
- (D) They both helped spread the ideas of the Italian Renaissance.

3 Why does the professor mention William Shakespeare?

- (A) To call him the greatest writer of the Renaissance
- (B) To stress the Italian influence on his works
- (C) To name some of his most famous plays
- (D) To say that he visited Italy to learn how to write

Summarizing   Fill in the blanks to complete the summary.

The professor mentions three main reasons that the Italian Renaissance spread to Northern Europe. First was
_____ . Second was the splitting of the Catholic Church and the _____ .
Third was the decline of feudalism. Monarchies also became stronger, so countries were unified. Monarchs
such as _____ enjoyed Italian things, especially architecture. Northern European
artists visited Italy to learn to paint. The literature in Northern Europe was also affected by Italy. For example,
_____ showed a strong Italian influence.

Mastering **Topics** with Lectures

Listen to part of a lecture in an archaeology class.

02-26

┌─────────────────── **The Clovis People** ───────────────────┐

The Clovis People:

First Theory against the Clovis People:

Second Theory against the Clovis People:

1   What aspect of the Clovis people does the professor mainly discuss?

    Ⓐ How they managed to spread out all over the Americas

    Ⓑ Where in the Americas their artifacts have been found

    Ⓒ Whether or not they were the first people to visit the Americas

    Ⓓ Why some people claim they were not very influential

2   According to the professor, where do the Clovis people get their name from?

    Ⓐ Folklore passed down from Native American tribes

    Ⓑ An area where their relics have been discovered

    Ⓒ Ancient books that used this name for them

    Ⓓ The type of strategy they used when they were in battle

3   What is the professor's opinion of the theory that only Clovis ideas spread through the Americas?

    Ⓐ He agrees with it.

    Ⓑ He disagrees with it.

    Ⓒ He has not made up his mind yet.

    Ⓓ He has no opinion on it.

Summarizing   Fill in the blanks to complete the summary.

The first people came to America across a land bridge during _____. They were hunter-gatherers following herds of animals. After a thousand years, humans had spread across both continents. _____ were the first in the Americas. Some of their artifacts are from _____. Their artifacts have been found everywhere. Some archaeologists think only _____, not people, spread. Others believe non-Clovis tribes settled parts of America. But scientific tests show that many Native Americans have similar DNA.

Mastering **Topics** with Lectures

Listen to part of a lecture in a psychology class.

02-27

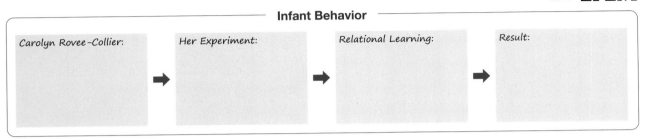

─── Infant Behavior ───

| Carolyn Rovee-Collier: | ➡ | Her Experiment: | ➡ | Relational Learning: | ➡ | Result: |

1 What is relational learning?

(A) Learning from a person that one is related to

(B) Doing an action by watching another person do it first

(C) Repeating a learned action based on one's memories

(D) Observing the ways that people both learn and behave

2 What can be inferred about Rovee-Collier?

(A) Her personality caused many people not to trust her work.

(B) She refused to give up when her theories were first rejected.

(C) She was never awarded a doctorate from a graduate school.

(D) She published several books after the 1960s.

3 Listen again to part of the lecture. Then answer the question.
What does the professor imply when he says this: 🎧

(A) He thinks Rovee-Collier was the greatest child behaviorist of the 1960s.

(B) He regards Rovee-Collier as his mentor with regard to child behavior.

(C) He believes Rovee-Collier's work demonstrates great understanding of infant behavior.

(D) He feels that Rovee-Collier could have done better research.

Summarizing Fill in the blanks to complete the summary.

The professor mentions that Carolyn Rovee-Collier is a leader in the field of early infant behavior. He describes
_____ . Her infant son learned how to make a mobile move. He _____
of how to do that. Rovee-Collier thought babies had the ability of _____ . She conducted
more experiments on how long the infants could remember certain tasks. She discovered they could keep their
memories for about _____ . At first, her work was rejected. But it was later accepted by
psychologists.

Mastering **Topics** with Conversations

Listen to part of a conversation between a student and a librarian.

02-28

─── **Service Encounter** ───

Librarian's Question:

➡

Student's Problem:

Student's Problem:

↖

Librarian's Solution:

➡

1   What are the speakers mainly discussing?

Ⓐ The student's first day of work

Ⓑ How the student needs to do his job

Ⓒ The best way to repair the computer

Ⓓ How to conduct a search for a library book

2   What is the librarian's attitude toward the student?

Ⓐ She is a little impolite to him.

Ⓑ She is concerned about him.

Ⓒ She is worried about his job performance.

Ⓓ She is interested in his personal life.

3   Why does the student mention the copier machine?

Ⓐ To say that he could not fix it

Ⓑ To find out who can repair it

Ⓒ To state that it has a paper jam

Ⓓ To tell the librarian that it is out of paper

Summarizing   Fill in the blanks to complete the summary.

The librarian asks the student how his _____ is going. He says that he likes it, yet he
has already gotten many difficult questions. There was _____, but he could not fix it.
The woman tells him to inform a librarian about that. There was also a problem _____
that he could not solve. She again tells him to speak with a librarian. She mentions that he should watch how
_____. Then, he will be able to do the same in the future.

02-29

Listen to part of a lecture in an archaeology class.

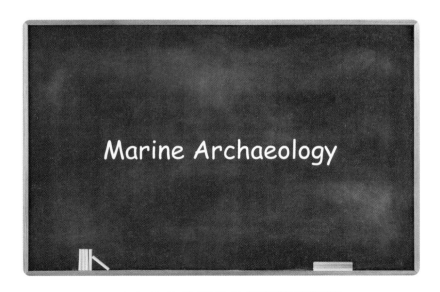

Marine Archaeology

1 What aspect of marine archaeology does the professor mainly discuss?
   (A) The dangers it holds for divers
   (B) The expenses required for it
   (C) Its relation to shipwrecks
   (D) The process involved in it

2 According to the professor, why do some archaeologists use a towed side-scanning sonar?
   (A) To make images of the bottom of the ocean
   (B) To identify the type of ship that sank
   (C) To collect artifacts off the ocean floor
   (D) To make video recordings under the water

3 How does the professor organize the information about finding shipwrecks that he presents to the class?
   (A) By showing the class slides to give them visual images
   (B) By emphasizing how difficult the entire process is
   (C) By describing the steps in the order that they are done
   (D) By having the class watch a video on how to locate shipwrecks

4 What will the professor probably do next?
   (A) Begin lecturing on ancient artifacts
   (B) Show the class some pictures
   (C) Demonstrate why some ships sink
   (D) Let the students look at some of his artifacts

5 Listen again to part of the lecture. Then answer the question.
   Why does the professor say this: 🎧
   (A) To change the topic of the discussion
   (B) To emphasize that the students heard him correctly
   (C) To let the students know what the lecture will be about
   (D) To apologize for making a mistake

6 Listen again to part of the lecture. Then answer the question.
   What does the professor mean when he says this: 🎧
   (A) He is currently involved in an archaeological dig.
   (B) It can take many years to find one sunken ship.
   (C) Finding a shipwreck site is complicated.
   (D) The students need to describe the process for their homework.

02-30

Listen to part of a conversation between a student and a professor.

1 Why does the student visit the professor?

  (A) To confirm the date on which his paper is due

  (B) To ask to borrow one of the professor's books

  (C) To get the professor to look at his research material

  (D) To find out if he has chosen an acceptable topic

2 What does the professor say about primary sources?

  (A) The student needs to use them.

  (B) One of the student's books includes them.

  (C) The best ones always include speeches.

  (D) They are more trustworthy than secondary sources.

3 What can be inferred about the professor?

  (A) He is impressed with the student's study ethic.

  (B) He has a large number of books in his library.

  (C) He has read most of the books on the student's topic.

  (D) He is willing to read the student's paper before he turns it in.

4 Listen again to part of the conversation. Then answer the question.
Why does the professor say this: 🎧

  (A) To encourage the student to work harder

  (B) To say that the paper looks good

  (C) To ask to see the student's outline

  (D) To compliment the student

5 Listen again to part of the conversation. Then answer the question.
What does the professor mean when he says this: 🎧

  (A) There is nothing new on that topic for the student to write on.

  (B) He thinks the student should rethink his decision.

  (C) He wants to know what exactly the student will write about.

  (D) He would like to propose some ideas to the student.

- **accurate** (adj) correct; precise
- **acquire** (v) to gain; to obtain
- **alter** (v) to change
- **ancestor** (n) a forebear; a precursor
- **anomaly** (n) a variance; an irregularity
- **architect** (n) a person who designs buildings
- **artifact** (n) a very old relic, often from an ancient civilization
- **baseline** (n) a benchmark
- **berserk** (adj) crazy; mad; in a frenzy
- **blame** (v) to place the responsibility for a mistake or problem on someone
- **biased** (adj) prejudiced
- **capacity** (n) an ability; a capability
- **comb** (v) to look at very closely; to scrutinize
- **concentrate** (v) to focus on or in
- **conclude** (v) to come to a decision; to decide; to believe to be true
- **counter** (v) to respond
- **countless** (adj) being a very large number; unable to be counted
- **credit** (v) to praise; to recognize
- **criticism** (n) the act of finding fault or making a negative statement
- **decline** (n) a downfall
- **devote** (v) to dedicate
- **disintegrate** (v) to fall apart into numerous very small pieces; to crumble
- **diverse** (adj) varied; assorted
- **embrace** (v) to accept; to approve of
- **encrusted** (adj) covered with; coated with
- **estimate** (v) to make an educated guess; to approximate
- **evidence** (n) proof
- **excavate** (v) to dig up; to unearth
- **expand** (v) to make larger; to enlarge
- **expose** (v) to lay open to danger or harm
- **flourish** (v) to grow; to become larger; to prosper
- **habit** (n) an act a person does regularly
- **habitation** (n) a dwelling; a home; a place where someone or something lives
- **identify** (v) to recognize; to classify
- **infant** (n) a young child; a baby
- **influence** (n) something that affects the thoughts, actions, or behavior of others
- **inhabit** (v) to live in; to reside; to dwell in
- **integral** (adj) very important; crucial
- **investigate** (v) to look at closely and carefully

- **judge** (v) to determine; to figure out
- **marine** (adj) relating to the water
- **misconception** (n) a misunderstanding; a fallacy
- **misspeak** (v) to say something incorrectly or improperly
- **monarchy** (n) a kingdom; a form of government in which the ruler is a king or queen
- **mood** (n) a feeling
- **nutritional** (adj) relating to nutrition or good health
- **occupy** (v) to take up; to live in
- **overweight** (v) being fat or weighing too much
- **outcome** (n) a result
- **pinpoint** (v) to determine something exactly
- **post** (v) to put something on the Internet
- **praise** (n) the act of expressing approval of something
- **precise** (adj) exact
- **proclaim** (v) to declare; to announce
- **promulgate** (v) to spread; to declare; to make known
- **propose** (v) to offer; to volunteer
- **ramification** (n) an effect
- **recipe** (n) cooking instructions
- **retain** (v) to keep; to maintain
- **reveal** (v) to show
- **revolve** (v) to go around; to rotate; to orbit
- **seabed** (n) the bottom of the sea; the seafloor
- **secular** (adj) not related to the church; worldly
- **selfie** (n) a picture one takes of oneself
- **serf** (n) a peasant; a peon; a poor farmer attached to the land
- **shipwreck** (n) the remains of a ship that has sunk
- **sling** (v) to hurl; to swing
- **solar system** (n) the sun and all of the planets that orbit it
- **span** (v) to go from one end to another
- **specific** (adj) exact; precise
- **split** (v) to divide
- **submersible** (n) a machine that can travel under the water
- **subscribe** (v) to believe to be true
- **succinct** (adj) very short; terse
- **suppress** (v) to put down; to stifle; to restrain
- **term** (n) an expression; a word
- **theory** (n) an idea; a hypothesis
- **unearth** (v) to dig up
- **wander** (v) to roam; to walk around with no intended destination
- **wane** (v) to decrease; to get smaller

Vocabulary **Review**

⛶ Choose the word with the closest meaning to each highlighted word or phrase.

1   People are much more conscious about the food they eat.

(A) aware
(B) interested
(C) ignored
(D) overt

2   The defendant countered by telling the judge that he was innocent.

(A) defended
(B) approached
(C) thought
(D) responded

3   Provide some specific details concerning what we can do to assist you.

(A) helpful
(B) unique
(C) costly
(D) exact

4   How much time do you estimate is left to complete the project?

(A) remember
(B) know
(C) guess
(D) request

5   I need to investigate this matter so that I can understand what is happening.

(A) examine
(B) consider
(C) approve
(D) determine

6   Your analysis is not accurate since you made several mistakes.

(A) correct
(B) appropriate
(C) acceptable
(D) legitimate

7   The monkeys are wandering through the jungle as they search for food.

(A) living
(B) expanding
(C) roaming
(D) hunting

8   The police found the evidence they needed to find the man guilty.

(A) proof
(B) hint
(C) plea
(D) site

9   Please retain your receipt in case you need to return this item.

(A) remove
(B) keep
(C) copy
(D) dispose of

10   The warrior became berserk and started attacking everyone in sight.

(A) skilled
(B) aware
(C) conscious
(D) crazy

⛶ Match each word with the correct definition.

11   acquire   •   •   (A) to gain; to receive

12   spear   •   •   (B) outstanding; impressive

13   orthodox   •   •   (C) to save; to keep from being destroyed

14   brilliant   •   •   (D) standard; approved; conventional

15   classify   •   •   (E) a long weapon with a sharp blade at its end

Part B

Chapter 04 **Social Sciences 2** | **Conversations**

history • archaeology • anthropology • economics • sociology • psychology •
education • geography • political science • linguistics

Listen to part of a lecture in an archaeology class.

02-31

TYPE 1 Why does the professor explain the story of the *Iliad*?

- (A) To provide some background information
- (B) To answer a student's question about it
- (C) To show why Heinrich Schliemann trusted Homer's writing
- (D) To prove that the Trojan War really happened

TYPE 2 Why does the professor discuss Heinrich Schliemann?

- (A) To compare his style with that of other archaeologists
- (B) To claim that his methods were not real archaeology
- (C) To describe the importance of his archaeological contributions
- (D) To explain why he was the only person who trusted Homer's accounts

TYPE 3 What does the professor imply about archaeology?

- (A) It attracts people who do not act in a professional manner.
- (B) It is one of the most difficult professions to make discoveries in.
- (C) Many of the people who practice it are highly learned.
- (D) It became more popular after Heinrich Schliemann's discoveries.

TYPE 4 Listen again to part of the lecture. Then answer the question.
What does the professor mean when he says this: 🎧

- (A) He believes that the matter is settled.
- (B) The student should speak up during discussion time.
- (C) He wants the student to ask her question.
- (D) He has finished speaking about that topic.

Summarizing   **Complete the summary by using the words in the box.**

interest in archaeology   using the *Iliad*   the Trojan War   field methods

The professor mentions that the *Iliad* tells part of the story of _____. He notes that people
once thought that Troy was mythical until Heinrich Schliemann discovered its ruins in 1873. A student comments
that Schliemann had awful _____, but the professor remarks that Schliemann got results.
His discoveries were very influential, and he increased the general public's _____. The
professor then states that it was by _____ as a guide that Schliemann was able to find Troy.

02-32

Listen to part of a lecture in a psychology class.

TYPE 5 What aspect of emotional intelligence does the professor mainly discuss?

- (A) Its definition
- (B) Its applications
- (C) The people who have it
- (D) How people manage it

TYPE 6 According to the professor, how can a person perceive emotions?
Click on 2 answers.

- (A) By watching a person's facial expressions
- (B) By reading books about emotions
- (C) By listening to a person describe emotions
- (D) By considering the person's environment

TYPE 7 What will the professor probably do next?

- (A) Discuss the second category of emotional intelligence
- (B) Hold a class discussion on the nature versus nurture argument
- (C) Ask the students to determine one another's emotions
- (D) Collect the homework that she assigned the students

TYPE 8 Listen again to part of the lecture. Then answer the question.
What does the professor imply when she says this: 🎧

- (A) She feels that nature has more importance than nurture in emotional intelligence.
- (B) She expects the students to know what she is talking about.
- (C) She will discuss that topic later in her lecture.
- (D) She wants someone to ask her what she means.

Summarizing Complete the summary by using the words in the box.

verbal and nonverbal	learned and developed	deal with emotions	the thinking process

The professor mentions that emotional intelligence is different from regular intelligence. It refers to a person's ability to _____ in various ways. Some psychologists believe people are born with emotional intelligence while others believe it can be _____ . There are four categories of emotional intelligence: perceiving emotions in others, using emotions in _____ , understanding the meanings of emotions, and managing emotions. The professor mentions that there are many ways to perceive emotions. These can be both _____ .

TYPE • **1** Gist-Content   TYPE • **2** Understanding Organization   TYPE • **3** Connecting Content   TYPE • **4** Speaker's Attitude

02-33

Listen to part of a lecture in a business management class.

TYPE ❶ What is the main topic of the lecture?

- (A) How to run a business in another country
- (B) Spoken and unspoken assumptions
- (C) The risks of making assumptions
- (D) The proper way to manage a business

TYPE ❷ How is the discussion organized?

- (A) The professor depends upon the students to answer her questions.
- (B) The professor uses examples of assumptions from real businesses.
- (C) The professor cites several case studies to prove her points.
- (D) The professor provides examples and then explains their importance.

TYPE ❸ What is the likely outcome of a businessperson from a developed country assuming that the rule of law will be followed in a foreign country?

- (A) The businessperson will make a large profit.
- (B) The businessperson will have to hire many foreign employees.
- (C) The businessperson's company will be unsuccessful.
- (D) The businessperson will learn by researching case studies.

TYPE ❹ What is the professor's attitude toward businesspeople from developed countries?

- (A) They make too many assumptions when doing business internationally.
- (B) They are often only successful in their home countries.
- (C) They fail to learn the languages of the countries they do business in.
- (D) They often develop the tendencies of businesspeople in foreign countries.

Summarizing   Complete the summary by using the words in the box.

conducting international business   spoken and unspoken   explicit and implicit   make assumptions

The professor claims that it can be very risky for businesses to ＿＿＿＿＿＿＿＿＿＿＿＿＿. A student comments
that making assumptions in business should guarantee failure, but the professor shows how that might not
happen. She claims that businesses must make assumptions when marketing new products. She mentions that
businesses make ＿＿＿＿＿＿＿＿＿＿ assumptions as well as ＿＿＿＿＿＿＿＿＿＿ assumptions.
She uses an example of people ＿＿＿＿＿＿＿＿＿＿＿. She says that people often assume that the
practices followed in their countries are the same in other nations.

Listen to part of a conversation between a student and a student activities center employee.

02-34

TYPE 5 What are the speakers mainly discussing?

(A) A recent problem on campus

(B) The need for better security

(C) A job opportunity for the student

(D) The student's missing item

TYPE 6 What does the man ask the student for?

(A) A copy of her class schedule

(B) A form of picture identification

(C) Proof that she is a university student

(D) A description of her backpack

TYPE 7 What can be inferred about the man?

(A) He is upset that the student's money is missing.

(B) He was the person who found the student's backpack.

(C) He has seen the student walking on campus before.

(D) He regrets not being able to fulfill the student's request.

TYPE 8 Listen again to part of the conversation. Then answer the question.
Why does the security guard say this: 🎧

(A) To imply that some of the student's possessions may be gone

(B) To stress that the student's backpack is in good condition

(C) To advise the student to file a complaint with the police

(D) To encourage the student to understand the situation

Summarizing Complete the summary by using the words in the box.

| some picture ID   the person's name   her money   her driver's license |

The student states that a person called to tell her that her missing backpack had been turned in. The man says he has the backpack but needs to see _____ . The student shows the man _____ , and he gives her the backpack. He tells her to check for any missing possessions. The student remarks that even _____ is still there. She wants to thank the person who turned in the backpack, but the man says he cannot give her _____ .

Listen to part of a lecture in a marketing class.

02-35

Product Testers

| Product Testers: | → | Beta Testers: |
| | | Reasons for Testing: |

---

1 Why does the professor explain what beta testers do?

- Ⓐ To emphasize their importance to the computer industry
- Ⓑ To complain that companies do not pay them enough
- Ⓒ To give an example of a freelance product tester
- Ⓓ To mention that she used to be one during her youth

2 According to the professor, why do companies do product testing?
Click on 2 answers.

- Ⓐ To make their products more popular with consumers
- Ⓑ To produce better products than their competitors
- Ⓒ To find out which features their customers prefer
- Ⓓ To ensure that the products they will sell are safe

3 What is the professor's opinion of product testers?

- Ⓐ They do important work.
- Ⓑ They offer some minor contributions.
- Ⓒ They are mostly unnecessary.
- Ⓓ Their opinions are undesirable.

Summarizing Fill in the blanks to complete the summary.

The professor discusses product testers. They are people who _____. There are
two types of product testers; some are companies that specialize in testing new products, and others
are _____. The professor states that beta testers for computer software are
freelancers. The testers give both _____ feedback to the company. This helps make
_____, so people will not get hurt or killed when using them. It also detects any problems
there may be with the products.

Mastering **Topics** with Lectures

Listen to part of a lecture in an economics class.

02-36

John Locke and Property Rights

John Locke:

➡

Labor Theory of Property:

Limits on the Theory:

---

1   What is the lecture mainly about?

Ⓐ The Founding Fathers' support of John Locke's ideas

Ⓑ What John Locke thought about property

Ⓒ The problems that existed in John Locke's philosophy

Ⓓ Why John Locke was a supporter of property rights

2   What will the professor probably do next?

Ⓐ Continue discussing John Locke's views on property rights

Ⓑ Show how the Founding Fathers utilized John Locke's theories

Ⓒ Ask the students their opinions on John Locke's work

Ⓓ Have the students read from a section in their textbooks

3   Listen again to part of the lecture. Then answer the question.
Why does the professor say this: 🎧

Ⓐ To criticize Locke's opinions

Ⓑ To quote from the book

Ⓒ To make an analogy

Ⓓ To answer a question

Summarizing   **Fill in the blanks to complete the summary.**

One must think about the relationships people have with things when considering property. _____,
an influential philosopher, thought about property rights. He based his ideas on the labor theory of property. He
believed that _____, so those who do the labor should control the property. He put limits on
that though. He thought people should only do so much labor and should leave _____. The
American _____ supported his work. But there were many contradictions in his work, which
the professor discusses.

Mastering **Topics** with Lectures

Listen to part of a lecture in a business class.

02-37

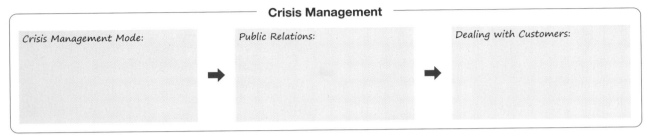

Crisis Management

| Crisis Management Mode: | ➡ | Public Relations: | ➡ | Dealing with Customers: |

1 According to the professor, what do public relations officials do?

  Ⓐ They handle communications with government agencies.

  Ⓑ They conduct interviews with members of the media.

  Ⓒ They try to improve the public image of their companies.

  Ⓓ They write editorials to appear in newspapers and magazines.

2 How is the discussion organized?

  Ⓐ The professor gives her opinion on the most effective ways to manage various crises.

  Ⓑ The professor provides actual examples of how companies engaged in crisis management.

  Ⓒ The professor calls on students to explain what they would do in certain situations.

  Ⓓ The professor shows how some companies failed in their attempts at crisis management.

3 Based on the information in the lecture, which companies do the following sentences refer to?
Click in the correct box for each sentence.

	Pan Am	Exxon	The Makers of Tylenol
1 It was the best at handling the media.			
2 It went bankrupt several years after the disaster.			
3 It tried to blame one person for the incident.			
4 It spent millions of dollars trying to recover its image.			

Summarizing Fill in the blanks to complete the summary.

The professor states that companies have many ways to overcome a crisis. One way is a product recall. She then says that disasters can make companies go into _____. She mentions the Pan Am terrorist bombing, the _____ running aground, and people dying after taking Tylenol. She notes that the makers of Tylenol _____ the best. Exxon and Pan Am both did poorly. She says that companies must make sure the same incident _____. Then she describes what happened to each company afterward.

Mastering **Topics** with Conversations

Listen to part of a conversation between a student and a professor.

02-38

Office Hours

Student's Problem:

→

Professor's Response:

Professor's Comment:

↖
→

Solution:

---

1 Why does the student visit the professor?

  Ⓐ To talk about an upcoming class

  Ⓑ To apply for an internship

  Ⓒ To give him some important news

  Ⓓ To ask about next semester's schedule

2 What can be inferred about the student?

  Ⓐ He is currently in his junior year.

  Ⓑ He will ask the professor to be his advisor.

  Ⓒ He needs to make money at the internship.

  Ⓓ He is planning to live at home in the summer.

3 Listen again to part of the conversation. Then answer the question.
What is the purpose of the student's response?

  Ⓐ To ask the professor to repeat himself

  Ⓑ To indicate his happiness with the resolution

  Ⓒ To show that he will think about his options

  Ⓓ To brag that he knew everything would work out fine

Summarizing   Fill in the blanks to complete the summary.

The student visits the professor to discuss _____ . The professor says that he is
looking forward to having the student in his class, but the student states that he cannot take it. He has
_____ , so he will be too busy to enroll in the class. The professor then tells the student that
he will teach the same class _____ . So the student should be able to do the internship in
the summer and _____ in the fall semester.

Listen to part of a lecture in an economics class.

02-39

Economics

1 What is the main topic of the lecture?

(A) The need for people to engage in bartering

(B) The best ways to ensure one's bartering is successful

(C) The reasons why people initially bartered with one another

(D) The various forms that bartering may take

2 Why does the professor explain how trade exchanges work?

(A) To show how some companies use it to avoid taxation

(B) To describe a modern-day form of bartering

(C) To compliment companies on their ingenuity

(D) To prove that bartering has changed little over time

3 What is triangular bartering?

(A) Bartering between three companies or individuals

(B) The most common type of bartering today

(C) Trading products on the international market

(D) The bartering of goods on a trade exchange

4 What is the professor's opinion of many people who barter?

(A) They know the value of the items they are trading.

(B) They should be using money instead of bartering.

(C) They should stop trying to avoid taxes.

(D) They are often not very effective at it.

5 Why does the professor discuss taxation?

(A) To mention when people had to start paying taxes

(B) To complain about the amount of taxes people must pay

(C) To say that bartering lets people avoid paying taxes

(D) To correct a mistaken belief that many people hold

6 Listen again to part of the lecture. Then answer the question.
Why does the student say this: 🎧

(A) To show his interest in the lecture topic

(B) To disagree with the professor's analysis

(C) To prove that he is familiar with the topic

(D) To ask the professor to elaborate on her point

02-40

Listen to part of a conversation between a student and a computer laboratory employee.

1   What are the speakers mainly discussing?

     (A) The employee's lack of ability concerning computers

     (B) The computer technicians' work schedules

     (C) The printers in the computer laboratory

     (D) The student's need to submit a paper soon

2   Why does the employee explain the student status of the computer technicians?

     (A) To indicate why they are not in the computer laboratory now

     (B) To excuse them for not being able to solve the student's problem

     (C) To let the student know when they are going to return

     (D) To keep the student from becoming overly upset

3   According to the employee, when will the ink for the printer arrive?

     (A) In the afternoon

     (B) In the evening

     (C) The next morning

     (D) The next afternoon

4   What will the student probably do next?

     (A) Visit her professor

     (B) Wait for a computer technician

     (C) Print her report

     (D) Fix the printer

5   Listen again to part of the conversation. Then answer the question.
        What is the purpose of the student's response?

     (A) To ask the man to stop joking

     (B) To indicate that she is angry

     (C) To express her disbelief

     (D) To make a joke about the situation

- **absolutely** (adv) totally; entirely; completely
- **approval** (n) acceptance; support
- **arguably** (adv) perhaps; possibly; questionably
- **argument** (n) a verbal fight
- **assume** (v) to believe to be true; to suppose; to think
- **barter** (v) to trade goods or services without using money
- **benefit** (n) an advantage
- **category** (n) a grouping; a class
- **clue** (n) a hint; a piece of a puzzle
- **conduct** (v) to do; to take part in
- **consider** (v) to think about; to give thought to
- **considerable** (adj) substantial; large
- **contradiction** (n) an inconsistency; an assertion of an opposite
- **contribute** (v) to add to something
- **crisis** (n) a catastrophe; a disaster
- **defender** (n) a person who guards, protects, or defends someone or something
- **devote** (v) to dedicate; to offer
- **disaster** (n) a catastrophe; a tragedy
- **enact** (v) to make law
- **encounter** (v) to meet; to face
- **ensure** (v) to guarantee
- **establish** (v) to found; to create
- **evaluate** (v) to appraise; to determine the value or worth of
- **excavate** (v) to dig up; to unearth
- **expert** (n) a highly skilled person
- **explicit** (adj) clear; spoken; open
- **express** (v) to state; to declare
- **factor** (n) a feature; an issue
- **fault** (n) blame
- **firsthand** (adj) personal; direct
- **flexible** (adj) moveable; elastic
- **force** (v) to obligate someone to do something
- **foremost** (adj) main; leading; primary
- **freelance** (adj) self-employed
- **guaranteed** (adj) definite; certain
- **handle** (v) to take care of; to tend to
- **heavily** (adv) greatly; deeply; seriously
- **ignore** (v) intentionally not to pay attention to someone or something
- **illuminating** (adj) enlightening
- **implicit** (adj) implied; understood; tacit
- **injury** (n) a wound; a hurt; damage
- **indicate** (v) to show

- **ludicrous** (adj) ridiculous; outrageous; inane
- **mass-manufactured** (adj) made on a large scale
- **master** (v) to become an expert at something
- **measure** (n) a means; a method
- **mode** (n) a manner; a style; a form
- **multilateral** (adj) many-sided
- **mythical** (adj) legendary; existing only in myths
- **nonverbal** (adj) unspoken; tacit
- **opponent** (n) a person who is opposed to another
- **perceive** (v) to identify
- **press** (n) the media
- **professional** (n) a person who does a certain skilled activity for a living
- **property** (n) anything that a person owns; a possession
- **psychologist** (n) a person who studies the human mind
- **reap** (v) to gain; to harvest
- **recall** (n) to remember
- **rely** (v) to depend upon
- **render** (v) to cause; to make
- **responsibility** (n) a duty; an obligation
- **restore** (v) to bring back
- **retrospect** (n) the contemplation of past events
- **rigorously** (adv) thoroughly; severely
- **risky** (adj) dangerous; perilous
- **scholar** (n) an academic; a person who studies a particular topic in depth
- **scope** (n) size; extent
- **serious** (adj) severe
- **shift** (v) to move; to change
- **spoil** (v) to rot; to go bad
- **state** (n) a condition
- **strictly** (adv) severely
- **survey** (n) a study; an analysis
- **test** (v) to sample; to try out; to examine
- **tough** (adj) difficult
- **transfer** (v) to shift; to move
- **ultimately** (adv) finally; in the end
- **unavoidable** (adj) inescapable; obligatory
- **unaware** (adj) oblivious; not knowing or recognizing something
- **unearth** (v) to dig up
- **unorthodox** (adj) unconventional; unusual; heterodox
- **volunteer** (n) a person who chooses to do something
- **wasteful** (adj) inefficient; extravagant

⌖ Choose the word with the closest meaning to each highlighted word or phrase.

1   You must ensure that nothing like this accident ever happens again.

   Ⓐ guess
   Ⓑ approve
   Ⓒ appear
   Ⓓ guarantee

2   Matt suffered a serious injury while he was hiking in the mountains.

   Ⓐ lethal
   Ⓑ minor
   Ⓒ uncommon
   Ⓓ severe

3   Please give me a clue so that I will know what I am looking for.

   Ⓐ hint
   Ⓑ answer
   Ⓒ puzzle
   Ⓓ term

4   John cannot recall what the bank robber looked like.

   Ⓐ say
   Ⓑ testify
   Ⓒ remember
   Ⓓ accuse

5   Janet is a master at handling contract negotiations.

   Ⓐ expert
   Ⓑ manager
   Ⓒ amateur
   Ⓓ boss

6   Mr. Jenkins transferred from the local branch to the company's headquarters.

   Ⓐ hired
   Ⓑ traveled
   Ⓒ shifted
   Ⓓ reported

7   What are the benefits of investing my money in that company?

   Ⓐ costs
   Ⓑ terms
   Ⓒ advantages
   Ⓓ awards

8   Your behavior is very risky, so you need to stop taking so many chances.

   Ⓐ dangerous
   Ⓑ childish
   Ⓒ ineffective
   Ⓓ late

9   The results indicate that our experiment was a complete success.

   Ⓐ form
   Ⓑ show
   Ⓒ estimate
   Ⓓ reap

10 I believe that she will be able to contribute to the repair effort.

   Ⓐ donate
   Ⓑ report
   Ⓒ respond
   Ⓓ add

⌖ Match each word with the correct definition.

11 report   •   •   Ⓐ a point; a dispute; a condition

12 issue   •   •   Ⓑ to make; to manufacture

13 admiration   •   •   Ⓒ an answer; a reaction

14 create   •   •   Ⓓ to admit to doing; to turn in

15 response   •   •   Ⓔ approval; acceptance; wonder

Part B

Chapter 05 **Physical Sciences 1 | Conversations**

astronomy • physics • chemistry • geology • environmental science • meteorology •
mineralogy • astrophysics • geophysics • physical chemistry

Mastering **Question Types**
with Lectures & Conversations

A1

TYPE • **1** Gist-Content   TYPE • **2** Understanding Organization   TYPE • **3** Connecting Content   TYPE • **4** Speaker's Attitude

02-41

Listen to part of a lecture in a geology class.

TYPE 1 What aspect of geysers does the professor mainly discuss?

(A) The places where they are most common on the Earth

(B) The requirements necessary for them to form

(C) The importance of geyserite to them

(D) The amount of heat required to create them

TYPE 2 Why does the professor discuss geyserite?

(A) To explain its relationship with molten rock

(B) To mention what contains the pressure in a geyser

(C) To talk about how a geyser's plumbing is created

(D) To describe how surface water collects underground

TYPE 3 What is the likely outcome of water collecting underground in a heated environment for a thousand years?

(A) A geyser will form.

(B) A volcano will erupt.

(C) A cave will be created.

(D) An underwater river will begin flowing.

TYPE 4 What is the student's attitude toward geysers?

(A) She was frightened by them.

(B) She thought they were not particularly interesting.

(C) She found them to be impressive.

(D) She believed they were similar to waterfalls.

Summarizing   **Complete the summary by using the words in the box.**

surface water	plumbing system	molten rocks	silica-rich rock

The professor asks if anyone has seen a geyser, and one student mentions that she has. He then states the factors necessary for a geyser to form. First, _____ must go belowground and accumulate for around 500 years. Next, there must be heat from _____. There must also be an underground _____ to act as a pressure chamber. And at the top, there must be a constriction for water to emerge from. Finally, geyserite—a _____—is necessary to contain the pressure in the geyser.

02-42

Listen to part of a lecture in a chemistry class.

TYPE 5 Why does the professor explain the Law of Conservation of Mass?

- Ⓐ To respond to a question by a student
- Ⓑ To focus on its importance to chemistry
- Ⓒ To describe its relation to phlogiston
- Ⓓ To argue that Lavoisier did not come up with it

TYPE 6 According to the professor, what is the importance of *Elementary Treatise of Chemistry*?

- Ⓐ It contained chemical equations.
- Ⓑ It explained the Law of Conservation of Mass.
- Ⓒ It announced the discovery of hydrogen.
- Ⓓ It was the first chemistry textbook.

TYPE 7 What will the professor probably do next?

- Ⓐ Dismiss the class for the day
- Ⓑ Return essays to the students
- Ⓒ Answer some questions
- Ⓓ Continue discussing Lavoisier

TYPE 8 Listen again to part of the lecture. Then answer the question.
What does the professor imply when she says this: 🎧

- Ⓐ She does not know much about the theory.
- Ⓑ The phlogiston theory was incorrect.
- Ⓒ The students do not need to know about phlogiston.
- Ⓓ People in the past did not know much about fire.

Summarizing **Complete the summary by using the words in the box.**

Law of Conservation of Mass   the French Revolution   chemistry textbook   phlogiston theory

The professor talks about Antoine Lavoisier. She says that he lived during the 1700s and was executed during _____. He was important to the field of chemistry for several reasons. He came up with the _____, which states that substances can change their state or form but not their mass. He also proved the _____ was wrong and showed that water is a combination of hydrogen and oxygen. Finally, he wrote the first _____, entitled *Elementary Treatise of Chemistry*.

Mastering **Question Types**
with Lectures & Conversations

TYPE • **1** Gist-Content   TYPE • **2** Understanding Organization   TYPE • **3** Connecting Content   TYPE • **4** Speaker's Attitude

Listen to part of a lecture in an astronomy class.

02-43

TYPE 1 What is the lecture mainly about?

(A) Solar flares

(B) Sunspots

(C) The surface of the sun

(D) The characteristics of the sun

TYPE 2 Why does the professor mention sunspots?

(A) To claim that they are similar to solar flares

(B) To mentions the kind of energy they release

(C) To respond to a question by a student

(D) To tell the class how they affect the Earth

TYPE 3 Based on the information in the lecture, which of the stages in a solar flare do the following sentences refer to?
Click in the correct box for each sentence.

	First Stage	Second Stage	Third Stage
1 Particles and rays are accelerated.			
2 It is also called the precursor stage.			
3 Magnetic energy is released.			
4 Soft X-rays begin to decay.			

TYPE 4 Listen again to part of the lecture. Then answer the question.
What does the professor mean when he says this: 🎧

(A) The material he is covering now will be on the test.

(B) He is willing to answer any questions about the exam.

(C) Their upcoming midterm exam will be difficult.

(D) He wants the students to perform well on their exam.

Summarizing Complete the summary by using the words in the box.

hydrogen bombs   midterm exam   three stages   radio transmissions

The professor tells the students to listen closely since they have a _____ coming soon. He states that solar flares are similar to fireworks. They are sudden, tremendous explosions on the sun's surface. They contain the power of millions of _____. He notes that sunspots and solar flares are different from each other. He explains the _____ in a solar flare: the precursor, impulse, and decay stages. Solar flares can also affect the Earth by interrupting _____ and causing power grid problems.

02-44

Listen to part of a conversation between a student and a professor.

TYPE 5 Why does the student ask to see the professor?

Ⓐ To pick up a paper from him

Ⓑ To get some information about a conference

Ⓒ To find out where another professor is

Ⓓ To apply for a study abroad program

TYPE 6 What does the student need from Professor Snyder?

Ⓐ A letter of recommendation

Ⓑ An application form

Ⓒ A handout from class

Ⓓ Her most recent paper

TYPE 7 Listen again to part of the conversation. Then answer the question.
What does the professor imply when he says this: 🎧

Ⓐ He is not always willing to help every student.

Ⓑ He does not have all of the forms that many students need.

Ⓒ He thinks that Professor Snyder may return earlier than expected.

Ⓓ He wants the student to get the paper from somewhere else.

TYPE 8 Listen again to part of the conversation. Then answer the question.
Why does the professor say this: 🎧

Ⓐ To encourage the student to go to the departmental office

Ⓑ To let the student know she is looking for the wrong person

Ⓒ To hint that he needs to ask the student for a favor

Ⓓ To indicate that he is about to surprise the student

Summarizing   Complete the summary by using the words in the box.

| deputy chair | study-in-Spain program | out of the state | application form |

The student tells the professor she is looking for Professor Snyder. The professor responds that Professor Snyder is _____ at a conference and will not return until Monday. The student mentions that she needs to see Professor Snyder about the summer _____ . She needs to complete an _____ by Friday. The professor then gives the student a form that he has in his office. He explains that he is the _____ of the department. Therefore, he has many forms students need.

Listen to part of a lecture in an environmental science class.

02-45

Diesel and Ethanol

Diesel Fuel:	→	Ethanol:

---

1 Why does the professor explain the advantages of ethanol?

- Ⓐ To emphasize how much it costs
- Ⓑ To comment that it is the best type of fuel
- Ⓒ To discuss where it is most commonly used
- Ⓓ To compare ethanol with diesel

2 Based on the information in the lecture, do the following statements refer to diesel or ethanol?
Click in the correct box for each sentence.

	Diesel	Ethanol
① It may become more expensive in winter.		
② Many military ships utilize it.		
③ It can be made from sugarcane and corn.		
④ It does not require spark plugs to run an engine using it.		

3 Listen again to part of the lecture. Then answer the question.
Why does the professor say this: 🎧

- Ⓐ To answer a question
- Ⓑ To give his opinion
- Ⓒ To correct a mistake
- Ⓓ To change the topic

Summarizing **Fill in the blanks to complete the summary.**

The professor compares diesel fuel and ethanol with each other. Diesel is any fuel used in a
_____, which needs no spark plugs. It may often come from soybeans and canola
oil. Ethanol is made from _____. Diesel is cleaner than gasoline and is often cheaper.
Ethanol produces _____ than gasoline and may be cheaper than it depending on where
_____. The material that diesel and ethanol are made of mostly determines which one is
better than the other as a fuel source.

Mastering **Topics** with Lectures

Listen to part of a lecture in a geology class.

02-46

Types of Volcanoes

Volcanoes and Their Characteristics:		The Effects of Volcanoes:

➡

---

1 According to the professor, what kind of volcanoes formed the Hawaiian Islands?

Ⓐ Shield volcanoes

Ⓑ Stratovolcanoes

Ⓒ Lava dome volcanoes

Ⓓ Cinder cone volcanoes

2 How is the discussion organized?

Ⓐ The professor encourages the students to provide answers of their own.

Ⓑ The professor goes over the book to talk about different volcanoes.

Ⓒ The professor describes each type of volcano while using slides.

Ⓓ The professor notes the damage that each type of volcano can do.

3 Listen again to part of the lecture. Then answer the question.
What can be inferred about the professor when she says this: 🎧

Ⓐ She has no time to stop the class to cover the book.

Ⓑ She does not know how to spell all of those names.

Ⓒ She will not repeat herself during the class.

Ⓓ She expects the students to look at their books.

Summarizing Fill in the blanks to complete the summary.

There are _____ of volcanoes. Stratovolcanoes are symmetrical, tall, and conical shaped.
Cinder cone volcanoes are low. _____ formed the Hawaiian Islands. They can be many
miles long. Lava dome volcanoes are round and form inside other volcanoes. _____ cause
extensive destruction. There was one in Yellowstone National Park in the U.S. _____ occur
underwater. And subglacial volcanoes are found under glaciers or icecaps.

Mastering **Topics** with Lectures

Listen to part of a lecture in an astronomy class.

02-47

Microbes in Outer Space

Microbes in Outer Space:		Theory:
	➡	First Experiment:
		Second Experiment:

---

1 What is the main topic of the lecture?

Ⓐ How the Earth was populated by microbes from space

Ⓑ The possibility of bacteria surviving in outer space

Ⓒ An experiment in space conducted by Swiss and German scientists

Ⓓ The manner in which bacteria could travel to other star systems

2 According to the professor, what happened to the spores on the Russian spacecraft? Click on 2 answers.

Ⓐ They were mixed with red sandstone.

Ⓑ They were exposed to infrared light.

Ⓒ Some managed to survive.

Ⓓ They lived for more than two centuries.

3 What does the professor imply about bacteria arriving on the Earth from other worlds?

Ⓐ It is totally impossible.

Ⓑ It has been confirmed as having happened.

Ⓒ It is something that could have happened.

Ⓓ It might happen sometime in the future.

Summarizing Fill in the blanks to complete the summary.

Some scientists are willing to accept that _____ may have come from outer space. It could have arrived on the Earth by bacteria or other spores that were attached to meteorites. Scientists discovered new forms of bacteria high _____ . Some believed the bacteria were from other worlds. Swiss and German scientists working with bacteria collected by _____ learned that the bacteria had traveled to many places and had lived for two centuries. Another experiment proved it was possible for bacteria to _____ .

Listen to part of a conversation between a student and a housing office employee.

02-48

--- Service Encounter ---

Student's Problem:

→ Employee's Response:

Student's Reaction:

→ Employee's Solution:

1 Why does the student visit the housing office?

- Ⓐ To discuss her dinner party
- Ⓑ To pay a repair bill
- Ⓒ To get something fixed
- Ⓓ To complain about a service

2 What is the student's attitude toward the man?

- Ⓐ She is very insulting toward him.
- Ⓑ She understands that he has a difficult job.
- Ⓒ She respects the work he is doing.
- Ⓓ She makes several demands to him.

3 What does the man imply about his friend?

- Ⓐ He might give the student a discount.
- Ⓑ He used to work at the university.
- Ⓒ He has an office located near the school.
- Ⓓ He charges rates that are higher than normal.

Summarizing   Fill in the blanks to complete the summary.

The student visits the housing office to complain that the _____ is not working. She wants
a repairman to fix it today. The man says he cannot send anyone until _____ because it
is already Friday afternoon. On Monday, his workers will be busy as well. The student claims she is having a
_____ and must have her oven fixed. The man gives her the number of a repair company.
So the student can call that and pay someone to _____.

02-49

Listen to part of a lecture in an astronomy class.

Astronomy

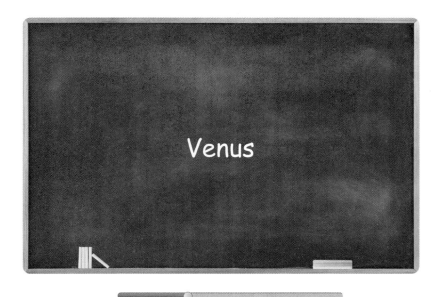

Venus

1   What is the lecture mainly about?

    Ⓐ The conditions that exist on Venus

    Ⓑ The formation of Venus

    Ⓒ A general overview of Venus

    Ⓓ The atmosphere of Venus

2   Why does the professor explain the rotation of Venus?

    Ⓐ To comment on how long its days are

    Ⓑ To mention why the planet is so hot

    Ⓒ To talk about its counterclockwise orbit

    Ⓓ To describe why it has so many clouds

3   Why is the greenhouse effect on Venus so powerful?

    Ⓐ Because of its nearness to the sun

    Ⓑ Because of the contents of its atmosphere

    Ⓒ Because of its dense cloud cover

    Ⓓ Because of its atmospheric pressure

4   How does the professor organize the information about the surface of Venus that he presents to the class?

    Ⓐ By discussing how the greenhouse effect has shaped Venus's surface

    Ⓑ By providing information in response to a student's question

    Ⓒ By comparing the surface of Venus to that of some other planets

    Ⓓ By showing pictures taken by some American and Russian probes

5   Based on the information in the lecture, do the following refer to aspects of Venus that are known or unknown?
Click in the correct box for each sentence.

	Known	Unknown
1 The existence of water		
2 Its average surface temperature		
3 The age of its surface		
4 The period of its rotation		

6   Listen again to part of the lecture. Then answer the question.
What does the professor imply when he says this: 🎧

    Ⓐ The temperature on Mercury is equivalent to that on Venus.

    Ⓑ In the future, Venus will become hotter than Mercury.

    Ⓒ Mercury should be hotter than Venus, but it is not.

    Ⓓ Some believe Mercury is the hottest planet in the solar system.

Listen to part of a conversation between a student and a professor.

1 Why does the professor ask to speak with the student?

  Ⓐ To make a proposal to him

  Ⓑ To give him back his paper

  Ⓒ To ask him to rewrite his paper

  Ⓓ To request that he be on time to class

2 According to the student, what school activity does he participate in?

  Ⓐ Intramural sports

  Ⓑ Student government

  Ⓒ The history club

  Ⓓ The photography club

3 What is the professor's opinion of the student's paper?

  Ⓐ It was an outstanding piece of writing.

  Ⓑ It requires a minor amount of editing.

  Ⓒ It can be published in its original form.

  Ⓓ It needs to be rewritten to get a better grade.

4 Listen again to part of the conversation. Then answer the question. What is the purpose of the student's response?

  Ⓐ To reject the professor's offer

  Ⓑ To complain about the amount of work involved

  Ⓒ To ask her for some advice

  Ⓓ To express his surprise

5 Listen again to part of the conversation. Then answer the question. What does the student imply when he says this: 🎧

  Ⓐ He has already made up his mind.

  Ⓑ He has no interest in rewriting his paper.

  Ⓒ He will probably accept the professor's offer.

  Ⓓ He thinks he needs to improve his résumé.

- **accelerate** (v) to increase in speed
- **accumulate** (v) to amass; to gather; to collect
- **accurate** (adj) correct
- **adequate** (adj) sufficient; enough
- **advantage** (n) a benefit
- **apparent** (adj) clear; obvious
- **atmosphere** (n) the air
- **attractive** (adj) appealing
- **author** (n) the writer of a book, story, article, or other written work
- **broad** (adj) wide
- **brilliant** (adj) very intelligent
- **buildup** (n) an accumulation; an increase
- **burst** (v) to explode
- **categorize** (v) to divide into separate groups
- **cavity** (n) a hole; a hollow space
- **clockwise** (adj) in the same direction that the hands of a clock move
- **combination** (n) two or more things united
- **combustion** (n) the act of burning
- **composition** (n) the makeup of something
- **compression** (n) the act of reducing the size of something
- **constriction** (n) restriction; restraint
- **counterclockwise** (adj) in the opposite direction that the hands of a clock move
- **credence** (n) believability; credibility
- **crush** (v) to squash; to press; to compress
- **definitive** (adj) ultimate; best
- **deprive** (v) to remove or take away something from others
- **descend** (v) to go down; to decline
- **devise** (v) to develop; to create; to come up with
- **disadvantage** (n) a detriment; a shortcoming; a drawback
- **discharge** (v) to release; to send out; to emit
- **disprove** (v) to show to be false or untrue
- **distinguish** (v) to show how two or more things are different; to differentiate
- **duration** (n) a length of time; a period
- **eject** (v) to toss out; to hurl; to spew
- **emission** (n) a discharge; a release; something that has been sent out
- **erupt** (v) to explode, as in a volcano
- **examination** (n) an investigation; a test
- **exposure** (n) contact; experience

- **flaming** (adj) on fire; shooting out flames
- **fluctuate** (v) to rise and fall; to go up and down
- **form** (n) an external appearance
- **function** (n) a use
- **generally** (adv) typically; usually; normally
- **harvest** (v) to reap; to collect crops from a field
- **home world** (n) the planet where someone or something is from
- **identical** (adj) being the same or very similar
- **ignite** (v) to light on fire
- **incinerate** (v) to burn completely
- **intensely** (adv) extremely; highly; powerfully
- **interrupt** (v) to break into; to disrupt
- **journey** (n) a very long trip; a trek
- **lava** (n) molten rock that is on the planet's surface
- **magma** (n) molten rock that is underneath the planet's surface
- **malfunction** (v) to work improperly; to break down
- **mass** (n) the quantity of matter
- **meteorite** (n) a rock from outer space that enters the Earth's atmosphere
- **mitigate** (v) to ease; to lessen
- **molten** (adj) melted and extremely hot
- **mounting** (adj) growing; increasing
- **organic** (adj) natural; relating to an organism
- **particle** (n) a very small piece of something
- **pollution** (n) contamination; dirt
- **porous** (adj) permeable
- **probe** (n) a satellite
- **replicate** (v) to duplicate; to imitate; to copy
- **retain** (v) to keep
- **soak** (v) to absorb
- **solar** (adj) relating to the sun
- **spew** (v) to shoot out; to expel
- **stage** (n) a phase; a period
- **submarine** (adj) underwater
- **symmetrical** (adj) balanced; proportioned
- **theorize** (v) to hypothesize; to come up with an idea or theory
- **toxic** (adj) poisonous; deadly
- **transmission** (n) a broadcast
- **tremendous** (adj) extremely large; huge; enormous
- **unstable** (adj) unbalanced; uneven; unsteady
- **vary** (v) to change
- **viscosity** (adj) thickness

⚷ Choose the word with the closest meaning to each highlighted word or phrase.

1   This appears to be a simple calculator, but it actually has many functions.

   Ⓐ batteries
   Ⓑ uses
   Ⓒ forms
   Ⓓ electronics

2   It was apparent to everyone that she was not telling the truth.

   Ⓐ possible
   Ⓑ acceptable
   Ⓒ shocking
   Ⓓ clear

3   Cobra venom is extremely toxic and can quickly kill a person.

   Ⓐ powerful
   Ⓑ poisonous
   Ⓒ rare
   Ⓓ unstable

4   That painting by Picasso is one of the gallery's invaluable treasures.

   Ⓐ priceless
   Ⓑ respected
   Ⓒ regarded
   Ⓓ appointed

5   Be careful as you descend the mountain since it can be dangerous.

   Ⓐ go around
   Ⓑ go down
   Ⓒ go toward
   Ⓓ go by

6   There are several probes exploring the solar system right now.

   Ⓐ satellites
   Ⓑ robots
   Ⓒ experiments
   Ⓓ tools

7   Mr. Taylor listed five advantages of getting a degree from a four-year college.

   Ⓐ drawbacks
   Ⓑ considerations
   Ⓒ benefits
   Ⓓ approaches

8   The check from the insurance company helped mitigate the loss of their home.

   Ⓐ assume
   Ⓑ repair
   Ⓒ accept
   Ⓓ ease

9   He often varies the way in which he drives his car to work.

   Ⓐ considers
   Ⓑ remembers
   Ⓒ changes
   Ⓓ forgets

10 When the volcano erupted, thousands of people were killed.

   Ⓐ exploded
   Ⓑ emerged
   Ⓒ approached
   Ⓓ formed

⚷ Match each word with the correct definition.

11 rotation   •   •   Ⓐ a combination of two or more substances

12 mixture   •   •   Ⓑ to initiate; to start; to spark

13 critical   •   •   Ⓒ to fall; to crumble; to break down

14 trigger   •   •   Ⓓ important; vital

15 collapse   •   •   Ⓔ the spin of an object

Part B

Chapter 06 Physical Sciences 2 | Conversations

astronomy • physics • chemistry • geology • environmental science • meteorology •
mineralogy • astrophysics • geophysics • physical chemistry

Mastering **Question Types**
with Lectures & Conversations

A1

TYPE • **1** Gist-Content   TYPE • **2** Understanding Organization   TYPE • **3** Connecting Content   TYPE • **4** Speaker's Attitude

Listen to part of a lecture in a chemistry class.

02-51

TYPE 1 What aspect of methane does the professor mainly discuss?

- Ⓐ Its effects on the environment
- Ⓑ Its chemical composition
- Ⓒ How people can detect it
- Ⓓ Its presence in the atmosphere

TYPE 2 Why does the professor discuss greenhouse gases?

- Ⓐ To tell the class what the most common ones are
- Ⓑ To describe how they benefit the planet
- Ⓒ To mention the average temperature on the Earth
- Ⓓ To encourage the students to ask him questions

TYPE 3 What is the likely outcome of filling an enclosed area with methane?

- Ⓐ Decomposition will occur.
- Ⓑ The area will become hotter.
- Ⓒ The area will explode.
- Ⓓ The methane will bond with oxygen.

TYPE 4 Listen again to part of the lecture. Then answer the question.
What does the student mean when she says this: 🎧

- Ⓐ She forgot an important chemistry term.
- Ⓑ She wants someone else to give an answer.
- Ⓒ She thinks her explanation was satisfactory.
- Ⓓ She cannot answer the professor's question.

Summarizing   **Complete the summary by using the words in the box.**

| it can explode | benefit the planet | infrared radiation | humans to breathe |

The professor describes methane as an odorless and lighter-than-air gas. He notes that it can be
dangerous since _____ when it is highly concentrated. Methane is also unsafe for
_____. The professor then states that greenhouse gases such as methane, carbon dioxide,
and water vapor _____. They keep the planet warm, which lets people survive. He explains
that greenhouse gases prevent some of the sun's _____ from leaving the atmosphere. This
is what keeps the planet warm.

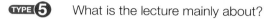

02-52

Listen to part of a lecture in a geology class.

TYPE 5 What is the lecture mainly about?

    (A) The best places to find stalactites and stalagmites

    (B) How stalactites are created

    (C) Calcium carbonate and stalagmites

    (D) Some formations that are found in caves

TYPE 6 What is calcite?

    (A) A chemical that limestone can form from

    (B) A mineral that contains carbon dioxide

    (C) The substance that forms stalactites and stalagmites

    (D) A material that transforms calcium carbonate into limestone

TYPE 7 Listen again to part of the lecture. Then answer the question.
What does the professor imply when she says this: 🎧

    (A) She has been asked this question in the past.

    (B) She uses a lot of technical language in her class.

    (C) The semester is about to come to an end.

    (D) The students are going to take a test soon.

TYPE 8 Why does the professor tell the students that stalactites hang from a cave's ceiling?

    (A) To explain why some of them are so long

    (B) To answer a question that a student asked

    (C) To differentiate them from stalagmites

    (D) To point out a fact while looking at a slide

Summarizing   Complete the summary by using the words in the box.

from the ceiling   many centuries   stalactites and stalagmites   dripping off stalactites

The professor tells the students that the formations found in some caves are called _____.
She says they grow in pairs and may sometimes combine to create a column. She then mentions that
stalactites grow _____. Both formations appear in limestone caves. They are formed
of calcite, or calcium carbonate. A combination of rainwater, carbon dioxide, and minerals creates them over
_____. As for stalagmites, they form because of water _____. This is
why stalagmites form underneath stalactites.

Mastering **Question Types**
with Lectures & Conversations

TYPE • **1** Gist-Content   TYPE • **2** Understanding Organization   TYPE • **3** Connecting Content   TYPE • **4** Speaker's Attitude

Listen to part of a lecture in an environmental sciences class.

02-53

TYPE 1 What is the main topic of the lecture?

- (A) The different types of permafrost
- (B) Permafrost and its characteristics
- (C) The places where permafrost is commonly found
- (D) The conditions required to create permafrost

TYPE 2 How does the professor organize the information about the types of permafrost that she presents to the class?

- (A) She shows pictures of each type as she describes its characteristics.
- (B) She has the students identify the characteristics of each type.
- (C) She names each type and the temperature that it needs to exist.
- (D) She tells the students where each type is most commonly found.

TYPE 3 Based on the information in the lecture, do the following places have large amounts of permafrost or small amounts of it?
Click in the correct box for each sentence.

	Large Amounts of Permafrost	Small Amounts of Permafrost
1 Siberia		
2 Scandinavia		
3 Antarctica		
4 Iceland		

TYPE 4 Listen again to part of the lecture. Then answer the question.
What can be inferred about the professor when she says this: 🎧

- (A) She has visited a place with cold permafrost before.
- (B) Her main topic of research is cold permafrost.
- (C) She enjoys telling stories about her past adventures.
- (D) She is a world-renowned expert in permafrost.

Summarizing   Complete the summary by using the words in the box.

soil, sediment, or rock   temperature in the area   1,000 meters deep   North and South poles

Permafrost is permanently frozen ground. It can be _____ . Permafrost may be less than
one meter deep or more than _____ . The amount of ice in it varies from thirty percent
to almost zero. According to the professor, there are several different types of permafrost depending upon the
_____ . These include warm permafrost and cold permafrost. It mostly appears at high
latitudes near the _____ . But there are many other places where there is permafrost.

02-54

Listen to part of a conversation between a student and an employee in the dean of engineering's office.

TYPE 5   Why does the student visit the dean of engineering's office?

    Ⓐ   To make an appointment

    Ⓑ   To ask for directions

    Ⓒ   To find a professor

    Ⓓ   To request a key

TYPE 6   Why does the student want to access the attic?

    Ⓐ   To look for a missing item

    Ⓑ   To pick up some equipment

    Ⓒ   To retrieve some documents

    Ⓓ   To find a quiet place to study

TYPE 7   What will the woman probably do next?

    Ⓐ   Finish some work she is doing

    Ⓑ   Call Professor Murdock

    Ⓒ   Give the student some instructions

    Ⓓ   Escort the student to the attic

TYPE 8   Listen again to part of the conversation. Then answer the question.

    Why does the man say this: 🎧

    Ⓐ   To confirm he has a letter

    Ⓑ   To ask the woman to repeat herself

    Ⓒ   To express his confusion

    Ⓓ   To agree with the woman's opinion

Summarizing   **Complete the summary by using the words in the box.**

| will accompany him   sensitive documents   retrieve some equipment   the key to the attic |

The student visits the office of the dean of engineering and requests _____. He has to _____ there for his professor. The woman asks for a letter and explains that access to the attic is controlled because _____ are stored there. The student remarks that the professor sent the woman an email. The woman tells the student that she _____ to the attic in ten minutes. She needs to see what he is doing while he is up there.

Listen to part of a lecture in a geology class.

02-55

Changes in the Earth's Features

Glaciers:

Floods:

Earthquakes:

1   What is the lecture mainly about?

- Ⓐ The ways the Earth's features may change naturally
- Ⓑ The differences between tsunamis and floods
- Ⓒ The movement patterns of glaciers
- Ⓓ The changes to the Earth that floods can cause

2   How does the professor organize the information about floods that she presents to the class?

- Ⓐ By stating where they most often occur
- Ⓑ By mentioning what usually causes them
- Ⓒ By focusing on their general effects
- Ⓓ By proving that they are more dangerous than tsunamis

3   Listen again to part of the lecture. Then answer the question.
What is the purpose of the professor's response?

- Ⓐ To correct the student
- Ⓑ To give the student a warning
- Ⓒ To indicate that she knows about tsunamis
- Ⓓ To entertain the students

Summarizing   Fill in the blanks to complete the summary.

The professor mentions that there are many ways the Earth's surface can change. One is by glaciers. Glaciers resemble rivers _____ . As they slowly move, they _____ below them. This can create lakes, widen valleys, and make new ones. Floods can _____ quickly or gradually. They may occur by rivers or oceans. Tsunamis, which are caused by _____ , sometimes shape the land. And earthquakes can cause massive amounts of destruction. But she also notes that most earthquakes are very weak.

Mastering **Topics** with Lectures

Listen to part of a lecture in a meteorology class.

02-56

The Causes of Rain

| The Water Cycle: | | The Causes of Rain: |

---

1 Why does the professor explain the water cycle?

- Ⓐ To mention the reason why monsoons occur
- Ⓑ To state that there would be no clouds without it
- Ⓒ To give the students some background information
- Ⓓ To note how often precipitation occurs because of it

2 Based on the information in the lecture, indicate which statements refer to precipitation caused by weather fronts and precipitation caused by seasonal weather phenomena.
Click in the correct box for each sentence.

	Weather Fronts	Seasonal Weather Phenomena
1 Results in monsoons in parts of Asia		
2 Are the most common reasons why rain falls		
3 May happen on the windward sides of mountains		
4 Can often cause floods when they occur		

3 Listen again to part of the lecture. Then answer the question.
What can be inferred about the professor when he says this: 🎧

- Ⓐ He believes he has given the students an important term.
- Ⓑ He thinks that many of his students are forgetful.
- Ⓒ He wants his students' grades to improve.
- Ⓓ He finds the study of meteorology fascinating.

Summarizing Fill in the blanks to complete the summary.

The professor explains _____ and how water evaporates, condenses, and falls to the ground as precipitation. He says there are many ways that rain can fall. Weather fronts cause rain. Sometimes cool temperatures make the air _____, so rain falls. Rain falls on the _____ of mountains, too. Convection is another cause of rain. In hot weather, thunderstorms may often result. Finally, _____ such as monsoons can cause rain. They may cause flooding, but the rain is needed for farming.

Mastering **Topics** with Lectures

Listen to part of a lecture in a geology class.

02-57

Earth's Inner and Outer Cores

Inner Core:

➡

Outer Core:

---

1 According to the professor, how is the Earth's magnetism related to the core?

- Ⓐ The core keeps the Earth's magnetism from becoming too powerful.
- Ⓑ The Earth's magnetism stops the core from splitting up.
- Ⓒ The core's movement creates the Earth's magnetism.
- Ⓓ The Earth's magnetism prevents the core from overheating.

2 Listen again to part of the lecture. Then answer the question.
Why does the professor say this: 🎧

- Ⓐ She just corrected herself.
- Ⓑ She dropped something while speaking.
- Ⓒ She made an error while writing on the board.
- Ⓓ She made a mistake.

3 Listen again to part of the lecture. Then answer the question.
What does the professor imply when she says this: 🎧

- Ⓐ She is finished talking about that particular topic for now.
- Ⓑ She does not know as much about the core as she should.
- Ⓒ She wants the students to trust the information she has given them.
- Ⓓ More research on the core needs to be done in the future.

Summarizing   Fill in the blanks to complete the summary.

The professor notes that the Earth has both inner and outer cores. Each is mostly _____ .
This is known because of various theories about the Earth's formation and from _____ done
on the cores. Both cores are very hot. The outer core is _____ , but the inner core is solid
despite being hotter than the outer core. The pressure in the inner core is very high. Both cores are responsible
for _____ . The revolving of the cores creates the Earth's magnetism.

Mastering **Topics** with Conversations

Listen to part of a conversation between a student and a professor.

02-58

Office Hours

Student's Problem:

➡

Professor's Response:

◤

Professor's Suggestion:

➡

Student's Response:

---

1 What are the speakers mainly discussing?

- Ⓐ The student's need to get a scholarship
- Ⓑ The desire of the student to become a journalist
- Ⓒ The possibility of the student changing schools
- Ⓓ The letters of recommendation that the student wants

2 What does the professor propose that the student should do?

- Ⓐ Get a double major in the two fields she likes
- Ⓑ Attend graduate school to study journalism
- Ⓒ Transfer to another university
- Ⓓ Take five years to graduate from school

3 Listen again to part of the conversation. Then answer the question. What can be inferred about the professor when she says this: 🎧

- Ⓐ She disagrees with the student's plan.
- Ⓑ She supports the student's desire to transfer.
- Ⓒ She thinks the student needs to calm down.
- Ⓓ She is confused by what the student said.

Summarizing Fill in the blanks to complete the summary.

The student appears upset when she visits the professor. She says she has to transfer. The professor asks why and states that she can _____ for scholarships if the student needs money. The student says it is not about money. She wants to _____, but the school has no Journalism Department. The professor mentions that, as a junior, it would be hard for the student _____. She suggests that the student stay at the school and then _____ to study journalism.

02-59

Listen to part of a lecture in a physics class.

Physics

1   Why does the professor explain microwaves?

   ⓐ To point out how dangerous they are to humans

   ⓑ To mention their usefulness in communications

   ⓒ To mention how effective they are at cooking food

   ⓓ To complain about how many people get injured by them

2   According to the professor, which of the following are characteristics of waves?
   Click on 2 answers.

   ⓐ They can move through anything.

   ⓑ They contain energy.

   ⓒ They have speed.

   ⓓ They are all audible to the human ear.

3   How does the professor organize the information about waves that she presents to the class?

   ⓐ She reads aloud from the text and encourages the students to ask questions.

   ⓑ She discusses some of the advances that humans have made by researching waves.

   ⓒ She covers waves in order from those with the highest frequency to the lowest.

   ⓓ She describes waves in general and then discusses them one by one.

4   Based on the information in the lecture, do the following refer to radio waves or microwaves?
   Click in the correct box for each sentence.

	Radio Waves	Microwaves
1 Have the longest wavelength on the electromagnetic energy spectrum		
2 May cause harm to humans		
3 Are highly used in long-distance telecommunications		
4 Have a very low frequency		

5   Listen again to part of the lecture. Then answer the question.
   Why does the professor say this: 🎧

   ⓐ To claim that some movies are not entirely realistic

   ⓑ To describe the effects of how sound travels in space

   ⓒ To imply that Hollywood movies actually employ scientific facts

   ⓓ To encourage the students to watch some Hollywood movies

6   Listen again to part of the lecture. Then answer the question.
   What does the professor mean when she says this: 🎧

   ⓐ She does not know the answer.

   ⓑ It is a difficult question to answer.

   ⓒ The student is trying to fool her.

   ⓓ She wants the student to answer his own question.

02-60

Listen to part of a conversation between a student and a financial aid office employee.

1   Why does the student visit the financial aid office?

    (A) To submit an application for a student loan

    (B) To apply for the school's work-study program

    (C) To find out how she can get some more assistance

    (D) To inquire about the results of her scholarship application

2   What does the man say that the student can do to remain in school?

    (A) Apply for a loan

    (B) Win a scholarship

    (C) Take a semester off

    (D) Find a part-time job

3   What does the man instruct the student to do?

    (A) Make an appointment to see his boss

    (B) Come back tomorrow to check on some results

    (C) Complete some forms and return them

    (D) Try to get an academic scholarship

4   What can be inferred about the student?

    (A) She gets good grades.

    (B) She has a part-time job.

    (C) She comes from a poor family.

    (D) She is a senior.

5   Listen again to part of the conversation. Then answer the question.
What does the student imply when she says this: 🎧

    (A) She has no plans for the future.

    (B) She is in desperate need of a job.

    (C) She is planning to quit school soon.

    (D) Her tuition is due in one week.

- **alter** (v) to change
- **altitude** (n) height above sea level
- **astronaut** (n) a person trained to go into outer space
- **cave** (n) a large opening in the earth, often in a mountain
- **composition** (n) a makeup
- **concentrated** (adj) focused
- **condensation** (n) the changing of water vapor into water droplets
- **confirm** (v) to guarantee to be true
- **crack** (n) a break; an opening; a fissure
- **decomposition** (n) the breaking down of an organic substance
- **deficient** (adj) lacking something
- **define** (v) to describe; to classify
- **density** (n) thickness
- **deposit** (n) a lode of ore or a mineral in the ground
- **destruction** (n) devastation
- **detect** (v) to identify; to find
- **displace** (v) to relocate; to move; to cause to move
- **disturbance** (n) a commotion; an ado
- **droplet** (n) a drop, often of water; a bead
- **drip** (v) to fall in drops; to trickle
- **dump** (v) to drop or let go suddenly
- **earth** (n) ground; dirt
- **earthquake** (n) the sudden shaking of the earth; a seism
- **emerge** (v) to come out of or from something
- **equator** (n) the imaginary line that runs horizontally around the center of the Earth
- **Eurasia** (n) the landmass that Europe and Asia are on
- **flood** (n) the overflowing of water; a deluge
- **frozen** (adj) solid; having turned solid because of the cold
- **glacier** (n) a huge sheet of ice
- **gradual** (adj) slow; happening over a long period of time
- **gravity** (n) the force that draws all objects back toward the Earth
- **hurricane** (n) a violent tropical storm
- **icicle** (n) a long, thin piece of ice
- **interaction** (n) communication; relations between two or more organisms
- **landmass** (v) a very large piece of land; a continent
- **landscape** (n) scenery
- **latitude** (n) the distance north or south from the equator that one is

- **literally** (adv) factually; actually; in truth
- **manure** (n) dung; the waste that is expelled from an animal
- **mechanical** (adj) related to machinery
- **medium** (n) a means
- **melt** (v) to change from a solid to a liquid form
- **moisture** (n) dampness; wetness
- **monsoon** (n) a seasonal event during which heavy rains fall
- **perceive** (v) to recognize; to distinguish
- **permanently** (adv) forever
- **phenomenon** (n) an event; an occurrence
- **plasma** (n) superheated gas
- **precipitation** (n) the falling of rain, snow, or ice
- **principle** (n) an idea; a belief; a theory
- **puffy** (adj) swollen; bloated
- **radiate** (v) to emit; to give off
- **range** (v) to vary; to change
- **recede** (v) to go back
- **reflect** (v) to bounce off; to echo; to return
- **release** (v) to let go
- **retreat** (v) to move back from
- **revert** (v) to change back to one's original form
- **rockslide** (n) the falling of a large number of rocks from a mountain
- **saturated** (adj) soaked; inundated; full
- **seasonal** (adj) recurring; cyclic
- **shake** (v) to move back and forth, often quickly
- **shift** (v) to change
- **simplified** (adj) basic; easy
- **stranded** (adj) stuck; marooned; trapped
- **strike** (v) to hit
- **structure** (n) a formation
- **sufficient** (adj) enough
- **thaw** (v) to defrost; to melt
- **thickness** (n) how wide or broad something is
- **trace** (adj) very small; minor
- **trickle** (v) to flow very slowly; to seep
- **uproot** (v) to pick up a tree or plant by its roots
- **valid** (adj) true; legitimate
- **vast** (adj) huge; enormous
- **ventilated** (adj) airy
- **vibration** (n) shaking
- **whisper** (v) to speak very softly
- **withstand** (v) to survive; to endure

Vocabulary **Review**

⚓ Choose the word with the closest meaning to each highlighted word or phrase.

1   The floodwaters began to recede a few hours ago.

   Ⓐ go up
   Ⓑ go to
   Ⓒ go back
   Ⓓ go with

2   Millions of people were displaced because of the war.

   Ⓐ moved
   Ⓑ killed
   Ⓒ frightened
   Ⓓ injured

3   This is one of the strangest phenomena that I have ever seen.

   Ⓐ creatures
   Ⓑ events
   Ⓒ organisms
   Ⓓ plants

4   Take the meat out of the freezer so that it can thaw.

   Ⓐ evaporate
   Ⓑ condense
   Ⓒ defrost
   Ⓓ precipitate

5   The earth in this region is very fertile and good for farming.

   Ⓐ soil
   Ⓑ sand
   Ⓒ mud
   Ⓓ stone

6   Your idea sounds valid, so I think that we should consider it.

   Ⓐ impossible
   Ⓑ creative
   Ⓒ difficult
   Ⓓ legitimate

7   Guards are not allowed to strike the prisoners at any time.

   Ⓐ speak with
   Ⓑ hit
   Ⓒ punish
   Ⓓ regard

8   How would you define the events that happened today?

   Ⓐ describe
   Ⓑ recall
   Ⓒ reveal
   Ⓓ stand

9   There is a vast amount of land that is still unsettled in that country.

   Ⓐ huge
   Ⓑ wild
   Ⓒ expensive
   Ⓓ distant

10 The hurricane caused an enormous flood that covered most of the city.

   Ⓐ seism
   Ⓑ avalanche
   Ⓒ tsunami
   Ⓓ deluge

⚓ Match each word with the correct definition.

11 core   •   • Ⓐ difficult to handle or deal with

12 dramatic   •   • Ⓑ constantly; regularly

13 continually   •   • Ⓒ the center of something

14 tricky   •   • Ⓓ present; recent

15 current   •   • Ⓔ sudden; spectacular

Part **B**

Chapter 07 **Arts 1** | **Conversations**

city planning • art history • literature • music • industrial design • visual arts • crafts •
architecture • film • photography

Mastering **Question Types**
with Lectures & Conversations

TYPE • 1 Gist-Content   **TYPE • 2** Understanding Organization   **TYPE • 3** Connecting Content   **TYPE • 4** Speaker's Attitude

02-61

Listen to part of a lecture in an art class.

TYPE 1   What is the lecture mainly about?

- (A) The differences between watercolors and oil paints
- (B) The styles that watercolor artists often use
- (C) The inventing of both watercolors and oil paints
- (D) The effects on paintings made with oil paints

TYPE 2   Why does the professor mention Jan van Eyck?

- (A) To praise his use of watercolors in his paintings
- (B) To claim that his oil paintings are very valuable
- (C) To describe his style of painting to the class
- (D) To name the man who invented modern oil paints

TYPE 3   Based on the information in the lecture, do the statements refer to oil paints or watercolors?
Click in the correct box for each sentence.

	Oil Paints	Watercolors
1 Were used in Japan in the eighth century		
2 Utilize opaque pigments		
3 Were first used by primitive men		
4 Are easy to make corrections with		

TYPE 4   Listen again to part of the lecture. Then answer the question.
What does the professor mean when he says this: 🎧

- (A) Most watercolor artists have no plan for how their works will look when finished.
- (B) Watercolor artists tend to make mistakes more often than do oil paint artists.
- (C) Unexpected mistakes happen with great frequency for even the best artists.
- (D) A mistake made with watercolors requires the artist to change the painting somehow.

Summarizing   **Complete the summary by using the words in the box.**

| invented by Jan van Eyck   about making mistakes   watercolors are not   their desired results |

The professor notes that watercolors were first utilized by primitive men. As for oil paints, they were used many centuries ago by the Greeks and Japanese, but modern oil paints were _____ in the fifteenth century. Oil paints are opaque while _____ . This affects how the artists must make their paintings. Oil painters can eventually get _____ , but watercolor painters have to be careful _____ . So they may have to improvise while making their paintings.

02-62

Listen to part of a lecture in an art history class.

TYPE **5**   What aspect of James Abbott McNeill Whistler does the professor mainly discuss?

- Ⓐ His early life
- Ⓑ His work *Whistler's Mother*
- Ⓒ The styles he used
- Ⓓ His most famous works

TYPE **6**   According to the professor, what did Whistler do in St. Petersburg, Russia?

- Ⓐ He held his first exhibition.
- Ⓑ He began taking painting lessons.
- Ⓒ He set up an art studio.
- Ⓓ He first saw Japanese art.

TYPE **7**   What will the professor probably do next?

- Ⓐ Talk about some aspects of Japanese art
- Ⓑ Discuss *Whistler's Mother* again
- Ⓒ Start talk about a different artist
- Ⓓ Show some more of Whistler's works

TYPE **8**   Listen again to part of the lecture. Then answer the question.
Why does the student say this: 🎧

- Ⓐ To express her surprise
- Ⓑ To make a joke
- Ⓒ To say the other student is wrong
- Ⓓ To ask for clarification

Summarizing   Complete the summary by using the words in the box.

| Japanese art   blue and light green   a professional artist   American Gilded Age |

The professor shows a painting, and a student identifies it as *Whistler's Mother*. The professor says that it was painted by James Abbott McNeill Whistler, an artist from the _____ . Whistler started taking art lessons in St. Petersburg, Russia, and decided to become _____ . His first exhibited work was *La Mere Gerard*. He often used _____ colors. He was influenced by _____ due to the monochromatic colors, cropped figures, and economical way the Japanese painted. His etchings clearly show this influence.

Mastering **Question Types**
with Lectures & Conversations

TYPE • **1** Gist-Content   TYPE • **2** Understanding Organization   TYPE • **3** Connecting Content   TYPE • **4** Speaker's Attitude

Listen to part of a lecture in a history of music class.

02-63

TYPE ① What aspect of music does the professor mainly discuss?

- Ⓐ The importance of musical instruments
- Ⓑ The role of music during ancient times
- Ⓒ The relationship of music with religion
- Ⓓ The first musical instruments to be used

TYPE ② Why does the professor discuss the Bible?

- Ⓐ To name some of her favorite psalms in it
- Ⓑ To describe what it mentions about music
- Ⓒ To show that music can be used for good
- Ⓓ To explain how music can elevate the soul

TYPE ③ Based on the information in the lecture, do the statements refer to the uses of music for religious purposes or secular purposes?
Click in the correct box for each sentence.

	Religious Purposes	Secular Purposes
1 Was sung by people doing manual labor		
2 Was used for various rites		
3 Was performed for street dancers		
4 Was able to inspire people		

TYPE ④ What is the professor's opinion of the first musical instruments?

- Ⓐ She finds them primitive.
- Ⓑ They make poor music.
- Ⓒ They are very well made.
- Ⓓ She appreciates them.

Summarizing   Complete the summary by using the words in the box.

biblical psalms	secular society	the human brain	both good and evil

The professor comments that biomusicologists believe _____ is wired for music. Vocals were important to ancient music. Music was used in many early religious ceremonies. _____ are the earliest known songs in Western culture. They were used in religious rites. The Bible notes that music can be used for _____. For good, it can inspire people and elevate their souls. Ancient music also had a role in _____, such as being used by manual laborers and street dancers.

02-64

Listen to part of a conversation between a student and a professor.

TYPE 5 Why does the student visit the professor?

- (A) To find out what time he needs to perform
- (B) To sign up for a music recital
- (C) To get permission to attend an audition
- (D) To apologize for not signing up for the recital

TYPE 6 According to the professor, what does the student need to do?

- (A) Show up for the tryouts by one thirty
- (B) Get the judges' permission to audition
- (C) Find out more about the music recital
- (D) Practice more until he improves

TYPE 7 What can be inferred about the professor?

- (A) She is a professional musician.
- (B) She teaches the student in one of her classes.
- (C) She assists with extracurricular activities.
- (D) She enjoys having the student as an advisee.

TYPE 8 Listen again to part of the conversation. Then answer the question.
What is the purpose of the student's response?

- (A) To show that he is serious about attending the audition
- (B) To explain why he missed the registration deadline
- (C) To try to understand what the professor means
- (D) To beg the professor to reconsider her decision

Summarizing Complete the summary by using the words in the box.

| she is a judge   try out last   an upcoming music recital   a second chance |

The student visits the professor to talk about an audition for _____. He never signed up for
a tryout time, and the auditions begin at one thirty. The professor says _____ at the tryouts.
The student asks to be permitted to audition. The professor tells him to show up at one thirty. If any student
misses the tryouts, he can take that student's spot. Otherwise, he can _____. The student
thanks the professor for giving him _____.

Mastering **Topics** with Lectures

Listen to part of a lecture in an art class.

02-65

Chinese Ceramics

Characteristics:		Firing Temperatures:
	→	Region:
		Period Made:

---

1 What aspect of Chinese ceramics does the professor mainly discuss?

- (A) The process commonly used to make them
- (B) The styles utilized to design early ceramics
- (C) Porcelain and how it was first created
- (D) The manner in which they are categorized

2 In the lecture, the professor describes a number of facts about Chinese ceramics. Indicate whether each of the following is a fact about Chinese ceramics.
Click in the correct box for each sentence.

	Fact	Not a Fact
1 Was used exclusively by the upper classes		
2 Has existed longer than any other ceramics industry in the world		
3 Can be divided into ceramics from two separate regions		
4 Was first created by making pots fired at very high temperatures		

3 Listen again to part of the lecture. Then answer the question.
What does the professor imply when he says this: 🎧

- (A) The students are not good at taking notes.
- (B) He used several technical terms in his definition.
- (C) The material he just discussed is difficult.
- (D) Several students are raising their hands to ask questions.

Summarizing Fill in the blanks to complete the summary.

The professor notes that China has the world's _____. The Chinese mostly made ceramics to serve as vessels to hold things. There are three ways to divide Chinese ceramics: by _____ they are fired at, by the locations of the materials used to make them, and by the era when they were made. Depending on the heat used, _____ can be made. Chinese ceramics are often either northern Chinese or southern Chinese. And the designs used on them _____.

Listen to part of a lecture in a music class.

02-66

Hip-Hop Music

Origins:

Influences:

Relationship with Rap Music:

1 Why does the professor discuss gangsta rap?

- (A) To talk about a new genre of hip-hop
- (B) To criticize the artists who perform it
- (C) To mention the backlash against it
- (D) To introduce the music the class will listen to

2 Based on the information in the lecture, do the statements refer to the influence on hip-hop from West Africa or from Jamaica?
Click in the correct box for each sentence.

	West Africa	Jamaica
1 Storytellers chanted in singsong voices.		
2 People used sound systems in place of live music.		
3 Slaves would make field calls while they were working.		
4 People had verbal sparring contests with one another.		

3 Listen again to part of the lecture. Then answer the question.
What does the student mean when he says this:

- (A) He is undecided about the question he just asked.
- (B) He wants the professor to state her opinion.
- (C) He believes that hip-hop and rap are identical.
- (D) There is not enough information available on that topic.

Summarizing Fill in the blanks to complete the summary.

The professor states that hip-hop began _____ in the 1970s and then spread across America and the world. It was initially an African-American genre, but people of all races enjoy it now. _____ are two similar genres. Singsong chants and field calls and responses from _____ were one influence on hip-hop. Jamaicans using sound systems instead of _____ was another. One new genre of hip-hop is gangsta rap. But there was a backlash against it because of the nature of its lyrics.

Mastering **Topics** with Lectures

Listen to part of a lecture in a literature class.

02-67

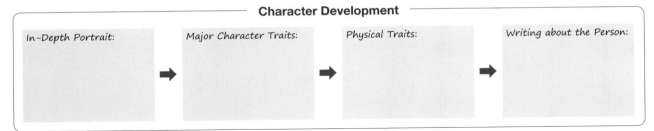

Character Development

| In-Depth Portrait: | Major Character Traits: | Physical Traits: | Writing about the Person: |

1   Why does the professor explain the need to determine a person's character traits?

    Ⓐ It will show the audience what the person looks like.

    Ⓑ Doing this will let the readers become attached to the character.

    Ⓒ Making the character's responses believable is important.

    Ⓓ It is necessary to make the individual a sympathetic character.

2   How is the discussion organized?

    Ⓐ The professor describes the traits of some famous characters in literature.

    Ⓑ The professor lists some important points and then expands on them.

    Ⓒ The professor tells the students some methods that they should avoid using.

    Ⓓ The professor asks questions that he expects the students to answer.

3   What will the professor probably do next?

    Ⓐ Make the students do a writing assignment

    Ⓑ Have the students submit their homework

    Ⓒ Dismiss the class for the day

    Ⓓ Have the students repeat the information he gave them

Summarizing   Fill in the blanks to complete the summary.

The professor mentions that writers must _____ in their stories to make them realistic. First, they can create _____ of the characters. These can include a character's background, career, family, interests, and goals. Next are the person's major character traits. These make a character's responses both _____. Physical traits should be developed, too. When writing, the author should not tell the readers what _____. Instead, the character's actions as well as dialogue can show readers what that person is like.

Mastering **Topics** with Converastions

Listen to part of a conversation between a student and a computer services office employee.

02-68

Service Encounter

Student's Problem:		Man's Response:

Student's Observation:		Man's Discovery:

---

1 Why does the student visit the computer services office?

- Ⓐ To apply for an additional email account
- Ⓑ To pay a fine that she owes the office
- Ⓒ To learn why she cannot access her account
- Ⓓ To see if the man there can fix her computer

2 According to the man, what is the student's problem?

- Ⓐ She has several library books that are overdue.
- Ⓑ Her account has been mixed up with another student's.
- Ⓒ She is typing her password incorrectly.
- Ⓓ The school's computer system is malfunctioning.

3 Why does the man ask the student for her school ID number?

- Ⓐ To access her account
- Ⓑ To clear her records
- Ⓒ To record the fine she just paid
- Ⓓ To confirm her identity

Summarizing Fill in the blanks to complete the summary.

The student visits the computer services office with a problem. When she tries to log in to her account, she gets an " _____ " message. The man tells her that she has _____ that she owes a fine on. The student claims she has not checked out a book that semester. The man gets _____ and learns the school has two students named Janet Lincoln. The other one has the overdue book. The man tells the student he will _____ with her account.

Listen to part of a lecture in an art history class.

02-69

Art History

1 What is the lecture mainly about?

    Ⓐ The characteristics of two separate types of architecture

    Ⓑ The manner in which Renaissance architects designed cathedrals

    Ⓒ The process of building a cathedral from the ground up

    Ⓓ An overview of the history of Renaissance architecture

2 Why does the professor explain Gothic architecture?

    Ⓐ To contrast it with Renaissance architecture

    Ⓑ To impress the students with his knowledge

    Ⓒ To show its similarity to ancient Greek architecture

    Ⓓ To note its influence on architecture in Italy

3 According to the professor, what did Gothic cathedrals often look like?

    Ⓐ They were based on mathematical precision.

    Ⓑ They had both high walls and tall spires.

    Ⓒ They displayed many statues and stained-glass windows.

    Ⓓ They resembled ancient Roman buildings.

4 Why does the professor tell the students about Florence Cathedral?

    Ⓐ To cite it as an ideal Renaissance cathedral

    Ⓑ To emphasize how long it took to build the cathedral

    Ⓒ To focus on the flying buttresses used in the cathedral

    Ⓓ To discuss a cathedral built in two separate styles

5 What can be inferred about Florence Cathedral?

    Ⓐ It contains mostly Renaissance images.

    Ⓑ It is a very high building.

    Ⓒ It was expensive to build.

    Ⓓ It is no longer standing.

6 What will the professor probably do next?

    Ⓐ Show another slide

    Ⓑ Wait for an answer

    Ⓒ Start reading from the book

    Ⓓ Continue his lecture

Listen to part of conversation between a student and a professor.

1   Why does the student visit the professor?

   Ⓐ To discuss a couple of historical figures
   Ⓑ To request that she get some bonus points
   Ⓒ To meet him for their scheduled appointment
   Ⓓ To show him some mistakes in the book

2   What is the professor's opinion of the publisher of the textbook?

   Ⓐ He thinks the mistakes it printed are understandable.
   Ⓑ He will never purchase books from that publisher again.
   Ⓒ He is upset by the mistakes that the publisher made.
   Ⓓ He is embarrassed that he bought the book from the publisher.

3   Why does the student mention Julius Caesar?

   Ⓐ He is one of her favorite people from history.
   Ⓑ The errors in the textbook concern his life.
   Ⓒ She needs to ask the professor some questions about him.
   Ⓓ She is writing a paper about his military background.

4   What is the professor going to do next?

   Ⓐ Schedule a meeting with the student
   Ⓑ Give the student the correct dates
   Ⓒ Call the publisher of the book
   Ⓓ Attend a staff meeting

5   Listen again to part of the conversation. Then answer the question.
   Why does the professor say this: 🎧

   Ⓐ To pay the student a compliment
   Ⓑ To complain about the textbook
   Ⓒ To indicate his happiness with the student's paper
   Ⓓ To give the student some career advice

- **aesthetically** (adv) in an artistic or pleasing manner
- **backlash** (n) a repercussion; a response
- **captivate** (v) to amaze; to entrance
- **century** (n) a period of 100 years
- **ceramics** (n) pottery
- **ceremony** (n) a rite; a ritual
- **chant** (n) an intonation; a song in which the words are spoken
- **clay** (n) a type of earth often used to make pottery
- **convey** (v) to express; to suggest; to communicate
- **craftsman** (n) an artisan
- **craftsmanship** (n) expertise; talent; skill
- **critical** (adj) important
- **cropped** (adj) having unwanted parts cut off or shortened
- **descendant** (n) offspring; a successor
- **desired** (adj) wanted
- **dialogue** (n) conversation; spoken lines between two or more people
- **diversify** (v) to spread; to expand; to make diverse
- **dominate** (v) to rule; to control
- **earthen** (adj) made from earth
- **economical** (adj) avoiding waste; efficient
- **elevate** (v) to raise; to lift
- **emotional** (adj) relating to feelings
- **enchanting** (adj) delightful; charming
- **enroll** (v) to sign up for a class
- **erect** (v) to put up; to build; to construct
- **etching** (n) an engraving; a print
- **exhibit** (v) to display; to show
- **facade** (n) a front wall
- **fire** (v) to heat
- **gallery** (n) a place where art is displayed
- **genre** (n) a category; a type; a kind
- **imitate** (v) to copy
- **improvise** (v) to adapt; to change; to make something new
- **incorporate** (v) to use; to utilize; to include
- **in-depth** (adj) detailed
- **indicator** (n) a sign; a market
- **influential** (adj) significant; important
- **inner-city** (adj) metropolitan
- **innocent** (adj) pure; naive
- **lyrics** (n) the words to a song
- **mainstream** (adj) normal; conventional; typical
- **majority** (n) the most; the bulk
- **mannerism** (n) a characteristic; a trait

- **monochromatic** (adj) of or having one color
- **motivate** (v) to inspire
- **opaque** (adj) unclear; obscure; thick
- **originate** (v) to be created; to start
- **perfect** (v) to make perfect or ideal
- **pervert** (v) to distort; to change the purpose or use of in a negative manner
- **pigment** (n) a color; a coloring
- **plantation** (n) a large farm, often where slaves were kept
- **porcelain** (n) an expensive white form of ceramics
- **portrait** (n) a picture of a person
- **portrayal** (n) a depiction
- **pose** (v) to get in a certain position for a picture or painting
- **poverty** (n) poorness; the state of having little or no money
- **primitive** (adj) basic; simple
- **professional** (adj) done in order to get paid or to make a living
- **proportion** (n) a ratio
- **prose** (n) any writing that is not poetry
- **psalm** (n) a religious hymn or song
- **psychological** (adj) relating to the mind
- **realistic** (adj) practical; sensible; pragmatic
- **relic** (n) an artifact
- **reveal** (v) to show; to display
- **rite** (n) a ceremony; a ritual
- **roughly** (adv) approximately; about
- **singsong** (adj) monotonous
- **solely** (adv) only
- **sparring** (adj) fighting
- **spire** (n) a steeple
- **stability** (n) steadiness; constancy
- **storyteller** (n) a bard; a narrator
- **symbolize** (v) to stand for; to represent
- **symmetry** (n) balance; evenness
- **talent** (n) skill; ability
- **tendency** (n) a habit; a custom
- **text** (n) a written work, such as a book
- **transparency** (n) openness; clearness
- **troupe** (n) a group of performers
- **unpredictable** (adj) random; changeable
- **uplift** (v) to elevate; to raise
- **verse** (n) poetry
- **vessel** (n) a container

⛩ Choose the word with the closest meaning to each highlighted word or phrase.

1   There, his parents recognized his talent for art.
   (A) considered
   (B) appreciated
   (C) expressed
   (D) noticed

2   I require an in-depth description of exactly what you plan to do next week.
   (A) approved
   (B) hasty
   (C) outstanding
   (D) detailed

3   The storyteller knows how to keep everyone's attention while he speaks.
   (A) linguist
   (B) narrator
   (C) professor
   (D) observer

4   We use those vessels to hold all kinds of different objects.
   (A) rafts
   (B) rooms
   (C) containers
   (D) warehouses

5   A true craftsman takes pride in the work that he does.
   (A) scientist
   (B) electrician
   (C) artisan
   (D) builder

6   The archaeologist found several ancient Egyptian relics at the dig site.
   (A) artifacts
   (B) texts
   (C) tomes
   (D) gems

7   Try to incorporate several types of materials in your design.
   (A) prepare
   (B) remember
   (C) avoid
   (D) include

8   The artist was known for using many different pigments in her works.
   (A) textures
   (B) colors
   (C) brushstrokes
   (D) ideas

9   Her music always uplifts our spirits and improves our moods.
   (A) affects
   (B) touches
   (C) elevates
   (D) passes by

10 Eric lost his entire fortune when his company suddenly went bankrupt.
   (A) wealth
   (B) fame
   (C) respect
   (D) job

⛩ Match each word with the correct definition.

11 achieve   •
12 portrait   •
13 primarily   •
14 role   •
15 prized   •

• (A) a duty; a job; a part
• (B) mostly; mainly
• (C) valued; desired
• (D) to attain
• (E) a picture; a description

Part **B**

Chapter 08 Arts 2 | **Conversations**

city planning • art history • literature • music • industrial design • visual arts • crafts • architecture • film • photography

Mastering **Question Types**
with Lectures & Conversations

TYPE • **1** Gist-Content   TYPE • **2** Understanding Organization   TYPE • **3** Connecting Content   TYPE • **4** Speaker's Attitude

02-71

Listen to part of a lecture in an art history class.

TYPE 1 What aspect of the Harlem Renaissance does the professor mainly discuss?

- Ⓐ Its founding and early years
- Ⓑ Its influence on African-American culture
- Ⓒ The different names that people gave it
- Ⓓ The most famous writers of that period

TYPE 2 How does the professor organize the information on the causes of the Harlem Renaissance that she presents to the class?

- Ⓐ She mentions the causes after she describes the effects that they produced.
- Ⓑ She makes a list of what she considers the most important points.
- Ⓒ She connects it with the entire situation in the United States at the time.
- Ⓓ She describes the economic situations of some individual people.

TYPE 3 Based on the information in the lecture, do the following sentences refer to the causes or effects of the Harlem Renaissance?
Click in the correct box for each sentence.

	Cause	Effect
1 African-Americans became proud of being black.		
2 Many African-Americans abandoned the rural South.		
3 African-Americans attempted to become more unified.		
4 The economy in parts of the country became depressed.		

TYPE 4 What is the professor's opinion of Langston Hughes?

- Ⓐ She likes some of his writing.
- Ⓑ She disagrees with his politics.
- Ⓒ She thinks he was the best writer of the 1900s.
- Ⓓ She believes he should have been a novelist.

Summarizing **Complete the summary by using the words in the box.**

| the Great Depression   were discriminated against   literature, art, and music   a more unified culture |

The Harlem Renaissance began in 1918 after World War I and lasted until _____.
It started because Southern African-Americans began moving north to look for economic opportunities.
The Harlem Renaissance was the reawakening of the cultural spirit of African-Americans. It affected
_____. Langston Hughes and Claude McKay were two notable poets from this time.
The writers focused on how African-Americans _____. They also tried to create
_____ around African-Americans. They wanted this to be a positive force.

02-72

Listen to part of a lecture in a film class.

TYPE 5   What aspect of montage does the professor mainly discuss?
- Ⓐ Which emotions it is expected to create in the audience
- Ⓑ How some filmmakers made use of it in the past
- Ⓒ When it was first utilized by movie directors
- Ⓓ What the most famous example of it in a movie is

TYPE 6   What is the example of montage in *Strike* that the professor mentions?
- Ⓐ People and cattle being killed simultaneously
- Ⓑ People protesting the government while politicians campaign
- Ⓒ Audience members watching a movie as it is being filmed
- Ⓓ A woman being murdered by a man trying to stab her

TYPE 7   What will the professor probably do next?
- Ⓐ Show the students some more film scenes
- Ⓑ Have the students think of some examples of montage
- Ⓒ Ask the students how they feel about montage
- Ⓓ Let the students take a short break from class

TYPE 8   Listen again to part of the lecture. Then answer the question.
What can be inferred from the professor's response to the student?
- Ⓐ The student must have read the book before class.
- Ⓑ She fully agrees with the student's definition.
- Ⓒ The student is most likely a film major.
- Ⓓ There is nothing else for her to tell the class about montage.

Summarizing   Complete the summary by using the words in the box.

enrage their audiences   strikers and cattle   form a new one   the woman is murdered

The professor defines montage as the putting together of different scenes to _____ .
He says that Russian filmmakers began using it in the 1910s for political purposes. They were trying to
_____ . Sergei Eisenstein used montage effectively in *Strike* in 1925. It showed scenes of
_____ being killed simultaneously. He then mentions that another famous montage is from
Psycho. It is the scene where _____ . The professor says that Alfred Hitchcock often used
montage to create suspense.

Mastering **Question Types**
with Lectures & Conversations

TYPE • **1** Gist-Content   TYPE • **2** Understanding Organization   TYPE • **3** Connecting Content   TYPE • **4** Speaker's Attitude

Listen to part of a lecture in a musicology class.

02-73

TYPE 1 What is the lecture mainly about?

(A) The capabilities of musical synthesizers

(B) Wendy Carlos and her relationship with the synthesizer

(C) The differences between synthesizers and pianos

(D) The types of music that synthesizers are used to create

TYPE 2 Why does the professor mention saxophone-style synthesizers?

(A) To prove that not all synthesizers are keyboards

(B) To claim that they produce sounds like real musical instruments

(C) To tell the students about the latest in synthesizer technology

(D) To complain about their overuse by some musicians

TYPE 3 What is the likely outcome of putting on a concert with a synthesizer?

(A) An electric failure could lead to problems during the concert.

(B) The audience will become upset since the music is not live.

(C) The music will sound like it does when it is being recorded.

(D) The singers can perform with the musicians more easily.

TYPE 4 Listen again to part of the lecture. Then answer the question.
What does the professor mean when she says this: 🎧

(A) She wants the student to play the synthesizer for the class.

(B) She would like for the student to answer her question.

(C) She believes that the student is not paying attention.

(D) She feels that the student does not know the answer.

Summarizing **Complete the summary by using the words in the box.**

a wide variety of sounds   a full orchestra or band   musical instruments   guitar synthesizers

A student identifies the music the class heard as coming from a synthesizer. A synthesizer is a musical instrument that can produce _____. It can make complex sounds produced from a variety of _____. But they are not always keyboards. Nowadays, there are both _____ and saxophone-style synthesizers. Wendy Carlos was the first person to use the synthesizer for modern-day music. Now, many musicians use it since they do not need _____ to accompany them when they perform.

02-74

Listen to part of a conversation between a student and a gymnasium employee.

TYPE 5 Why does the student visit the gymnasium?

(A) To play squash with one of her friends
(B) To report for her work shift
(C) To ask about booking a room there
(D) To attend a class that she is taking

TYPE 6 What does the student say she is going to do?

(A) Take part in a competition
(B) Try out for a sports team
(C) Work out to get in shape
(D) Practice yoga with a friend

TYPE 7 What can be inferred about the gym?

(A) Students are hired to do various jobs at it.
(B) Its facilities can be used by faculty members.
(C) People must pay money to use certain rooms in it.
(D) It closes late in the evening most days of the week.

TYPE 8 Listen again to part of the conversation. Then answer the question.
What does the student imply when she says this: 🎧

(A) She wants to book a room for this evening.
(B) She is not happy a room is unavailable now.
(C) She needs to eat dinner before she works out.
(D) She plans to return with a friend in the evening.

Summarizing Complete the summary by using the words in the box.

| her ID card | making multiple bookings | visits the gymnasium | mirrors and padded floors |

The student _____ and asks the man about booking a room. Because she is
a full-time student, she can do that. She is competing in a dance contest and wants a room with
_____ to practice in. There is a room available now, but she plans to return in the evening.
She asks about _____, and the man responds that she can do that. She then gives the
man _____ in order to book a room for this evening.

Listen to part of a lecture in an industrial design class.

02-75

┌─────────────────────────── Albert Kahn ───────────────────────────┐
│   │
│ His Life: ➡   His Work: │
│   │
└───┘

1 What aspect of Albert Kahn does the professor mainly discuss?

　Ⓐ The buildings that he designed in Detroit

　Ⓑ The various types of work that he did

　Ⓒ The reasons why he became an architect

　Ⓓ His early life in the world of architecture

2 According to the professor, what best describes Albert Kahn's style?

　Ⓐ He created many abstract designs.

　Ⓑ He had an easily recognizable style.

　Ⓒ He preferred to use exotic materials.

　Ⓓ His designs were quite practical.

3 Listen again to part of the lecture. Then answer the question.
Why does the professor say this: 🎧

　Ⓐ He forgot what he was talking about.

　Ⓑ He does not remember an important fact.

　Ⓒ He cannot recall where he is going.

　Ⓓ He thinks he needs to finish the lecture.

Summarizing Fill in the blanks to complete the summary.

Albert Kahn was a famous designer of industrial buildings. He lacked a formal education but worked at
an architectural firm as a boy, which started him in architecture. Many of Kahn's works are in Michigan,
particularly Detroit. He used ＿＿＿＿＿＿＿＿＿＿＿＿＿＿ and basic materials and did not overspend. He had
no ＿＿＿＿＿＿＿＿＿＿＿＿＿＿ but did what was needed to finish a job. Kahn often got work from abroad,
including from ＿＿＿＿＿＿＿＿＿＿＿＿＿＿. Many of his buildings were used to manufacture war material during
＿＿＿＿＿＿＿＿＿＿＿＿＿＿.

Mastering **Topics** with Lectures

Listen to part of a lecture in an art class.

02-76

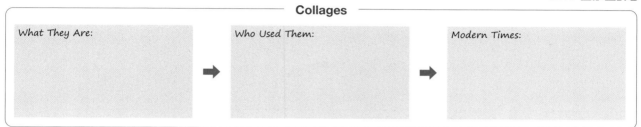

Collages

| What They Are: | Who Used Them: | Modern Times: |

1 What can be inferred about the professor?

   Ⓐ She is unfamiliar with much of the history of collages.

   Ⓑ She enjoys the works made during the Dada art movement.

   Ⓒ She gives the students grades on everything they do in class.

   Ⓓ She believes that collages should be considered art.

2 Why does the professor mention Picasso?

   Ⓐ To note his role in legitimizing collages

   Ⓑ To say that his collages sell for millions of dollars

   Ⓒ To state that he worked with Georges Braque

   Ⓓ To associate him with the Dada art movement

3 Listen again to part of the lecture. Then answer the question.
What does the professor imply when she says this: 🎧

   Ⓐ The students should understand how to make a collage.

   Ⓑ Some materials used in collages are rarer than others.

   Ⓒ She has not mentioned all of the materials used in collages.

   Ⓓ There is nothing more for her to say about collages.

Summarizing Fill in the blanks to complete the summary.

The professor describes collages as an art form that uses many things to make a single work of art.
Artists _____ things to paper, cardboard, or canvas. Collages were used in China,
Japan, and medieval Europe. In the 1800s, collage-making became a hobby for many people. In 1912,
_____ began using the collage. He worked on them together with Georges Braque.
Artists in _____ used collages as well. The collage later came to be accepted as
_____ .

Listen to part of a lecture in an art history class.

02-77

Paracas and Nazca Art

Paracas Art:

➡️

Nazca Art:

---

1 Why does the professor explain the burial practices of the Paracas?

- Ⓐ To mention how they were different from those of the Nazca
- Ⓑ To claim that the Paracas were the only South Americans to use that method
- Ⓒ To account for the good condition of the artifacts that have been found
- Ⓓ To talk about why many Paracas artifacts have death motifs

2 What are the Nazca lines?

- Ⓐ Lines that were made by aliens long ago
- Ⓑ Naturally forming lines in the Nazca's territory
- Ⓒ Lines that create large shapes in the desert
- Ⓓ Lines that were used as roads by the Nazca

3 Based on the information in the lecture, do the following sentences refer to Paracas art or Nazca art? Click in the correct box for each sentence.

	Paracas Art	Nazca Art
1 Their pottery was colored first and then fired.		
2 They made double spouts on their pottery.		
3 They made single spouts on their pottery.		
4 Their pottery has some cat-like shapes.		

Summarizing Fill in the blanks to complete the summary.

In pre-Columbian times in the area in modern-day Peru, there were two main groups of people: the Paracas and the Nazca. Much Paracas art is well preserved. Many artworks are _____ textiles. Much of their pottery has cat-like shapes on it. The Nazca also made _____. Their pots had double spouts, but the Paracas' pots _____. The Nazca's textiles resembled those of the Paracas. The Nazca also made _____ that show various shapes. No one knows their purpose.

Mastering **Topics** with Conversations

Listen to part of a conversation between a student and a professor.

02-78

─── Office Hours ───

Student's Problem:		Professor's Response:
	➡	
Student's Question:	↙	Professor's Response:
	➡	

1 Why does the student visit the professor?

- Ⓐ To submit her short paper
- Ⓑ To ask him some questions
- Ⓒ To inquire about the midterm exam
- Ⓓ To get the professor's class notes

2 What can be inferred about the professor?

- Ⓐ He has been working hard all day long.
- Ⓑ He must attend a meeting in a few minutes.
- Ⓒ He enjoys speaking with his students.
- Ⓓ He does not give many assignments in his classes.

3 Listen again to part of the conversation. Then answer the question.
What is the purpose of the professor's response?

- Ⓐ To grant the student's request
- Ⓑ To tell her that he heard her the first time
- Ⓒ To indicate that he has a hearing problem
- Ⓓ To ask her to speak loudly

Summarizing Fill in the blanks to complete the summary.

The professor asks the student if she is waiting to talk to him, and she says yes. The student apologizes for missing class and offers to show the professor _____ . Then, she asks the professor _____ he gave the class. The student wants to know more about the paper the professor assigned. The professor tells her that they must write about a topic that was covered in class during _____ . And the paper should be about _____ long.

02-79

Listen to part of a lecture in an art history class.

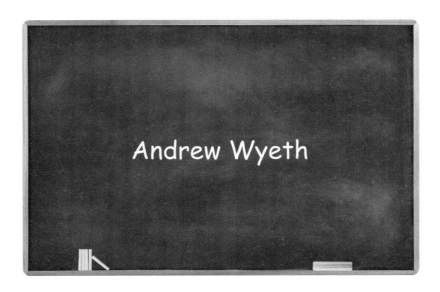

Andrew Wyeth

1 What is the lecture mainly about?

    (A) The influence of Andrew Wyeth on modern painters

    (B) *Christina's World* and the Helga paintings

    (C) Andrew Wyeth's relationship with art critics

    (D) The life and paintings of Andrew Wyeth

2 According to the professor, what do some of Andrew Wyeth's detractors say about his artwork?

    (A) They claim there is nothing special about his paintings.

    (B) They believe that he used too many bright colors.

    (C) They feel that some of his work is too abstract.

    (D) They dislike the appearances of the models that he hired.

3 How is the discussion organized?

    (A) The professor focuses primarily on Andrew Wyeth's most famous works.

    (B) The professor introduces a chronological selection of Andrew Wyeth's paintings.

    (C) The professor asks the students to look at some pictures in the book while she speaks.

    (D) The professor provides criticism of several famous paintings that Andrew Wyeth made.

4 Based on the information in the lecture, do the following sentences refer to *Christina's World* or the Helga paintings?
Click in the correct box for each sentence.

	Christina's World	The Helga Paintings
1 Contained some nudity		
2 Featured a woman with a disability		
3 Depicted a woman with red hair		
4 Took a long time to complete		

5 Listen again to part of the lecture. Then answer the question.
What does the professor imply when she says this: 🎧

    (A) She dislikes having only art history majors in her class.

    (B) Andrew Wyeth was somewhat visually impaired.

    (C) Andrew Wyeth avoided the abstract style of painting.

    (D) One of her favorite artists is Andrew Wyeth.

6 Listen again to part of the lecture. Then answer the question.
What does the professor mean when she says this: 🎧

    (A) It took a long time to convince Andrew Wyeth to exhibit the Helga paintings.

    (B) There was a lot of publicity surrounding the Helga paintings.

    (C) People were upset because some Helga paintings were nudes.

    (D) Andrew Wyeth preferred to paint with watercolors.

Listen to part of a conversation between a student and a housing office employee.

1 Why does the student visit the housing office?

   (A) To complain about the amount of noise near her dormitory

   (B) To ask to be assigned a new roommate

   (C) To request a room in a different dormitory

   (D) To find out whom she will be rooming with in the summer

2 In the conversation, the man makes several suggestions to solve the student's problem. Indicate whether each of the following is a suggestion that the man makes.
Click in the correct box for each sentence.

	Suggestion	Not a Suggestion
1 Select a triple room in a dormitory away from the noise		
2 Go to the library to study		
3 Live somewhere off campus during the summer		
4 Ask her roommate not to invite students into their room		

3 Why does the man ask the student the reason she does not want a double room?

   (A) To determine her opposition to having a roommate

   (B) To find a weak point in her argument so that he can convince her to move

   (C) To justify letting her move into a single room elsewhere

   (D) To write her answer on the complaint form he is filing

4 What does the man imply about the school?

   (A) It is in the middle of erecting several new buildings on campus.

   (B) It does not consider the housing needs of its students.

   (C) It has few places available for students to live.

   (D) It has more students than usual on campus in the summer.

5 What can be inferred about the student?

   (A) She needs to improve her grades in her major.

   (B) She has no interest in socializing during the summer.

   (C) She cannot afford to move to a place off campus.

   (D) She frequently complains about her housing situations.

- **accept** (v) to approve; to consider
- **admirer** (n) a person who likes someone or something else
- **appeal** (n) an attraction
- **architect** (n) a person who designs buildings
- **attach** (v) to connect one thing to another
- **audience** (n) the people watching a performance
- **canvas** (n) a type of material upon which artists often paint
- **central** (adj) major; most important; main
- **class** (n) a division; a ranking
- **clipping** (n) something cut out from a newspaper or magazine
- **coin** (v) to make something new, often a word
- **commission** (n) an order to make or design something
- **commonplace** (adj) ordinary; usual; regular
- **contemporary** (adj) modern; current; recent
- **continuous** (adj) ongoing
- **convey** (v) to communicate; to express; to spread a message
- **credit** (v) to acknowledge; to praise
- **criticize** (v) to point out the faults of
- **decade** (n) a period of ten years
- **depressed** (adj) low; miserable
- **despise** (v) to hate; to dislike very much
- **detractor** (n) a critic; a person who does not like someone or something else
- **discriminate** (v) to show favoritism; to treat a person poorly for being different from others
- **distinctive** (adj) unique; individual
- **downtown** (n) the center of a city
- **dull** (adj) drab; muted; boring
- **elaborate** (adj) complex; complicated
- **enrage** (v) to become very angry
- **entitle** (v) to give a title to
- **ethnic** (adj) racial; national
- **experiment** (v) to practice
- **exhibition** (n) a display; an exhibit; a show
- **extant** (adj) existing
- **excel** (v) to do very well
- **filmmaker** (n) a person who makes films; a director
- **generate** (v) to make; to create
- **glue** (v) to attach with glue or paste
- **handmade** (adj) made by a person, not a machine
- **illustrator** (n) a person who makes drawings or illustrations
- **impressive** (adj) remarkable; outstanding

- **incite** (v) to make angry; to anger; to arouse
- **influx** (n) an invasion; an arrival
- **literary** (adj) relating to literature
- **manipulate** (v) to control; to direct; to influence
- **master** (n) an expert; a professional
- **mimic** (v) to imitate
- **novelist** (n) a person who writes novels
- **poet** (n) a person who writes poetry
- **pose** (v) to stand or sit for a picture or drawing; to remain in a certain position
- **potential** (adj) possible
- **practical** (adj) sensible; reasonable
- **persevered** (adj) saved
- **pottery** (n) ceramics; stoneware; earthenware
- **prominent** (adj) well-known; famous
- **realize** (v) to recognize; to notice
- **reawaken** (v) to revive; to renew
- **reputation** (n) a name; a status; a standing
- **reveal** (v) to show; to point out
- **revolution** (n) a rebellion; a fight against authority
- **scrapbook** (n) an album; a book of memories
- **shock** (v) to surprise; to stun
- **site** (n) a location; a place
- **slaughter** (v) to kill a large number of people or animals, often in a bloody manner
- **societal** (adj) relating to society
- **specialize** (v) to focus on one particular skill or field
- **spirit** (n) heart; soul
- **stage** (n) a raised platform on which people perform for others
- **stylized** (adj) formal
- **suspense** (n) tension; anticipation; expectation
- **synthesize** (v) to combine; to blend; to bring together
- **talented** (adj) skilled
- **technique** (n) a style; a method; a manner
- **textile** (n) a kind of fabric; cloth
- **tomb** (n) a place where a person is buried
- **united** (adj) together
- **upheaval** (n) a disturbance; turmoil
- **vision** (n) an idea; an image
- **weave** (v) to sew thread or yarn together
- **widespread** (adj) common; general
- **worship** (v) to pray to someone or something as if it were a god
- **wrap** (v) to cover; to enclose

✍ Choose the word with the closest meaning to each highlighted word or phrase.

1 The central point of her argument was found to be incorrect.

- Ⓐ primary
- Ⓑ ultimate
- Ⓒ damaging
- Ⓓ distinctive

2 We were shocked to learn that the time of the game had changed.

- Ⓐ disappointed
- Ⓑ surprised
- Ⓒ upset
- Ⓓ enraged

3 That famous filmmaker is going to release a new movie next month.

- Ⓐ actor
- Ⓑ cameraman
- Ⓒ editor
- Ⓓ director

4 Many contemporary artists never become famous during their lives.

- Ⓐ abstract
- Ⓑ hardworking
- Ⓒ current
- Ⓓ amateur

5 Dr. Taylor is one of the most talented men at the hospital.

- Ⓐ noteworthy
- Ⓑ considerate
- Ⓒ practical
- Ⓓ skilled

6 What is the appeal of snowboarding? I don't know why he likes it so much.

- Ⓐ danger
- Ⓑ attraction
- Ⓒ theory
- Ⓓ credit

7 Jason is a prominent member of the community who knows many people.

- Ⓐ well-known
- Ⓑ wealthy
- Ⓒ popular
- Ⓓ miserly

8 The union leaders are trying to incite their members to become violent.

- Ⓐ arouse
- Ⓑ request
- Ⓒ appeal
- Ⓓ affect

9 Harry has many detractors, but they are afraid to criticize him in public.

- Ⓐ friends
- Ⓑ drawbacks
- Ⓒ disadvantages
- Ⓓ opponents

10 You showed a lot of spirit when you tried as hard as you could.

- Ⓐ mind
- Ⓑ heart
- Ⓒ brain
- Ⓓ idea

✍ Match each word with the correct definition.

11 creative   •

12 friendship   •

13 perform   •

14 education   •

15 frequency   •

• Ⓐ schooling; what a person has learned

• Ⓑ intimacy; the act of being friendly with someone

• Ⓒ the rate at which something happens

• Ⓓ original; imaginative

• Ⓔ to act

Part C

Experiencing the TOEFL iBT Actual Tests

CONTINUE | VOLUME

Listening Section Directions

03-01

This section measures your ability to understand conversations and lectures in English.

The Listening section is divided into separately timed parts. In each part, you will listen to 1 conversation and 1 or 2 lectures. You will hear each conversation or lecture only **one** time.

After each conversation or lecture, you will answer some questions about it. The questions typically ask about the main idea and supporting details. Some questions ask about a speaker's purpose or attitude. Answer the questions based on what is stated or implied by the speakers.

You may take notes while you listen. You may use your notes to help you answer the questions. Your notes will not be scored.

If you need to change the volume while you listen, click on **Volume** at the top of the screen.

In some questions, you will see this icon: 🎧 This means that you will hear, but not see, part of the question.

Some of the questions have special directions. These directions appear in a gray box on the screen.

Most questions are worth 1 point. If a question is worth more than 1 point, it will have special directions that indicate how many points you can receive.

A clock at the top of the screen will show you how much time is remaining. The clock will not count down while you are listening. The clock will count down only while you are answering the questions.

Set A

Listening Directions

03-02

In this part, you will listen to 1 conversation and 2 lectures.

You must answer each question. After you answer, click on **Next**. Then click on **OK** to confirm your answer and go on to the next question. After you click on **OK**, you cannot return to the previous questions.

You may now begin this part of the Listening section. You will have **10 minutes** to answer the questions.

Click on **Continue** to go on.

03-03

1 Why does the student visit the professor?

Ⓐ To discuss a recent discovery

Ⓑ To talk about his future plans

Ⓒ To ask to go to a dig site

Ⓓ To get the professor's opinion

2 What does the student say about the site?

Ⓐ It is located far from the city limits.

Ⓑ It was damaged by the construction crew.

Ⓒ It may be thousands of years old.

Ⓓ It does not have many artifacts.

3 What can be inferred about the student?

Ⓐ He has been on several digs in the past.

Ⓑ He is writing a paper for the professor.

Ⓒ He is concerned about protecting the site.

Ⓓ He hopes to get class credit for the dig.

4 What does the professor tell the student to bring?
Click on 2 answers.

Ⓐ Some digging tools

Ⓑ Food and water

Ⓒ A digital camera

Ⓓ A map

5 Listen again to part of the conversation. Then answer the question.
What does the professor imply when she says this: 🎧

Ⓐ The student is welcome to accompany her to the site.

Ⓑ She wants the student to do some research tomorrow.

Ⓒ She believes the student has classes the following day.

Ⓓ Her classes on the following day will be canceled.

03-04

Marine Biology

6 What is the lecture mainly about?

   Ⓐ The physical characteristics of dolphins and porpoises

   Ⓑ The eating habits of most baleen whales

   Ⓒ The similarities between whales and sharks

   Ⓓ The characteristics of some whale subclasses

7 According to the professor, what do many sperm whales eat?

   Ⓐ Giant squid

   Ⓑ Krill

   Ⓒ Various types of fish

   Ⓓ Plankton

8 Based on the information in the lecture, indicate which statements refer to toothed whales and baleen whales.
Click in the correct box for each sentence.

	Toothed Whales	Baleen Whales
1 Consume marine life such as plankton		
2 Include blue whales and humpback whales		
3 Include dolphins and porpoises		
4 May eat fish and large animals		

9 What will the professor probably do next?

     Ⓐ Continue his lecture

     Ⓑ Dismiss the class

     Ⓒ Show the class a video

     Ⓓ Assign some homework

10 Listen again to part of the lecture. Then answer the question. What does the professor imply when he says this: 🎧

     Ⓐ The students did not do the class reading.

     Ⓑ He wants the students to be able to pronounce the word.

     Ⓒ He understands that the word is difficult to spell.

     Ⓓ The students' knowledge of marine biology is low.

11 Listen again to part of the lecture. Then answer the question. What does the professor mean when he says this: 🎧

     Ⓐ The student should stop asking questions.

     Ⓑ He dislikes the student's constant interruptions.

     Ⓒ He is pleased with the questions the student is asking.

     Ⓓ The student should be able to answer her own question.

03-05

12 What is the main topic of the lecture?

Ⓐ How artists can use light and dark in their works

Ⓑ Rembrandt's use of shadows in his paintings

Ⓒ Leonardo da Vinci and his usage of sfumato

Ⓓ The use of chiaroscuro and tenebrism

13 What is tenebrism?

Ⓐ A positive effect that can create various shadows

Ⓑ An illusion caused by both reflected and refracted light

Ⓒ An extreme contrast between dark and light colors

Ⓓ The softening of the transition between light and dark

14 Why does the professor tell the students about the *Mona Lisa*?

Ⓐ To let them know that Leonardo da Vinci painted it

Ⓑ To note that it uses sfumato and chiaroscuro

Ⓒ To contrast it with *Self Portrait as St. Paul*

Ⓓ To emphasize how famous the painting is

15 How is the discussion organized?

    Ⓐ The professor shows some pictures and then explains what they mean.

    Ⓑ The professor encourages the students to ask questions about the topic.

    Ⓒ The professor asks questions that he then answers himself.

    Ⓓ The professor explains some concepts and then shows examples of them.

16 What can be inferred about the professor?

    Ⓐ Rembrandt is one of his favorite artists.

    Ⓑ He has been teaching this class for years.

    Ⓒ He is getting ready to finish the class.

    Ⓓ Painting is a hobby of his.

17 Listen again to part of the lecture. Then answer the question.
What does the professor mean when he says this: 🎧

    Ⓐ He wants the student to quit speaking.

    Ⓑ The student is not paying enough attention.

    Ⓒ The student should turn off the lights.

    Ⓓ He would like the student to answer his question.

Listening Directions

03-06

In this part, you will listen to 1 conversation and 2 lectures.

You must answer each question. After you answer, click on **Next**. Then click on **OK** to confirm your answer and go on to the next question. After you click on **OK**, you cannot return to the previous questions.

You may now begin this part of the Listening section. You will have **10 minutes** to answer the questions.

Click on **Continue** to go on.

03-07

1 What are the speakers mainly discussing?

    Ⓐ The student's qualifications

    Ⓑ A job opening at the museum

    Ⓒ The work that the man does

    Ⓓ The student's relationship with Dr. Lucas

2 Why does the student visit the school museum?

    Ⓐ To deliver a note from her advisor

    Ⓑ To submit some forms she has filled out

    Ⓒ To apply for a job that was advertised

    Ⓓ To ask about the qualifications for a position

3 Which of the following is a requirement for the job in the curator's office?
Click on 2 answers.

    Ⓐ The applicant must be a junior or senior.

    Ⓑ The applicant must be an archaeology major.

    Ⓒ The applicant's grades must be good.

    Ⓓ The applicant must have a faculty recommendation.

4 What can be inferred about the student?

    Ⓐ She is well liked by her advisor.

    Ⓑ She gets high grades in her major.

    Ⓒ She is working on a double major.

    Ⓓ She is attending school on a scholarship.

5 Listen again to part of the conversation. Then answer the question.
What does the man imply when he says this: 🎧

    Ⓐ The student is unqualified for the position.

    Ⓑ The student has a good chance of getting hired.

    Ⓒ The student is talking to the wrong person.

    Ⓓ The student is applying for a high-level position.

03-08

Astronomy

6 What aspect of exoplanets does the professor mainly discuss?

    (A) Where in the galaxy they are typically located

    (B) How large they often tend to be

    (C) What the chances of life existing on them are

    (D) How astronomers attempt to find them

7 Why does the professor explain the concept of transit?

    (A) To prove that there are no exoplanets near Earth

    (B) To demonstrate the effectiveness of some new telescopes

    (C) To insist that the existence of alien life is highly likely

    (D) To show one way that exoplanets may be discovered

8 According to the professor, what is the main problem with using the Doppler wobble to detect exoplanets?

    (A) It can take up to three years to confirm an exoplanet's existence.

    (B) It is difficult for astronomers to see changes in a star's movement.

    (C) Only planets that are thousands of times larger than Earth can be detected.

    (D) It is unable to confirm that life exists on the exoplanets it is used to find.

9 How does the professor organize the information about exoplanet detection methods that she presents to the class?

Ⓐ By describing each according to its popularity

Ⓑ By discussing them according to their likelihood of success

Ⓒ By going into detail about each type of method

Ⓓ By covering them in the order of their importance

10 What will the professor probably do next?

Ⓐ Lecture on the habitable zone

Ⓑ Talk about some special telescopes

Ⓒ Show pictures of some exoplanets

Ⓓ Continue describing the Doppler wobble

11 Listen again to part of the lecture. Then answer the question.
What does the professor imply when she says this: 🎧

Ⓐ Jupiter may be a brown dwarf.

Ⓑ Saturn is a large planet.

Ⓒ Gas planets may have life on them.

Ⓓ Jupiter is larger than most exoplanets.

03-09

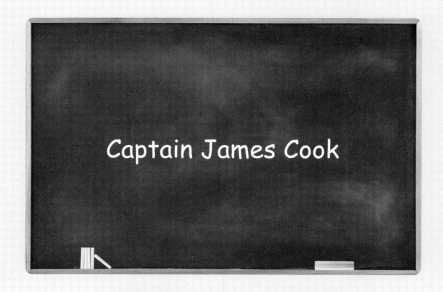

Captain James Cook

12 What aspect of James Cook's life does the professor mainly discuss?

Ⓐ His connection with the First Age of Exploration

Ⓑ The maps of various places that he made

Ⓒ The major voyages that he went on

Ⓓ The manner in which his life ended

13 What was a result of the First Age of Exploration?

Ⓐ Much of Australia and New Zealand was mapped.

Ⓑ People visited and explored places in the Arctic.

Ⓒ Many islands in the Pacific Ocean were discovered.

Ⓓ Some European colonies were established in Asia.

14 How does the professor organize the information about James Cook's voyages that he presents to the class?

Ⓐ By covering them according to their importance

Ⓑ By discussing them in chronological order

Ⓒ By going from the shortest voyage to the longest

Ⓓ By focusing on the voyages in the Indian Ocean

15 Based on the information in the lecture, which of the voyages of James Cook do the following sentences refer to?

Click in the correct box for each sentence.

	First Voyage	Second Voyage	Third Voyage
1 Parts of Australia's east coast were mapped.			
2 An attempt to find the Northwest Passage was made.			
3 A scientist was transported to Tahiti.			
4 Cook and his men tried to find Antarctica.			

16 According to the professor, where was James Cook killed?

(A) Hawaii

(B) Australia

(C) Easter Island

(D) New Zealand

17 Listen again to part of the lecture. Then answer the question.

Why does the student say this: 🎧

(A) To express her confusion

(B) To bring up a new topic

(C) To apologize for interrupting class

(D) To correct the professor's mistake

CONTINUE   VOLUME

03-10

Listening Section Directions

This section measures your ability to understand conversations and lectures in English.

The Listening section is divided into separately timed parts. In each part, you will listen to 1 conversation and 1 or 2 lectures. You will hear each conversation or lecture only **one** time.

After each conversation or lecture, you will answer some questions about it. The questions typically ask about the main idea and supporting details. Some questions ask about a speaker's purpose or attitude. Answer the questions based on what is stated or implied by the speakers.

You may take notes while you listen. You may use your notes to help you answer the questions. Your notes will not be scored.

If you need to change the volume while you listen, click on **Volume** at the top of the screen.

In some questions, you will see this icon: 🎧 This means that you will hear, but not see, part of the question.

Some of the questions have special directions. These directions appear in a gray box on the screen.

Most questions are worth 1 point. If a question is worth more than 1 point, it will have special directions that indicate how many points you can receive.

A clock at the top of the screen will show you how much time is remaining. The clock will not count down while you are listening. The clock will count down only while you are answering the questions.

Listening Directions

In this part, you will listen to 1 conversation and 2 lectures.

You must answer each question. After you answer, click on **Next**. Then click on **OK** to confirm your answer and go on to the next question. After you click on **OK**, you cannot return to the previous questions.

You may now begin this part of the Listening section. You will have **10 minutes** to answer the questions.

Click on **Continue** to go on.

03-12

1 Why did the professor ask to see the student?

   Ⓐ To give the student a new class assignment

   Ⓑ To tell the student to attend a makeup lab class

   Ⓒ To criticize the student's class performance

   Ⓓ To discuss the student's recent accident

2 According to the professor, what must the student do?

   Ⓐ Pay for the damage that he caused

   Ⓑ Submit a written apology to the department

   Ⓒ Retake the class the next semester

   Ⓓ Attend another lab class that afternoon

3 What will the student probably do next?

   Ⓐ Attend his mathematics class

   Ⓑ Go to the Chemistry Department office

   Ⓒ Eat lunch

   Ⓓ Visit the chemistry laboratory

4 Listen again to part of the conversation. Then answer the question.
   What does the student mean when he says this: 🎧

   Ⓐ He suffered some minor injuries.

   Ⓑ He incurred lasting psychological trauma.

   Ⓒ He has no significant physical injuries.

   Ⓓ His feelings were hurt by the accident.

5 Listen again to part of the conversation. Then answer the question.
   What is the purpose of the professor's response?

   Ⓐ To request that the student wait a moment

   Ⓑ To indicate that the student needs to hurry

   Ⓒ To tell the student to ask his question

   Ⓓ To advise the student to be more careful

Botany

6   What is the main topic of the lecture?

Ⓐ The regions that giant sequoias and redwoods grow in

Ⓑ The necessary conditions for trees growing to great heights

Ⓒ The features of giant sequoias and redwoods

Ⓓ The importance of protecting large, ancient trees

7   How does the professor organize the information about giant sequoias and redwoods that she presents to the class?

Ⓐ By stressing the similarities between the trees

Ⓑ By contrasting the two trees

Ⓒ By mostly talking about the habitats of the trees

Ⓓ By focusing on the life cycles of the trees

8   What does the professor imply about the students?

Ⓐ Almost all of them failed to submit their midterm papers.

Ⓑ Most of them cannot differentiate between giant sequoias and redwoods.

Ⓒ They are going to be tested on the material she covers in the class.

Ⓓ Many of them will have difficulty understanding the day's lesson.

9 Why does the professor mention the Sierra Nevada Mountains?

Ⓐ To say that redwoods are common there

Ⓑ To note how often forest fires happen there

Ⓒ To point out where giant sequoias grow

Ⓓ To describe the habit there in detail

10 According to the professor, what stands out the most about giant sequoias?

Ⓐ The sizes of their trunks

Ⓑ The color of their bark

Ⓒ The lengths of their needles

Ⓓ The speed that they grow

11 Based on the information in the lecture, indicate which statements refer to giant sequoias and redwoods.

Click in the correct box for each phrase.

	Giant Sequoias	Redwoods
1 Can have hundreds of seeds in a single cone		
2 Have bark that is dull chocolate brown in color		
3 Need cool temperatures and plenty of water to grow		
4 Have thick trunks which do not taper off		

03-14

Archaeology

12 What is the main topic of the lecture?

    Ⓐ The type of people who were able to use the quipu

    Ⓑ The way to record and understand information on the quipu

    Ⓒ The manner in which the quipu was developed

    Ⓓ The reason why there are few existing quipus today

13 According to the professor, what did a quipu look like?

    Ⓐ It was a long string with other strings attached to it.

    Ⓑ It had colorful animal hairs that were tied in knots.

    Ⓒ It was a rope that had ribbons and braids on it.

    Ⓓ It was one long string that was tied into smaller knots.

14 Why does the professor tell the students to look in their books?

    Ⓐ So that she can more easily answer the student's question

    Ⓑ So that they can follow along with her lecture

    Ⓒ So that they can see a picture of a quipu

    Ⓓ So that she can show them a guide to the Incan language

15 Why does the professor mention the Spanish?

- Ⓐ To compare their writing system with the Inca's
- Ⓑ To say why they never translated very many quipus
- Ⓒ To explain how they managed to conquer the Incas
- Ⓓ To state why there are few quipus in existence

16 What does the professor imply about her research interests?

- Ⓐ She has attempted to translate some quipus.
- Ⓑ She focuses mostly on Incan archaeology.
- Ⓒ She is a world expert on the Incan language.
- Ⓓ She knows how to read many of the existing quipus.

17 Listen again to part of the lecture. Then answer the question.
What can be inferred about the professor when she says this: 🎧

- Ⓐ She enjoys trying to make the students laugh.
- Ⓑ She wants the students to ask her some questions.
- Ⓒ She thinks that the topic she is covering is humorous.
- Ⓓ She believes the material she just discussed is difficult.

MEMO

MEMO

MEMO

TOEFL® MAP Listening

New TOEFL® Edition

Intermediate

Answers, Explanations, and Scripts

DARAKWON

TOEFL® MAP Listening

New TOEFL® Edition

Intermediate

Answers, Explanations, and Scripts

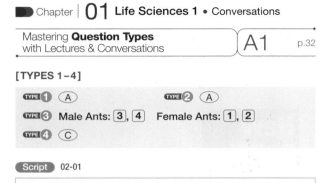

Part B

Building Background Knowledge of TOEFL Topics

■▶ Chapter | 01 Life Sciences 1 • Conversations

Mastering **Question Types**
with Lectures & Conversations

A1 p.32

[TYPES 1–4]

TYPE❶ Ⓐ   TYPE❷ Ⓐ

TYPE❸ Male Ants: ③, ④ Female Ants: ①, ②

TYPE❹ Ⓒ

Script 02-01

M Professor: Now, I want to talk about ant behavior. Like many other insects, ants have a social structure. They live together in large groups, and certain ants have, uh, specific positions and jobs. Ants also often cooperate to perform tasks, such as, uh, such as finding food.

But first, let's look at how they live. Ants live in an ant colony. A colony can have a few dozen ants or millions. It depends upon the species. Again, depending on what species the ants are, the colony's shape and size may also vary. It's located mostly belowground but can have a distinctive mound shape aboveground. Within the colony, there are three main types of ants: the queen, males, and females. The queen is a fertile female, so she mates with the males and lays eggs. There is typically only one queen per colony. Some species, however, may have multiple queens. As for males, most colonies have only a few. They're called drones, and their sole task is to mate with the queen. They have short life spans . . . often living only a few weeks.

That leaves the female ants, which do all of the work. They're often divided into worker classes. Some are soldier ants that deal with the colony's enemies and are also sent out to forage for food. Others are simple worker ants. They help build the colony, care for the eggs, and do other tasks as well.

Part of ant social behavior is their ability to direct thousands . . . and sometimes millions . . . of ants to do the same tasks. They accomplish this by communicating with chemical smells called pheromones. You're familiar with them, right . . .? Excellent. These smells can be used to direct ants to do tasks together. For example, one pheromone can mark a trail for ants to follow to a food source. After gathering the food, they can follow the trail back to

their colony. By working together with one another like this, ants are able to develop stronger colonies. Since all of the ants have specific chores to do, there's no duplication involved. Amazing, isn't it?

TYPE❶ [Rhetorical Purpose Question]

The professor mostly focuses on the roles of ants and how they behave with one another. He describes how they act socially.

TYPE❷ [Understanding Organization Question]

The professor mentions the queen, males, and females. Then, he describes the duties of each of them in order.

TYPE❸ [Connecting Content Question]

According to the lecture, male ants only have one task: to mate with the queen. Males are also called drones. As for female ants, they care for the queen's eggs, and they are also the ants that search for food.

TYPE❹ [Speaker's Attitude Question]

When talking about the specific chores that ants do, the professor says, "By working together with one another like this, ants are able to develop stronger colonies. Since all of the ants have specific chores to do, there's no duplication involved. Amazing, isn't it?" Clearly, he is impressed by ants.

Summarizing

The professor first describes ant colonies and says they may have different shapes and sizes. He then mentions that all colonies have a queen, males, and females. The queen lays eggs. Males mate with the queen. And females do work such as guarding the colony, foraging for food, and taking care of the eggs. Ants communicate what work needs to be done by using pheromones. These help ants work together to do tasks such as gathering food and bringing it back to the colony.

[TYPES 5–8]

TYPE❺ Ⓑ   TYPE❻ Ⓑ

TYPE❼ Ⓒ   TYPE❽ Ⓓ

Script 02-02

W Professor: Now that we've examined the structure of the human body's cells, I want to move on and examine how the body actually produces energy. The key is small organelles . . . uh, extremely small organs . . . in each cell called mitochondria. They're so tiny that hundreds, even thousands, of mitochondria may exist in one human cell. Different parts of the body contain different amounts of mitochondria. For example, the muscles have more mitochondria per cell since they need more energy . . . and need it more quickly . . . to do heavy work.

M Student: Professor Mitchell, I'm sorry, but what are mitochondria?

W: Oh, sorry. I got a bit ahead of myself. Mitochondria form something like, um, an energy factory in a cell. They have two membranes: the outer membrane and the inner membrane. The outer membrane is like a protective covering. Interestingly, the inner membrane is much larger, but it's folded many times to fit inside the outer membrane. This folding gives it a large surface area, so it enables the inner membrane to perform its task better. Now, before you ask, let me tell you that its task is to convert nutrients into energy for the cell and, thus, be utilized by the body.

Imagine that mitochondria are like a, um, a cell's digestive system. [8]What happens is that oxygen combines with the nutrients in the inner membrane of the mitochondria, and then energy for the body is created in the form of an energy-rich molecule called the ATP molecule. ATP is an abbreviation for a longer scientific name. **Look it up if you're interested in knowing it.** The term for this process is cellular respiration. Yes, respiration, as in breathing.

Every cell in your body has mitochondria. However, some cells have more than others since they do more work and therefore require more energy. Fat cells also have lots of mitochondria because they store energy for the body. In other cells, mitochondria do very little or might even be dead. For example, hair has few mitochondria since it produces no energy for the body. Some layers of skin have few mitochondria, too.

TYPE 5 [Gist-Content Question]

The professor mostly focuses on the benefits of mitochondria for humans.

TYPE 6 [Detail Question]

The professor states, "Fat cells also have lots of mitochondria because they store energy for the body."

TYPE 7 [Making Inferences Question]

First, the professor says, "What happens is that oxygen combines with the nutrients in the inner membrane of the mitochondria, and then energy for the body is created in the form of an energy-rich molecule called the ATP molecule." Then, she says, "Some layers of skin have few mitochondria, too." Thus, it can be inferred that skin does not create energy.

TYPE 8 [Understanding Function Question]

When the professor tells the students to look up what ATP stands for, she is implying that she is not going to tell them what it means.

Summarizing

The professor starts discussing mitochondria and mentions how small they are. A student interrupts and asks what they are. The professor explains that mitochondria are like energy factories in cells. They have an inner and outer membrane, which convert nutrients to energy for the cells. The mitochondria use oxygen to create ATP molecules, which contain energy. All cells in the body have mitochondria. Some—such as fat cells—have many, but others—such as hair and skin—have few mitochondria.

Mastering **Question Types**
with Lectures & Conversations

A2   p.34

[TYPES 1–4]

TYPE 1 C   TYPE 2 A
TYPE 3 A   TYPE 4 D

Script 02-03

M Professor: Another aspect of plants is called photosynthesis. It's the process by which plants use carbon dioxide, water, and sunlight to create sugar and oxygen. [4]Plants extract carbon dioxide from the atmosphere, and they get water either from the ground or rainfall. Once photosynthesis occurs, the plants then absorb the sugar—called glucose—they create and use it for food. They also release oxygen as a byproduct. **Photosynthesis is a mysterious, yet crucial, process, without which life as we know it on the Earth, well, simply couldn't exist.**

That was a rather simplistic explanation of a complex chemical process. So let me delve into it a little more deeply, okay . . .? Now, plants have green parts—their stems and leaves in particular. The green pigment in plants is chlorophyll. It's absolutely crucial to photosynthesis since it lets plants absorb the sunlight necessary for the process to occur. Now, plants' membranes . . . especially those in their green leaves . . . contain hundreds of thousands of small parts called chloroplasts. These are what absorb sunlight. Take a look at this picture here . . . It's a view of some plants from above. Notice how their leaves are spread out so that they're all in position to absorb the maximum amount of sunlight possible. Here's another picture . . . and another . . . So as plants' leaves collect sunlight, photosynthesis can occur.

Perhaps you're wondering why photosynthesis is so important. Well, plants and animals are all interconnected. Without plants, animals couldn't survive. Without animals, plants couldn't survive. And the key is photosynthesis. Animals exhale carbon dioxide, which plants inhale and then transform into oxygen, which animals then inhale. That's how the cycle works. In addition, eons ago, there was no free oxygen on the Earth, nor were there any complex life forms. However, simple plant forms slowly emerged billions of years ago and started the photosynthesis process. This released oxygen into the atmosphere. It took millions of years for a large supply of oxygen to be created. But as the oxygen level increased, oxygen-dependent life forms evolved. The more oxygen there was, the more complex life became. Finally, humans emerged. And photosynthesis is a major reason for that.

TYPE 1 [Gist-Content Question]

The professor mostly discusses photosynthesis and how important it is to the planet.

TYPE 2 [Understanding Organization Question]

As soon as the professor mentions chloroplasts, he says, "These are what absorb sunlight."

TYPE 3 [Connecting Content Question]

The professor declares, "Now, plants have green parts—their stems and leaves in particular. The green pigment in plants is chlorophyll." Thus, he implies that chlorophyll is found in leaves.

TYPE 4 [Speaker's Attitude Question]

When the professor says, "Life as we know it on the Earth, well, simply couldn't exist," he means that photosynthesis is what keeps all organisms alive. So life on the Earth would die without plants being able to undergo it.

Summarizing

The professor explains that plants undergo photosynthesis. This happens when they use carbon dioxide, water, and sunlight to make sugar and oxygen. The professor mentions that chlorophyll gives plants' leaves and stems their green color. And plants have chloroplasts, which allow them to absorb sunlight. The professor then states why photosynthesis is so important. Billions of years ago, the Earth had no free oxygen until plants started producing it. As more oxygen was created, more complex life forms were able to evolve.

[TYPES 5–8]

TYPE 5	B	**TYPE 6**	D
TYPE 7	A	**TYPE 8**	C

Script 02-04

W Professor: Good afternoon, Chris. Thanks for coming in. I remember you telling me that Thursdays are your busiest days.

M Student: Good afternoon, Professor Taylor. Yes, that's correct. I have three classes and a lab during the day, and then I go to my part-time job in the evening. But I have free time now.

W: That's great to hear. So . . . I reviewed your thesis proposal. Overall, I think it's quite original and should produce a quality thesis.

M: Thank you for saying that.

W: However, I believe your topic is a bit broad and needs to be narrowed down somewhat.

M: How so?

W: Well, you're proposing to research how the reproductive habits of butterflies have been affected by environmental changes. That's a great topic which I don't believe anyone has looked into yet. [8]However, your proposal mentioned seven species, which is just too many.

M: Really? I thought it might not be enough.

W: Chris, this is a senior thesis. If you pursue a topic like this for a master's or doctoral degree, sure, you can look at a large number of different species. However, for this project, I suggest studying only two or maybe three species.

M: Ah, okay. I'll select the ones that I think are the most promising, and then I will present you with a rewritten proposal by tomorrow afternoon. Oh, are there any other issues?

TYPE 5 [Gist-Purpose Question]

The professor says, "I reviewed your thesis proposal. Overall, I think it's quite original and should produce a quality thesis."

TYPE 6 [Detail Question]

The professor tells the student, "Overall, I think it's quite original and should produce a quality thesis."

TYPE 7 [Making Inferences Question]

At the end of the conversation, the student asks the professor, "Oh, are there any other issues?" So the professor will probably respond to the student's question.

When the professor says, "Chris, this is a senior thesis," she is implying that the student does not need to study so many different species of butterflies. She is therefore indicating that a senior thesis does not require too much research.

Summarizing

The professor asks to see the student to discuss the proposal he turned in for a senior thesis. She says that the idea is original and should produce a quality thesis. However, she says that the topic is too broad and needs to be narrowed down. Instead of studying the effects of the environment on the reproductive habits of seven butterfly species, she wants him to research two or three species. The student agrees and says he will rewrite the proposal and submit it the next day.

Mastering **Topics** with Lectures (B1) p.36

1 Ⓑ 2 Ⓒ 3 Ⓑ

Script & Graphic Organizer 02-05

W Professor: As we know, plants not only live on land but also in the ocean. One of the biggest of these ocean plants is the giant kelp. It's a type of seaweed. Actually, seaweed is a more commonly used term than kelp. Anyway, let's go over a few details about giant kelps right now.

Giant kelps can be found in the Pacific Ocean on the west coast of Canada, California, and parts of Mexico. What's unique about them is that they may be up to 200 feet long . . . Yeah, that's impressive, isn't it? They grow rapidly—sometimes up to a foot a day. Another of their unique features is that they grow in kelp forests. By that, I mean that they grow in large groups. When underwater, the kelps stand erect, making them look like trees. What makes this possible are their large bladders. These bladders are like, uh, air pockets, so they enable the kelps to float in an upright position.

Now, let's look at the conditions they require in order to grow. First, they need shallow water. They typically grow in water between fifteen and 120 feet deep. So when kelps grow to be very big . . . say, uh, over 100 feet long, parts of them usually float on the ocean surface. These sections can form a very dense canopy of vegetation. It's almost similar to the canopy in a rainforest in some cases. Second, giant kelps require temperatures between, um, forty and seventy-two degrees Fahrenheit. They frequently die if the water temperature increases beyond that. Finally, they need a rocky bottom to anchor themselves to the ground. This is called a holdfast.

[3]Kelps reproduce by releasing spores. A single giant kelp can release up to a trillion spores per year. **That number is almost unimaginable, isn't it?** Now, you're probably wondering why the oceans aren't covered in giant kelp, aren't you? Here's the answer . . . Very few spores actually survive. Many get buried in sand or mud and can't find a holdfast anywhere. Others get consumed by ocean animals. Still others find rocky bottoms and begin growing, yet they lack enough sunlight, space, or nutrients, so they fail to mature. In fact, only about one out of every 100,000 young giant kelps reaches adulthood.

Once kelps start growing in ideal conditions, they develop quickly. Their central stalk is called the stipe. Offshoots, or leaves, called fronds, grow from the stipe. Each frond lives for about six months and then dies. But they're replaced by new fronds after they fall off. Oh, and kelps live around four to ten years, which makes them perennials.

Many aquatic life forms live in giant kelp forests. But humans also make use of kelps. In fact, many people harvest them. Yeah, just like farmers. Typically, people in boats cut away the top layer of a kelp forest. By only cutting their tops, they don't kill the kelps, which will continue to grow. Talk about a renewable resource, huh? Anyway, kelps are used to make additives for foods, cosmetics, and drugs. But overharvesting is becoming a problem. So the giant kelp has been classified as an endangered species in some places. This affords it some protections. For instance, in California, kelp harvesting is regulated, and harvesters aren't permitted to uproot entire plants.

Giant Kelp

Characteristics:

- *Can be up to 200 feet long*
- *Found in the Pacific Ocean*
- *Grow in shallow water*
- *Can form a dense canopy similar to a rainforest*
- *Grow in water 40 to 72 degrees Fahrenheit*
- *Need rocky bottoms to anchor themselves to*

Spores:

Reproduce by releasing spores; release 1 trillion a year; most do not survive; those that find a holdfast grow very quickly

Kelp Harvesting:

Humans cut away top layers; use for foods, cosmetics, and drugs; are being overharvested; are regulations on how to harvest them

1 [Gist-Content Question]

The professor mostly focuses on how giant kelps grow.

2 [Understanding Organization Question]

About the bladders of giant kelps, the professor states, "These bladders are like, uh, air pockets, so they enable the kelps to float in an upright position."

3 [Understanding Attitude Question]

When the professor says that the number is "almost unimaginable," she means that it is a very high number.

Summarizing

Giant kelps are a type of seaweed found in the eastern Pacific Ocean. They can be up to 200 feet long and grow in kelp forests that resemble tropical rainforests. The top parts of kelps often float on the ocean's surface. The kelps can release a trillion spores a year, but most spores do not develop for various reasons. Some people harvest kelps to use as additives for foods, cosmetics, and drugs. Because kelps are becoming endangered, kelp harvesting is now regulated in some places.

Mastering **Topics** with Lectures | B2 | p.37

1 Ⓓ   2 Color Blindness in Humans: ①, ③
Color Blindness in Monkeys: ②, ④

3 Ⓐ

Script & Graphic Organizer 02-06

M Professor: Humans are sometimes unable to distinguish between certain colors. For instance, some people can't tell the difference between green and red. This is called color blindness. This problem also exists in the animal kingdom. For example, some species of monkeys lack the ability to see certain colors. I just read an article about how researchers have used a special type of therapy to restore some monkeys' ability to see colors . . . Yes?

W Student: Is that therapy available for humans, too?

M: [3]According to the article, the scientists hope to help humans but not just to overcome color blindness. They want to cure blindness as well. **Okay, but that's a topic for a later day.** Now let's get back to color blindness, shall we . . . ? First, color blindness in humans can take many forms. Some people can only see certain colors while others can't

see any colors at all. In addition, genetic factors are often responsible for color blindness in humans. However, other people have developed color blindness after suffering either head or eye injuries.

As for monkeys, it's believed that their color blindness issues are also genetic. The main question scientists ask is why nature has made some species of monkeys . . . but not others . . . color blind. One theory is that the kinds of foods they eat may cause color blindness. For example, some monkeys only eat insects and small animals. Thus, they develop more important senses, such as, uh, smell, to help them find and catch their meals. Their sense of sight is therefore less important to them, so color blindness doesn't negatively affect them. Other monkeys, however, eat fruit and other plants. They must be able to see in color in order to, well, to distinguish between various types of plants. And they need to be able to separate colors from the background green of their jungle homes. Think about it. Being able to see colors lets them identify ripe fruit to eat.

Here's an example . . . Male squirrel monkeys have problems seeing red and green, yet they can see blue and yellow with no problems. A recent experiment in the United States . . . get this . . . reversed the color blindness in two male squirrel monkeys. The researchers injected the monkeys with a gene. This particular gene creates a protein that gets released when certain wavelengths of light hit the retina in the eye. The protein tells the brain what color is being seen. At first, the two squirrel monkeys couldn't distinguish between red and green. However, after five months of treatment, they could regularly pick out red- and green-colored objects. Apparently, like humans, some monkeys have genetic problems that give them color blindness.

What's difficult for researchers now is finding out exactly what happened in the monkeys' eyes and brains. One theory is that the new gene caused physical changes in their brains and eyes. These changes then enabled the monkeys to see red and green. Another, more likely, theory is that there were no changes at all. The monkeys' eyes and brains already had the ability to distinguish between red and green. What was lacking was the gene necessary to make the protein that allowed the connection between the eyes and the brain. Scientists obviously need to conduct more research. But, hopefully, what they learn while researching monkeys will be applied to help humans overcome their color blindness as well.

Color Blindness in Monkeys

Color Blindness in Humans:	Color Blindness in Monkeys:
- Some people cannot tell the difference between green and red	- Some species are color blind while others are not
- Is often caused by genetic factors	- Often has to do with the food they eat
- Can sometimes be caused by head or eye injuries	- Some monkeys have been cured by medical experiments on them

1 [Gist-Purpose Question]

After discussing the experiment with the male squirrel monkeys, the professor comments, "Apparently, like humans, some monkeys have genetic problems that give them color blindness."

2 [Connecting Content Question]

According to the lecture, humans can get color blindness because of head injuries. They may also not be able to see any colors at all. As for monkeys, their color blindness has been corrected in an experiment, and it may be caused by the absence of a protein in their bodies.

3 [Understanding Function Question]

When the professor says that it is "a topic for a later day," he is telling the students that he will cover that subject in another lecture.

Summarizing

Many humans are color blind, but the professor says that animals such as monkeys may be color blind, too. For humans, genetic factors and injuries to their head or eyes can cause color blindness. Some monkey species are color blind while others are not. The foods monkeys eat often determine whether they will be harmed by being color blind or not. In an experiment with male squirrel monkeys, they were cured of their color blindness after receiving gene therapy. But scientists do not know exactly why they were cured.

Mastering **Topics** with Lectures   B3   p.38

1 Ⓐ   2 Ⓓ   3 Ⓑ

Script & Graphic Organizer   02-07

W Professor: Fish achieve propulsion either by moving their bodies or by using a tailfin. This

tailfin is called the caudal fin. There are different types of caudal fins. They vary in their shapes and compositions. First, how does a fish use its caudal fin? By rapidly moving its caudal fin back and forth, a fish can achieve movement. Keep in mind that fish do not usually steer with their caudal fin. Instead, the pectoral fins, which are on the fish's sides, are used for steering.

Now, let me show you some pictures of a few different caudal fins. By seeing them, you'll be able to understand the differences better. Caudal fins are vertical, so they go back and forth from right to left . . . Ah, okay, yes, whales have horizontal tailfins, but remember that they aren't fish. They're mammals. There's a difference. A big one . . . Now, back to caudal fins. There are eight main types, and the shape is the main difference between them. Here they're all on the screen . . . First, we have the pointed tail right here. It's not really a fin, but it's in the rear and swishes back and forth to help with movement. Next is the pointed caudal fin here . . . As you can see, it's slightly wider than the pointed tail. It also has raised parts on the top and bottom that are obviously fin-like in nature.

Third . . . is the round caudal fin. It's triangular in shape, but as its name indicates, its end is rounded. Next is the truncate caudal fin . . . here. It's similar to the rounded fin except that its end is not rounded but is more square-like. Fifth . . . is the emarginated caudal fin. It's also triangular in shape, but the end of the fin is not quite squared off. Instead, it's more fork-like. The sixth one is the forked caudal. Again, notice the triangular shape, but the fork right here . . . is very pronounced. You can see two distinct forks in the fin. Seventh is the lunate caudal fin. It's also forked, but the forks are thinner, and its shape is like the, uh, like the moon in its crescent stage. [3]Finally, the last type is the heterocercal fin. It too is forked, but notice here . . . that the top fork is longer than the bottom fork. Usually, in these fins, the top fork has cartilage, which gives it more strength. **Sharks typically have this type of fin.**

Please remember that some fish can achieve propulsion without the use of a caudal fin. For example, some eels have one long, continuous fin where the dorsal fin, or back fin, and the caudal fin would be on a fish. And some eels have no fins at all. All eels swim by moving their bodies back and forth like a snake on land. This type of movement is called u-u-u-undulation . . . Sorry. That's undulation. Additionally, undulation isn't unique to snakes and eels. Many fish use it in conjunction with their caudal fins to propel themselves through the water.

Now, let's look at some other creatures . . . First,

the seahorse. Notice the large dorsal fin. Seahorses move from a vertical position, not from a horizontal one like most fish do. Thus, the seahorse's dorsal fin operates in the same manner that the caudal fin does for fish.

The Caudal Fins of Fish

Characteristics:	Differences in Fins:
- Are the tailfins of fish	The main difference between them is their shapes
- Help fish achieve propulsion	
- Move caudal fins back and forth to go forward	Eels:
- Are always vertical	Do not need caudal fins to move but move by undulation instead
- Are eight main types of caudal fins	
	Seahorses:
	Move in the vertical position so have their dorsal fin act like caudal fin

1 [Detail Question]

The professor says, "By rapidly moving its caudal fin back and forth, a fish can achieve movement."

2 [Understanding Organization Question]

Throughout her lecture, the professor shows slides of various caudal fins so that the students can see exactly what she is talking about.

3 [Making Inferences Question]

The professor notes that the heterocercal fin gives fish more strength. She then states that sharks "typically have this type of fin." It can therefore be inferred that many sharks are powerful swimmers.

Summarizing

Fish propel themselves through the water by using their tailfin, which is called the caudal fin. They move their caudal fin back and forth quickly to create movement. The caudal fins of fish are always vertical. There are eight main types of caudal fins. These fins mostly differ in their shapes. For example, some caudal fins are forked while others are not. Some fish do not need a caudal fin to move. In addition, eels have no caudal fin but move through undulation.

Mastering **Topics** with Conversations p.39

1 Ⓒ   2 Ⓒ   3 Ⓑ

W Student: Good afternoon, sir. Are you the person I need to speak with to get something printed?

M Printing Office Employee: I sure am. My name's David Chun. What can I assist you with today?

W: Well, I'm a student in the Math Department, and I'm trying to find some tutoring jobs. I could really use the extra money.

M: Um, okay. But, uh, how exactly is that important to me?

W: Oh, uh, right. I need to make some advertisements to post all around campus . . . you know, like on bulletin boards and stuff . . . uh, so I came here to get some flyers printed. But I, er, need some information first.

M: Sure. What do you want to know?

W: Well, are you able to make color copies here?

M: Yes, we can do that. We have several state-of-the-art color copiers here, so you'll get the best quality available. But they cost more than just plain black and white copies.

W: Oh, I see . . . What are your rates?

M: [3]Assuming that you're making copies on regular-sized paper, we charge ten cents a page for each black-and-white copy. And we charge twenty cents a page for each color copy. **I'd say that's a pretty good bargain.**

W: You're right. That's not bad at all. I was expecting you to charge me a lot more than that for color copies. A store off campus asked me to pay double that price.

M: Yeah, they do that sometimes. By the way, you can actually get a cheaper rate than the one I just quoted you. If you make 100 or more copies, we'll reduce the price of color copies to fifteen cents a page.

W: Wow, that's awesome. That's precisely the number of copies I need. Here's my flyer. How soon, uh, how soon do you think you can run these off in color?

M: Well . . . I've got a couple of other jobs to do first, so why don't you leave the flyer with me and come back here after lunch? Everything will be ready by then.

Service Encounter

Reason for Visiting:	Result:
Wants to make copies of a tutoring advertisement	Employee tells her the costs of making black-and-white and color copies
Student's Decision:	Man's Response:
Wants to make 100 color copies of her flyer	Tells her to return after lunch to pick up her copies

1 [Gist-Purpose Question]

The student tells the employee, "I need to make some advertisements to post all around campus . . . you know, like on bulletin boards and stuff . . . uh, so I came here to get some flyers printed. But I, er, need some information first."

2 [Making Inferences Question]

The employee tells the student to come back after lunch. So it can be inferred that she will leave the printing office.

3 [Understanding Function Question]

When the man says, "I'd say that's a pretty good bargain," he has just finished comparing the prices at his printing office with the prices at another place.

Summarizing

The woman visits the printing office because she wants to make some flyers. She asks the man if he can make color copies, and he responds positively. Then, she asks for the rates, and he tells her the prices of printing black-and-white and color copies. The woman is surprised by how cheap color copies are. The man says that if she prints 100 or more copies, she can get an even cheaper price. The woman agrees and gives the man her flyer.

TOEFL **Practice Tests**   C1   p.40

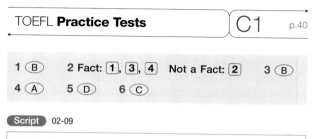

1 Ⓑ   2 Fact: 1, 3, 4   Not a Fact: 2   3 Ⓑ
4 Ⓐ   5 Ⓓ   6 Ⓒ

`Script` 02-09

M Professor: Our next reptile is the alligator. It's one of the oldest life forms on the Earth and has remained practically the same since it evolved millions of years ago. There are two types of alligators. They are the Chinese and the American alligator, but the latter is much more common. In fact, sadly, the Chinese alligator is virtually extinct now.

W Student: Professor Ringo, I'm curious . . . What's the difference between an alligator and a crocodile?

M: If you don't mind, I'll cover that in a moment. Okay? But, first, I'd like to describe some physical characteristics of alligators. Just so you know, most of what I plan to discuss concerns the American alligator. First, their size . . . Adult alligators can grow up to fourteen feet in length. Er, those are males. Females are smaller, being, um, about nine or ten feet long. Males average between 800 and 1,000 pounds, so they're extremely heavy while females are lighter on average. Alligators typically live for thirty to forty years, but some captive specimens have survived as long as seventy-five years. Now, to answer your question, Michele . . . Most notably, alligators have wide U-shaped snouts while crocodiles have narrower V-shaped snouts. There are, of course, other differences, but that's a quick and easy way to tell them apart.

American alligators are found in Florida and the other states abutting the Gulf of Mexico. They spend lots of time in the water, but they, uh, they can't breathe underwater. Swampy land is their favorite habitat. They breed in spring starting at around the age of ten. After mating, the female builds a mound-shaped nest made of mud, leaves, twigs, and other vegetation. It's high because it needs to be above the water. After building the nest, the female digs a hole in the middle and lays around twenty to forty eggs.

The eggs take about, oh, sixty-five days to hatch. The female doesn't sit on the nest like a bird, but she does remain close by to guard her eggs. Small animals like raccoons often try to dig up the eggs and eat them. When the eggs are ready to hatch, the baby alligators start making, uh, chirping noises, which attract the mother. She digs up the eggs and helps them hatch. When they hatch, the baby alligators are eight to ten inches long and are black with yellow stripes. This color scheme helps them hide among vegetation from predators. Mother alligators also stay with their young and protect them for up to two years. However, many young die, and only one in twenty survives to adulthood.

Alligators' diets consist of small fish, shellfish, turtles, frogs, snakes, and animals that venture too close to the water. On land, they're slow, but in the water, they're quite swift. They normally lie in wait with only their nostrils and eyes above water. Check out the picture on page forty-nine in your texts . . . Look . . . You can barely see it, can't you? Suddenly, when its prey is near, the alligator strikes and grips it in its jaws. If its catch is small, the alligator eats it whole. But sometimes the alligator must crush it first.

This is frequently the case for turtles and shellfish. For larger prey, such as deer, the alligator simply rolls over in the water and drowns its victim. But remember that alligators don't eat that often. They're coldblooded, so they don't need food to maintain their body temperature. In fact, females can go for months without food while they're protecting their eggs.

W: ⁶Do alligators ever attack people?

M: Yes, and you should be wary of them. **However, they're not as aggressive as crocodiles.** Alligator attacks are rare, and deaths are even rarer. For example, since 1948, only around twenty people have been killed by alligators in Florida. In fact, alligators have more to fear from humans than we do from them. People sometimes steal their eggs for alligator farms. People also eat alligator meat and use their skins to make leather products. However, most alligators used by people are raised on farms. It's also estimated that there are about a million American alligators in the wild. The Chinese alligator, however, is endangered. It lives in the Yangtze River, and it's believed that only a few dozen remain. Here's a picture of one.

1 [Gist-Content Question]

Throughout the lecture, the professor mostly describes the physical characteristics of alligators and their feeding habits.

2 [Detail Question]

According to the lecture, alligators' diets mostly consist of animals. There are also about a million of them in the wild, and they have U-shaped snouts that are wide. It is not a fact that alligators sit on their eggs to guard them.

3 [Understanding Organization Question]

The professor says, "If its catch is small, the alligator eats it whole. But sometimes the alligator must crush it first. This is frequently the case for turtles or shellfish. For larger prey, such as deer, the alligator simply rolls over in the water and drowns its victim." So he is letting the students know how alligators kill and eat their prey.

4 [Connecting Content Question]

The professor states, "Most notably, alligators have wide U-shaped snouts while crocodiles have narrower V-shaped snouts."

5 [Making Inferences Question]

At the end, the professor declares, "The Chinese alligator, however, is endangered. It lives in the Yangtze River, and it's believed that only a few dozen remain. Here's a picture of one." Since he is showing a picture

of the Chinese alligator, it is likely that he will talk about it some more.

6 [Understanding Function Question]

When the professor notes that alligators are "not as aggressive as crocodiles," it can be inferred that crocodiles attack humans more often than alligators.

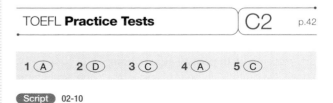

TOEFL **Practice Tests** C2 p.42

1 (A)   2 (D)   3 (C)   4 (A)   5 (C)

Script 02-10

M Student: Professor Richardson, do you have some time to spare?

W Professor: Charles, come in, please . . . What can I do for you?

M: Are you, uh, sure you aren't too busy? It looks like you've got a lot of, uh, papers on your desk.

W: Oh, don't mind all these. I'm just going over my lecture notes for the graduate-level class I'm teaching this afternoon. Those grad students are sharp, so I need to make sure I have my facts right. Anyway, what can I do for you?

M: I need some advice . . . You see, uh, I'm trying to make up my mind about next semester's classes.

W: Ah, yes. You register for classes next week, don't you?

M: That's correct. I've already decided on most of the classes I'm going to take. Here . . . Take a look at my schedule.

W: Let me take a look . . . Economics . . . That's a good choice. Ah, an astronomy class. Fulfilling your course requirements, I see.

M: Exactly. Plus, I've heard that Professor Mumford's class is a lot of fun.

W: Oh, yes, he's a fascinating lecturer who not only knows his field well but also makes the material come alive. Okay, let me see . . . Ah, yes, I see the problem.

M: Yeah, it's between journalism and marketing. I want to take both classes, but there's a time conflict. The journalism class starts thirty minutes before the marketing class finishes. So, uh, what do you think I should do?

W: That's a good question. Let me think for a moment . . . Hmm . . . The journalism class is an introductory one, but the marketing one isn't, right?

M: Yes. I've been considering getting a minor in journalism, so that would be a good class to take. It would introduce me to the field. The marketing is an upper-level class though.

W: So the marketing class doesn't get offered every semester, does it?

M: Oh . . . I see. You're right. I might have to wait a year to take that marketing class again, and it's crucial to my major.

W: Bingo.

M: But what about the journalism class? Don't you think I should take it?

W: Charles, you stayed on campus and worked here last summer, right? If you're planning to do that again this year, why don't you take the journalism class during summer school? That way, you'd get to take both classes. And you'd be able to determine if you're interested in pursuing journalism as a minor, too.

M: Say, that's a great idea. ⁵But, uh, are you positive that the journalism class is being offered in the summer?

W: I'm totally sure. I have lunch with Professor Madsen every week, and he mentioned to me that he's teaching it this summer. **So you're all set.**

1   [Gist-Content Question]

Concerning his problem, the student mentions, "Yeah, it's between journalism and marketing. I want to take both classes, but there's a time conflict. The journalism class starts thirty minutes before the marketing class finishes."

2   [Understanding Function Question]

Since the marketing class is an upper-level class, it does not get offered every semester. So the student might have to wait a while to take it. The professor is therefore encouraging him to take the marketing class so that he does not have to wait a year to enroll in it.

3   [Understanding Organization Question]

The student thinks the professor looks busy because of all of the papers on her desk. She responds that she is just preparing for a graduate-level class that she is teaching in the afternoon.

4   [Making Inferences Question]

The student goes to the professor for advice about his classes. It can be inferred from this that she is the student's advisor.

5   [Understanding Attitude Question]

Saying, "So you're all set," indicates that there are no more problems. So the professor is telling the student that if he follows her plan, he will not have any problems with his schedule.

Vocabulary **Review**   p.45

1 (B)   2 (B)   3 (C)   4 (D)   5 (A)
6 (B)   7 (D)   8 (A)   9 (D)   10 (B)
11 (B)   12 (C)   13 (E)   14 (D)   15 (A)

▶ Chapter │ **02** Life Sciences 2 • Conversations

Mastering **Question Types**
with Lectures & Conversations   **A1**   p.48

[TYPES 1–4]

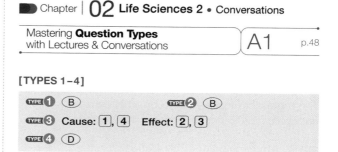

TYPE**1** (B)   TYPE**2** (B)
TYPE**3** Cause: [1], [4]   Effect: [2], [3]
TYPE**4** (D)

Script 02-11

W Professor: For our first topic today, I'd like to cover eutrophication. Oh, it's written on page, uh, page fifty-six in your texts if you're interested in the spelling. So eutrophication . . . Can anyone explain what it means?

M Student: Doesn't it, uh, have to do with the increased growth of plant life in lakes?

W: Correct, Thomas. I'm glad to see you've been keeping up with your reading . . . Uh, yes, that's one important aspect of eutrophication. Yet there's more to it than what you just said.

What is eutrophication? Basically, it's the increased production of algae caused by the buildup of key nutrients that control the amount of plant growth in a body of water. In general, we talk about eutrophication happening in lakes. But it can take place in any aquatic environment. For instance, uh, estuaries, ponds, and even, um, streams. Be sure to remember that. All right?

What causes eutrophication? It's mostly caused by an increase in nitrates and phosphates in a body of water. Humans are typically responsible for this. How? Well, many fertilizers contain nitrates and phosphates. When water runs off farmland with fertilizer in it, nitrates and phosphates can enter the water. Oh, and animal and human waste with these nutrients can enter the water, too.

What happens next? The nutrients essentially, uh, fertilize the water, which quickly causes an increase in algae growth. This creates an algae bloom. That's a dense, visible patch of algae located near the water's surface. Now, you'd think that increased algae growth would be a good thing. But that's not always true. Why not? Well, it prevents light from getting to the deeper areas of the water. This can kill some fish, but it also causes a more serious problem when the algae die. Then, oxygen-using bacteria start decomposing the algae. Because the water has so much algae, the bacteria multiply and start depleting the water of oxygen. Without oxygen, the fish in the water literally suffocate and die.

Obviously, eutrophication is harmful. How can we stop it? There are several ways. Let me tell you about some.

TYPE 1 [Gist-Content Question]

The professor focuses mostly on what causes eutrophication to occur and what its effects are.

TYPE 2 [Understanding Organization Question]

Throughout the lecture, the professor asks questions. Then, she proceeds to answer them herself.

TYPE 3 [Connecting Content Question]

According to the lecture, eutrophication is caused when nitrates enter the water and the water gets fertilized. Among its effects are that the oxygen supply disappears from the water and an algae bloom may be created.

TYPE 4 [Speaker's Attitude Question]

The professor tells the student, "I'm glad to see you've been keeping up with your reading," so she is giving him a compliment.

Summarizing

The professor asks the class about eutrophication. A student gives her a partial definition. The teacher explains that eutrophication is the increased production of algae in water such as lakes. Nitrates and phosphates enter the water. This fertilizes it, so algae grow quickly. This forms an algae bloom. When the algae die, bacteria begin eating them. But there are so many algae that the bacteria increase tremendously and remove the oxygen from the lake. This kills all of the fish in the water.

[TYPES 5–8]

| TYPE 5 | B | TYPE 6 | D |
| TYPE 7 | B | TYPE 8 | D |

Script 02-12

M Professor: I've described features of fish living in fresh water, and we've also covered fish that live in salt water and their characteristics. Now, um, let me discuss fish that can handle living in both fresh and salt water. There are not many of these euryhaline fish. By the way, that's spelled E-U-R-Y-H-A-L-I-N-E.

In general, there are two types of euryhaline fish. First are those that swim upstream to spawn. These are sea fish which spend the majority of their lives in salt water. Second are those that migrate to the sea to spawn. These are river fish, which include certain types of eels.

Arguably the best-known euryhaline sea fish is the salmon. There are many species of salmon, nearly all of which spend time in fresh and salt water. First, salmon hatch from eggs in freshwater rivers and streams. After a couple of years, they migrate to the ocean, where they live for years. Near the ends of their lives, they depart their saltwater homes, return to where they were born, reproduce, and then die. Uh, just so you know, some other euryhaline sea fish are various species of sturgeon, mackerel, and sea bass.

Another fish—one much more dangerous than salmon—that lives in both environments is the bull shark. The bull shark . . . ah, here's a picture of it on the screen . . . is an aggressive shark that is incredibly dangerous. It frequently swims in shallow water near beaches. It also attacks more humans than great white sharks.

So, uh, anyway, bull sharks are often found swimming in rivers. Not so long ago, two bull sharks were found near St. Louis in the Mississippi River. In case you don't know, that's approximately 1,100 miles away from the saltwater Gulf of Mexico. Bull sharks have also been found about that far upriver in the Amazon in South America.

How do their bodies manage to process both salt water and fresh water? Let me tell you what happens . . .

TYPE 5 [Gist-Content Question]

In his lecture on fish, the professor focuses on those that can survive in both freshwater and saltwater environments.

TYPE 6 [Detail Question]

The professor states, "First are those that swim upstream to spawn. These are sea fish which spend the majority of their lives in salt water."

TYPE 7 [Making Inferences Question]

The professor says, "Near the ends of their lives, they depart their saltwater homes, return to where they were born, reproduce, and then die." Since salmon return to where they were born in order to reproduce and then die after reproducing, the professor implies that salmon reproduce only one time in their lives.

TYPE 8 [Understanding Function Question]

The professor emphasizes how far upriver bull sharks can go in stating, "Not so long ago, two bull sharks were found near St. Louis in the Mississippi River. In case you don't know, that's approximately 1,100 miles away from the saltwater Gulf of Mexico. Bull sharks have also been found about that far upriver in the Amazon in South America."

Summarizing

The professor discusses euryhaline fish, which can survive in freshwater and saltwater environments. There are euryhaline sea fish and river fish. The salmon hatches in fresh water but lives most of its life in the ocean. Later, it returns to the river or stream where it was born, reproduces, and dies. The bull shark is another euryhaline fish. It is dangerous and attacks more people than great white sharks. Bull sharks have been found swimming more than 1,000 miles from the ocean in the Mississippi River and the Amazon River.

Mastering **Question Types**
with Lectures & Conversations

A2   p.50

[TYPES 1-4]

TYPE 1 (A)   **TYPE 2** (D)
TYPE 3 (B)   **TYPE 4** (B)

Script 02-13

M Professor: As I hope you remember, your homework was to read about enzymes in the text. However, it's my experience that enzymes can be, well, a little difficult to understand. So I want to talk about enzymes now. You know, uh, in case you didn't understand what you read.

At the most basic level, enzymes are proteins created in various organisms. Without them, it would

simply be impossible for an organism to live. Why is that? Well, enzymes are basically catalysts for the body. What they do is help accelerate a variety of chemical reactions in the body. Remember that, uh, every second, there are thousands of chemical reactions taking place in our bodies. And thanks to enzymes, these reactions happen both smoothly and quickly.

There are three main types of enzymes. The first are metabolic enzymes. These help, uh, run the body I guess we could say. The second are digestive enzymes. I'm sure you can figure out from their name that they help digest food. The third are food enzymes. These enable the body to start the digestion process. These enzymes are actually found in raw foods. When foods with them get cooked, these enzymes get destroyed. That's one reason why nutritionists advise us to eat some uncooked foods.

Okay, uh, let's get back to the roles of enzymes. As I'm sure you noticed, among their primary functions is to help with the processing and digesting of food. Essentially, they help convert the food we eat into chemical substances that can enter the bloodstream. This then allows the body to make use of the vitamins, minerals, and other nutrients contained in the food. Enzymes have other roles as well, but digestion is, uh, I would say, their most crucial one. The reason why is that, without enzymes, the body would take hours to break down food. Enzymes, meanwhile, can do the same thing in a matter of minutes. And enzymes don't get destroyed or changed during the chemical process. So the body can use them again and again.

TYPE 1 [Gist-Content Question]

The professor mostly talks about the roles that enzymes have in the body.

TYPE 2 [Understanding Organization Question]

The professor talks about the three main types of enzymes, and the first that he discusses is metabolic enzymes.

TYPE 3 [Connecting Content Question]

The professor mentions, "At the most basic level, enzymes are proteins created in various organisms."

TYPE 4 [Speaker's Attitude Question]

The professor starts by saying, "As I hope you remember, your homework was to read about enzymes in the text. However, it's my experience that enzymes can be, well, a little difficult to understand." He is implying that the homework may have been too advanced for the students.

The professor comments on the difficulty of the students' reading assignment. So he says he will go over what enzymes are. He identifies them as proteins and states that a body cannot live without them because of the chemical reactions that they help accelerate. There are three types of enzymes: metabolic, digestive, and food enzymes. All three of these enzymes have unique roles. Mostly, enzymes help the body process and digest food. They also release nutrients such as vitamins and minerals that the body can use.

[TYPES 5–8]

TYPE 5 (B)   TYPE 6 (A)
TYPE 7 (C)   TYPE 8 (C)

Script 02-14

M1 Student: Good afternoon. I have a problem with my dorm room, so I hope that you can give me some assistance.

M2 Housing Office Employee: Sure. I'll do my best. What seems to be the problem?

M1: I just checked into my new room, and, uh . . . well, there's no desk in it. I've got a single room in Bush Hall. It's got a bed and a dresser but not a desk.

M2: Well . . . That's certainly a big mistake. I can't believe that happened.

M1: So, uh, what do I do about this situation? I don't want to go an entire school year without a desk you know. That wouldn't be fun.

M2: [8]Of course. I wouldn't advise that. But, uh, don't worry. We have a procedure for this.

M1: This happens a lot?

M2: Not a lot, but it happens enough times that we know what to do to solve the problem. You need to fill out this form here . . . and you should get your desk sometime tomorrow before lunch.

M1: That's it? Are you, uh, sure about that? I mean, you're really not going to make me wait for a week or something?

M2: No, no. Not at all. Like I said, we know what to do in this situation. We'll take care of your problem as soon as possible. We always try to make life as easy as possible for our students here. Now, why don't you get started on that form?

TYPE 5 [Gist-Purpose Question]

The student tells the employee, "I just checked into my

new room, and, uh . . . well, there's no desk in it."

TYPE 6 [Detail Question]

The employee tells the student, "You should get your desk sometime tomorrow before lunch."

TYPE 7 [Making Inferences Question]

At the end of the conversation, the employee says, "Now, why don't you get started on that form?" The student will therefore probably complete the form.

TYPE 8 [Understanding Function Question]

When the student asks, "This happens a lot?" he is expressing his surprise that the school has a procedure for dealing with missing furniture.

The student visits the housing office to complain about a problem in his dormitory room. His room is missing a desk. The student says that he does not want to go the entire semester without a desk. The employee remarks that there is a procedure for the student to follow. He tells the student that a desk will be delivered. The student is surprised by how quickly he will get his desk. The employee then asks the student to fill out a form.

Mastering **Topics** with Lectures   B1   p.52

1 (C)   2 (A)   3 (D)

Script & Graphic Organizer 02-15

M Professor: Now that we've discussed the wolf, let's move on to a similar animal: the coyote. Coyotes are fascinating dog-like animals that live exclusively in North and Central America. They reside as far north as Alaska and as far south as Panama. There are nineteen species of coyotes, but they all share similar traits.

The upper parts of coyotes' fur are either grayish brown or grayish yellow. Their lower bodies tend to be whitish in color. Sometimes their legs and parts of their heads are reddish in appearance. Some actually look quite nice. Most coyotes are between two and three feet long, and each has a foot-long tail. On average, they weigh about, oh, thirty pounds. Obviously, they're not particularly big, but they have sharp claws and teeth and strong jaws. They're also swift runners and have been clocked at speeds of up to forty miles per hour. That, by the way, is faster than humans can run.

As for their habitats, well, coyotes are highly adaptable. I say that because they live in virtually every possible land ecosystem. That includes deserts, tundra, forests, and plains. Males, females, and cubs all live together in packs. They tend not to migrate but instead make their homes—called dens—in burrows underground, among rocky crevices, and in caves. On occasion, coyotes may find a den another animal has abandoned and make it their own. But that's not particularly, uh, common.

Let's see . . . What else? Ah, yes. Coyotes are nocturnal, so they hunt at night. They're mostly carnivorous, but some species supplement their diets with fruit and berries. Coyotes typically hunt in pairs. However, when pursuing large game, such as deer, they may hunt in packs. They also attack livestock, including sheep, cattle, and goats. As a result, ranchers frequently shoot them on sight. Many ranchers also trap and poison coyotes in attempts to control their numbers.

As for their mating habits, females tend to select one male and mate with him for several years. But they're not always monogamous. Nor do male and female coyotes form bonds for life as wolves do. Coyotes mate in the early spring and bear litters with anywhere from one to, uh . . . get this . . . nineteen pups. Six, however, is the average number. Coyotes reach maturity rapidly, as evidenced by the fact that males often leave the pack when they're anywhere from six to nine months old. Females, however, remain with their mother's pack for life. It's a harsh world for the male pups. Many die while on their own. In fact, only around fifty percent of them survive to adulthood. Yes? You have a question?

W Student: Yes, Professor Kirk, I do. What about the way they communicate? I've heard that coyotes can bark like dogs. Is that true?

M: Indeed it is. Actually, coyotes use many different sounds to communicate with one another. Barks are one of them. For instance, uh, a short bark may indicate the presence of danger. On the other hand, a long howl may let the rest of the pack know where the coyote is. Males use a variety of growls to show who the alpha male, uh, you know, the leader of the pack, is. And both males and females make various sounds when selecting their mates.

Coyotes

Coyote Characteristics:	Mating Habits:
- Are small dog-like animals	Females may mate with the same male for several years; have litters averaging 6 pups
- Have fur and long tails	
- Can live in many habitats	
- Live in packs	**Communication:**
- Have homes in dens	Use many different sounds, including barks; may also howl and make many different growls
- Often hunt together in pairs	

1 [Gist-Content Question]

The professor covers many aspects of coyotes, so he gives an overview of them.

2 [Understanding Attitude Question]

The professor's lecture is sympathetic toward coyotes, and he even says, "Some actually look quite nice," while describing them. Thus, he has some positive feelings toward them.

3 [Making Inferences Question]

The professor mentions, "I say that because they live in virtually every possible land ecosystem. That includes deserts, tundra, forests, and plains." Deserts are typically very hot while tundra is very cold. So the professor implies that coyotes can survive in all kinds of temperatures.

Summarizing

Coyotes are dog-like animals that live in North and Central America. They have grayish-brown or grayish-yellow fur and grow to be about three feet long. They are adaptable animals that can live in many different habitats. They live together in packs but often hunt in pairs. They may sometimes hunt in packs when chasing large animals. When they breed, the average litter has six pups. Only about half of all coyotes live to adulthood. They also use different sounds to communicate with one another.

Mastering **Topics** with Lectures | B2 | p.53

1 Ⓐ   2 Ⓒ   3 Ⓑ

Script 02-16

M Professor: Let me turn your attention now to the negative environmental impacts of dams. Dams can have a tremendous impact on the environment, both near and far from where they're situated. There are three major issues we need to focus on.

To begin, once a dam is built, it can have a huge impact on the fish that live in the river that's been, uh, dammed. Many species of fish swim upstream to breed and to lay eggs. Take the salmon as an example. Salmon are well known for returning to the places they were born, where they lay their eggs and then die. But, uh, what happens if there's a dam in the way? This can prevent salmon—and other fish as well—from reaching their breeding grounds . . . Er, yes?

W Student: But don't most dams have fish ladders that allow fish to swim around the dam and then continue upriver?

M: For the most part, yes, but many older dams lack them. In addition, not all fish can successfully navigate these fish ladders. Uh . . . I see some puzzled looks. You're curious about fish ladders, right? I've got a picture here . . . See . . . They're merely manmade watery pathways that allow fish to pass over or around a dam. Most have a series of steps that make them look like ladders, hence the name.

Now, the second issue . . . Excuse me. Rivers carry silt, which is dirt and other particles that are suspended in the water. Further downriver, the flow of silt decreases, so it often falls to the bottom of the river. This forms river bottoms and banks, and near the ocean or sea, it may create a delta. Silt is rich in nutrients, so the areas along a river's banks or in deltas are prime farmland. Consider, uh, consider the Nile River in Egypt. For thousands of years, its waters brought rich silt downriver. This permitted farmers to grow crops to feed the Egyptian people. However, when a dam gets built across a river, like the Egyptians did to the Nile in the late 1960s, then the flow of silt gets disrupted. This can lead to the loss of river banks, deltas, and fertile farmland. Additionally, the silt may build up behind a dam. This can block a dam's floodgates, which control the flow of water escaping a dam.

The third primary issue with dams is the flooding of the land upstream from them. Typically, a large lake forms behind a dam once it's built. While the lake may provide some benefits, which we've already discussed, it may also have many drawbacks. For instance, for the people and animals living in the flooded area, a dam may be disastrous. More than a decade ago, the Chinese constructed a massive dam—the, uh, the Three Gorges Dam—on the Yangtze River. While it's used to produce hydroelectric power, it has dislocated millions . . . yes, millions . . . of people. And when huge lakes form, wildlife must move to new habitats. Some wildlife may even die because their food sources disappear. Now, let's take an in-depth look at how the Aswan Dam across the Nile has affected the land and the people of Egypt. I think you'll find this fascinating.

The Negative Effects of Dams

First Effect:	Second Effect:	Third Effect:
- Can impact fish living in the river	- Decrease the flow of silt downriver	- Land upstream gets flooded
- Fish like salmon cannot swim upstream to lay eggs	- Silt is nutrient rich so is good for farmers	- People and animals living there must move
- Must build fish ladders for fish to use	- Dam on the Nile River stops Egyptians farmers from getting silt	- Can dislocate millions of people
		- Wildlife may even die

1 [Gist-Purpose Question]

About the Three Gorges Dam, the professor states, "For instance, for the people and animals living in the flooded area, a dam may be disastrous. More than a decade ago, the Chinese constructed a massive dam—the, uh, the Three Gorges Dam—on the Yangtze River. While it's used to produce hydroelectric power, it has dislocated millions . . . yes, millions . . . of people."

2 [Detail Question]

Concerning fish ladders, the professor says, "They're merely manmade watery pathways that allow fish to pass over or around a dam. Most have a series of steps that make them look like ladders, hence the name."

3 [Understanding Organization Question]

The professor explains, "Consider, uh, consider the Nile River in Egypt. For thousands of years, its waters brought rich silt downriver. This permitted farmers to grow crops to feed the Egyptian people. However, when a dam gets built across a river, like the Egyptians did to the Nile in the late 1960s, then the flow of silt gets disrupted." He is commenting on the Nile's relationship with silt.

Summarizing

The professor describes the negative effects of dams. First is that they can adversely impact fish, such as salmon, that travel upriver to lay their eggs. He points out there are fish ladders, however, that fish use to get by dams. Second is that dams prevent nutrient-rich silt from going downriver. He notes that the dam across the Nile River is disrupting the flow of silt. Third is that dams flood the land upstream. So people and animals often get displaced and have to move or may even die.

Mastering **Topics** with Lectures B3 p.54

1 (A) 2 Vocalization: [2], [4] Echolocation: [1], [3] 3 (C)

Script & Graphic Organizer 02-17

W Professor: So how do marine animals communicate and navigate in the oceans? Let's look at dolphins for our first case study. Dolphins are widely considered among the most intelligent marine animals. They use their intelligence both to communicate with one another and to navigate while underwater. How do they do this? There are two major ways: vocalization and echolocation. I'm sure you can guess that vocalization means using voices to make sounds. But please note that dolphins lack vocal cords like many land animals have. Instead, they use muscles in their blowholes to make clicks and whistles.

M Student: Ah, I beg your pardon, but what's a . . . a blowhole?

W: It's the round hole at the top of a dolphin's head that it uses to breathe. Remember that dolphins are mammals, not fish, so they have no gills. Like whales, they must surface constantly to breathe. Got it . . . ? So, uh, back to vocalization . . . Anyway, when a dolphin forces air out of its blowhole, some muscles inside it contract. This, in turn, lets the dolphin make various sounds. Thanks to a great deal of observation and experimentation conducted by marine biologists, we think we know the purposes of some of these sounds. [3]First, dolphins use whistle-like sounds to communicate with other dolphins. One of these is an identification sound. Each dolphin has its own unique whistle identification sound. **Think of it as a dolphin's uh, personal ID card.** This is created very early in a dolphin's life. So dolphins can recognize one another just from that sound. These sounds are also used to identify a particular pod, which is what we call a group of dolphins.

M: Can dolphins actually talk to each other and, uh, you know, give commands and stuff?

W: Er, not really. Okay, let me clarify that. Some people have carried out experiments and learned that dolphins can recognize some human words. In that sense, they're kind of like, er, dogs and cats in their amount of understanding. But as to whether or not dolphins can actually, uh, talk to one another, well, that's currently unknown. Still, they employ body language with one another. They may show their teeth, slap their tails, and butt heads with other dolphins. So we can consider body language a definite form of dolphin communication.

Dolphins also use sound to navigate. They can emit high-pitched clicking sounds at rapid rates. Marine biologists have determined that these clicks are a form of echolocation, which is a navigation method. Basically, it's a way for dolphins to locate objects when visibility in the water is poor. It's sort of like radar, or, I should say, sonar. You know, like what bats use on land. Dolphins emit these clicks at frequencies of up to 200 kilohertz. The sound waves bounce off objects and return to them. Inside every dolphin's head is an organ called the melon. This sensory organ picks up the sound waves. Then, the brain interprets the distance, direction, and size of the object. As dolphins near certain objects of interest, they emit clicks more rapidly. Some have been measured at up to 700 clicks per second. This lets them identify whatever they're homing in on.

Dolphin Communication and Navigation

Dolphin Communication:	Dolphin Navigation:
- *Use their blowholes to make sounds* - *Communicate with other dolphins by making whistle-like sounds* - *Use body language such as showing their teeth, slapping their tails, and butting heads with other dolphins*	- *Use sound to navigate* - *Is a form of echolocation* - *Rapidly emit high-pitched clicks* - *Use the their melon to know the distances, directions, and sizes of objects*

1 [Understanding Organization Question]

When describing the process of dolphin navigation, the professor discusses the science that makes it possible.

2 [Connecting Content Question]

According to the lecture, vocalization is caused by contracting muscles and relies upon a dolphin's blowhole. As for echolocation, the melon in the dolphin's head interprets the clicks, and it works much like sonar does.

3 [Understanding Function Question]

By mentioning a "personal ID card," the professor is making a comparison between an ID card and the whistling sounds of dolphins.

The professor says that dolphins are intelligent, so they can communicate with each other. They can vocalize by using their blowholes. By forcing air out of its blowhole, a dolphin can make some muscles contract. This lets it make different sounds. Dolphins also make whistling sounds and use body language to communicate with each other. As for navigating, dolphins emit high-pitched clicking sounds. These are a form of echolocation. Dolphins use a kind of sonar to see underwater and to identify whatever they are pursuing.

Mastering **Topics** with Conversations (B4) p.55

1 (B)   2 (D)   3 (A)

Script & Graphic Organizer 02-18

W Student: Professor Patterson, may I come in? I have a couple of questions for you.

M Professor: Of course, Sheila. Please come in and make yourself comfortable. Have a seat in that chair.

W: Thank you so much, sir. So, uh, I have a question about our most recent assignment.

M: Do you mean the reading? Oh, that's easy. All you have to do is read chapter 4 by the time we have our next lecture.

W: Oh, no, sir. I'm not here about the reading. I'm here about the project you assigned last week. You know, uh, the script that we're supposed to write for you.

M: Ah, yes. Sure. So, uh, what exactly do you want to know about it?

W: Well, um . . . I'm kind of confused. Let me see if I understand . . . You want us to write a script for a scene in a movie, right?

M: Exactly. But, of course, it has to be an original script. I don't want you to, uh, just copy a scene from some movie that's already been released. You need to make your own movie.

W: All right. That's what I was planning to do. But I'm having problems with it.

M: Like what?

W: Even though I'm just writing a single scene, I have to think about the entire movie. At first, I thought this would be a simple assignment. But, now, I'm having problems with it. I have to create a bunch

of characters and then give them personalities, background stories, and everything else.

M: Ah, yes. [3]Now you can see how tough it really is to write a movie script. But here . . . Let me give you a little hint on what to do.

W: A hint? Awesome. What is it?

M: Start with scene one in the movie. That way, you won't have to do quite as much work as you would with, say, the final scene in a movie. Oh, and since your final project is to write a complete movie script, you can use this first scene as part of that movie.

Office Hours

Reason for Visiting:	Result:
Wants to confirm her writing assignment	Professor confirms that she must write an original scene from a movie
Student's Complaint:	Professor's Response:
Creating characters for a new movie is very difficult	Write the opening scene from a movie she makes up

1 [Gist-Purpose Question]

The student says, "So, uh, I have a question about our most recent assignment."

2 [Detail Question]

When the student asks, "You want us to write a script for a scene in a movie, right?" the professor responds by saying, "Exactly."

3 [Understanding Attitude Question]

When the student responds by saying, "Awesome," she is showing how pleased she is that the professor is going to give her a hint.

The student visits the professor to ask about her assignment. The professor tells her to read chapter 4. The student says she is there about a different assignment. She wants to confirm that she should write one scene from a movie. He says she is right. The student complains that it is difficult to do this assignment. The professor says to make the scene the opening one since that will be easier. He then mentions that she can use that scene as a part of her final project.

1 Ⓒ   2 Ⓓ   3 Ⓑ   4 Flowers: ②, ③, ④

Fruits and Berries: ①   5 Ⓐ   6 Ⓒ

Script 02-19

W Professor: Every spring, we see all kinds of beautiful flowers blooming everywhere. What I'd like to address now is why many flowers bloom during spring in temperate climates. In order to answer this question, we need to know what the, uh, the purpose of a flower is. Let's find out, shall we?

Plants reproduce from seeds. In flowering plants, these seeds are present in fruits and berries. Inside the flower is the plant's reproductive system. The male part, which contains pollen, is the stamen. The female part, which contains ovules, or eggs, is the pistil. When the pollen meets the eggs, fertilization occurs, and reproduction begins. The result is the growth of fruits and berries, which contain the seeds. However, the stamen and pistil are not in close proximity, relatively speaking, to each other. They need help to meet. Sometimes the wind or the rain can do this. But animals such as insects do a much better job of pollinating plants. And this is where blooming flowers become important. Essentially, blooming flowers attract birds and insects such as, oh, bees and butterflies. These animals can all pollinate plants and therefore enable them to reproduce.

Here's what the flowers do . . . First, they attract animals with their sweet nectar. Bees, for example, suck the nectar of flowering plants and use it to make honey. The smell of the nectar attracts many animals. In addition, the colorful petals of many blooming flowers act as attractors. Essentially, they're like big neon signs on restaurants that read, "Eat here. Delicious food." You see, birds and bees have color vision, so they can recognize the colorful flower petals. So once attracted, either by smell or color, the animals arrive and move around inside the flower while extracting the nectar. Their movements spread the pollen from the stamen to the pistil, thereby fertilizing the plants' ovules.

The tasty fruits and berries also attract other animals and humans. When someone or something plucks and eats the fruits and berries, some seeds may get dropped on the ground or moved to new locations, where they may subsequently fall to the earth. In this manner, some of these seeds many germinate and begin growing. As a result, there are more new flowering plants. As you can see, without blooming flowers, most plants would not survive since they wouldn't be able to reproduce.

Now, uh, back to my initial question: Why do most flowers bloom in spring in temperate climates that have four seasons? Well, flowers bloom then since they need to be pollinated and require time to produce seeds before colder fall and winter weather arrives. Simply put, most fruits and berries can't survive in cold weather. In fact, sometimes cold snaps in spring may damage or even kill newly growing seeds.

Of course, not every flower blooms in spring. Let's see . . . hydrangeas, lilies, and sunflowers produce no fruit, so they never evolved to bloom in spring. Instead, they bloom in summer. That season's hot weather gives them enough time to produce the seeds that will ensure their survival. Other plants are tough enough to survive early winter frosts, so they bloom later in the year. There are also plants such as orchids, which grow in tropical climates. They can bloom at any time during the year since the weather is fairly consistent and the risk of damage from cold weather is, uh, nonexistent. As you can likely surmise from what I've just said, not all flowers bloom at the same time. Each species has its own cycle and timing. The amounts of heat, sunlight, and rain all play significant roles in determining the cycle.

[6]**But keep this in mind, please . . .** Even if a flower blooms, gets pollinated, produces fruits or berries, and has some seeds fall to the ground, there's no guarantee these seeds will become new plants. Sometimes there's not enough rain, so the seeds don't grow. Other times, there's too much, so the seeds get washed away. Some seeds may get parched when it's too hot. And seeds must compete with other plants, including non-flowering plants like, uh, grasses. They all vie for sunlight, water, and nutrients in the soil. The seeds often win. But they sometimes lose.

1 [Gist-Content Question]

The professor mainly focuses on flower reproduction throughout her lecture.

2 [Gist-Purpose Question]

The professor says, "First, they attract animals with their sweet nectar. Bees, for example, suck the nectar of flowering plants and use it to make honey. The smell of the nectar attracts many animals. In addition, the colorful petals of many blooming flowers act as attractors. Essentially, they're like big neon signs on restaurants that read, 'Eat here. Delicious food.'" While explaining nectar, she stresses the attraction of animals to it.

3 [Detail Question]

The professor mentions, "There are also plants such as orchids, which grow in tropical climates. They can bloom at any time during the year since the weather is fairly consistent and the risk of damage from cold weather is, uh, nonexistent."

4 [Connecting Content Question]

According to the lecture, flowers usually bloom in the spring, produce nectar that animals consume, and attract animals because of their colors. As for fruits and berries, they may get dropped on the ground and then germinate later.

5 [Making Inferences Question]

The professor notes the importance of insects to pollinating plants. Thus, it can be inferred that bees, which are insects, are crucial to the pollination process.

6 [Understanding Function Question]

When the professor says, "Keep this in mind," and then pauses, she is letting the students know that she is about to make an important point.

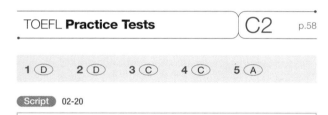

TOEFL **Practice Tests** C2 p.58

1 Ⓓ   2 Ⓓ   3 Ⓒ   4 Ⓒ   5 Ⓐ

Script 02-20

W Bookstore Employee: Hello. I'm the manager of the bookstore. One of my employees said that you're looking for me. What can I do for you?

M Student: Ah, yes. Hi. I'm, uh, I'm trying to return this book, but your employee won't let me.

W: May I see your receipt, please? You have the receipt with you, right?

M: Of course I do. I've got it right here. See . . . It's this book right here. The, uh, the third one on the list. It cost me 12.99 dollars. All I want is my money back, but your employee won't give it to me. And the book is in perfect condition . . . See. Here it is. Look at it. It's perfect.

W: Okay, sir, I understand why the employee wouldn't refund your money.

M: Yeah? You do?

W: You see, um, you purchased this book on September 2. There's the date up at the top of the receipt.

M: Yeah, right. That was the first day of class. I purchased all of my books on that day.

W: Yes, I can see that here. It's a long receipt. But today is September 21. So it's been nineteen days since you purchased that book.

M: Okay . . . Uh, so what? I don't get it.

W: Well, the bookstore has a two-week return policy. That means you can only return a book for a refund two weeks after you purchase it. If you wait any longer than that, we can't give you your money back. So, unfortunately, I cannot refund your money.

M: You've got to be kidding me. The bookstore only has a two-week return policy? That's not very fair.

W: What do you mean?

M: Well, I'm returning this book because I dropped the class. So, uh, obviously, I don't need the book anymore. But most students don't drop their classes until the third or fourth week of school.

W: Perhaps you should have waited to buy your books.

M: Why would I do that? If I take a class, I want to buy the books immediately. What kind of student would I be if I didn't buy the books?

W: Yes, you make a good point. I totally see what you mean.

M: Great. So, uh, then you're going to refund my money?

W: No, I can't do that. But I will talk to my supervisor. I'll see if I can get him to change the store's policy. That's the best I can do. [5]Why don't you write down your name and contact information? I'll let you know what happens.

M: Okay. I guess that's better than nothing.

1 [Gist-Content Question]

The student is trying to get his money back for a book that he purchased at the bookstore.

2 [Gist-Purpose Question]

The manager tells the student about the policies of the bookstore because she is trying to explain why the student cannot return the book: He is returning it too late.

3 [Understanding Attitude Question]

The student says, "You've got to be kidding me. The bookstore only has a two-week return policy? That's not very fair."

4 [Understanding Organization Question]

The student states, "Well, I'm returning this book because I dropped the class. So, uh, obviously, I don't need the book anymore."

5 [Understanding Function Question]

When the student declares, "That's better than nothing," he is agreeing to do what the manager requests.

Vocabulary Review   p.61

1 Ⓓ   2 Ⓑ   3 Ⓓ   4 Ⓒ   5 Ⓐ
6 Ⓒ   7 Ⓓ   8 Ⓓ   9 Ⓐ   10 Ⓑ
11 Ⓑ   12 Ⓔ   13 Ⓒ   14 Ⓐ   15 Ⓓ

▶ Chapter | **03** Social Sciences 1 • Conversations

Mastering **Question Types** with Lectures & Conversations   **A1**   p.64

[TYPES 1–4]

TYPE❶ Ⓓ   TYPE❷ Ⓒ
TYPE❸ Geocentricism: ①, ②   Heliocentricism: ③, ④
TYPE❹ Ⓓ

Script   02-21

W Professor: As we all know, there have been various theories of Earth's place in the universe. Two such theories are heliocentricism and geocentricism. Are any of you aware of what these terms mean? Craig, do you want to take a guess?

M Student: Yes, ma'am. I'm pretty sure that geocentricism is the belief that Earth is at the center of the solar system. As for heliocentricism, I think that theory puts the sun at the center of the solar system instead.

W: ⁴**That's a pretty succinct answer, Craig.** Now, let me give you a few of the details concerning each. First, please be aware that the ancients knew Earth was round. Don't believe all that stuff about people thinking Earth was flat. Sure, some people did, but most knew better. Anyway, uh, sorry for that digression. Okay, now, both geocentricism and heliocentricism were proposed by the ancient Greeks. However, the majority of ancient Greeks subscribed to the geocentric model. This included, by the way, Aristotle and Ptolemy. Basically, they

believed the sun, moon, planets, and other stars all revolved around Earth.

This essentially became, hmm, shall we say, orthodox thinking for almost two thousand years. After all, who was going to challenge Aristotle in terms of scientific knowledge? No one, right? Thus it wasn't until the sixteenth century that anyone began seriously to challenge the geocentric theory. The first person to state that the sun was at the center of the solar system was Nicolaus Copernicus. He presented a mathematical formula that showed Earth orbited the sun, not the other way around. Well, Johannes Kepler took Copernicus's work and expanded upon it. Finally, Galileo Galilei used his telescope to further confirm that the heliocentric model was correct.

Since this isn't a science class, we won't get into how he did it. However, Galileo's work had huge social ramifications. One of them was that he really upset the Roman Catholic Church with his theories. So the Church made an effort to suppress Galileo's findings. And that's what we need to get into right now.

TYPE❶ [Gist-Content Question]

The professor mostly discusses geocentricism and heliocentricism, which are two models of the solar system.

TYPE❷ [Understanding Organization Question]

During her lecture, the professor names the two theories on the solar system, and then she discusses both of them.

TYPE❸ [Connecting Content Question]

According to the lecture, geocentricism was believed by Aristotle and dominated scientific thought for 2,000 years. As for heliocentricism, Nicolaus Copernicus believed that theory, and it was confirmed thanks to the telescope.

TYPE❹ [Speaker's Attitude Question]

When the professor notes that the student gave "a pretty succinct answer," he is indicating that the answer was well stated.

Summarizing

The professor asks the students what geocentricism and heliocentricism are. A student answers that geocentricism places Earth at the center of the solar system while heliocentricism puts the sun at the center of the solar system. The professor explains that most ancient Greeks believed in the heliocentric model. This included Aristotle and Ptolemy. So this model dominated for 2,000 years.

Then, Nicolaus Copernicus proposed the heliocentric model. Johannes Kepler expanded on the idea. And Galileo Galilei used a telescope to prove it was correct.

[TYPES 5-8]

TYPE **5** Ⓑ TYPE **6** Ⓒ
TYPE **7** Ⓒ TYPE **8** Ⓓ

Script 02-22

M Professor: [8]Please be sure to pay close attention and take good notes, everyone. **The information I'm about to give you will be on next week's midterm exam.** I'd like to give you a brief overview of the Celts before going into detail on their history. One common misconception people have about the Celts concerns their identity. Most people believe the Celts were merely the ancestors of the Irish and the Scots. While true, in fact, the Celts comprised many other groups of people. What these groups had in common was that they all spoke various Celtic languages, of which there were several. Irish, Cornish, Welsh, and Breton are four.

As you can see, the Celts were a diverse group of people. They occupied lands that spanned the European continent. However, they were mostly concentrated in Central and Western Europe. The earliest archaeological evidence of the Celts was unearthed in Hallstatt, Austria, and dates to around 1200 B.C. Included in the artifacts uncovered there were iron weapons. This indicates that the Celts were among the first . . . perhaps even the first . . . people on the European continent to use iron.

Most of what we know about Celtic history comes from Greek and Roman sources. Please note, though, that the Greeks and the Romans were both biased against the Celts as they considered them to be, uh . . . violently insane.

W Student: Huh? How so?

M: It came from the Celts' approach to warfare. You see, the Celts fought, in the words of many commentators, like, uh, wild beasts. They went sort of, shall we say, berserk when they fought. They slung their weapons around violently and killed anything around them. They also tended to regard warfare as sport, which made them less than civilized in the minds of most Greeks and Romans. Of course, since the Celts had no written tradition, they have left behind no writings to defend their actions. So we have to rely on others instead. Okay, enough of that. Now, you've probably heard of Druids, right? They were an integral part of Celtic culture. Let me go over them now.

TYPE **5** [Gist-Purpose Question]

The professor states, "Most of what we know about Celtic history comes from Greek and Roman sources. Please note, though, that the Greeks and the Romans were both biased against the Celts as they considered them to be, uh . . . violently insane."

TYPE **6** [Detail Question]

The professor mentions, "The earliest archaeological evidence of the Celts was unearthed in Hallstatt, Austria, and dates to around 1200 B.C. Included in the artifacts uncovered there were iron weapons."

TYPE **7** [Making Inferences Question]

The professor says, "Now, you've probably heard of Druids, right? They were an integral part of Celtic culture. Let me go over them now." So he is going to discuss another aspect of the Celts.

TYPE **8** [Understanding Function Question]

When the professor remarks that the information will be on the upcoming midterm, he is indicating that the material he is going to cover is important.

Summarizing

The professor declares that he wants to give a short overview of the Celts. He says that the Celts comprised many groups of people. They all spoke Celtic languages such as Irish, Cornish, Welsh, and Breton. The Celts lived all over Central and Western Europe. They were among the first people in Europe to use iron. The Greeks and the Romans wrote about the Celts but disliked them. They thought the Celts fought like wild beasts and were uncivilized. The Celts had no written tradition, so they left no records of themselves.

Mastering **Question Types**
with Lectures & Conversations

A2 p.66

[TYPES 1-4]

TYPE **1** Ⓐ TYPE **2** Ⓒ
TYPE **3** Advantage: ①, ②, ④ Disadvantage: ③
TYPE **4** Ⓑ

Script 02-23

M Professor: Technology has changed modern lives in numerous ways. We can fly to places around the world and even visit outer space these days. Computers and the Internet have altered how people learn, work, and get entertained. But I don't want to discuss those changes that technology has caused. Instead, I want to discuss something different. I'd like to cover how technology has changed how people consume food.

Let me give you one example. How many of you take pictures of your meals and post them onto social media . . . ? Yeah, just about everyone's hand went up. Sylvia? You have a comment?

W Student: I frequently post selfies with food, but I'm not sure how that has changed my eating habits.

M: Actually, social media has a huge influence on what people eat. Do you show pictures of junk food or healthy, nutritious food?

W: The latter. I wouldn't dare post a picture of me with a candy bar. Oh . . . I get your point.

M: Wonderful, Sylvia. You see, people are much more conscious about the food they eat since others on social media pages are likely to make comments. Nobody wants criticism. Instead, people want praise for their choices. So eating habits have improved.

In addition, you should consider how the Internet has changed eating habits . . . Many years ago when I was growing up, my mother had a single cookbook that she got recipes from. Today, there are countless ways to obtain recipes. There are cooking blogs, for instance. People randomly post recipes as well. It's also simple to acquire nutritional information about the food you're preparing and eating thanks to modern technology. None of that was accessible a mere thirty years ago.

Here's another point . . . You've probably noticed that many young people are overweight. Well . . . we can blame technology for that, too. Young people are often glued to computer games and TV shows, so they don't cook much. Many of them are making poor food choices. They're consuming convenience store food, frozen food, and other food with low nutritional value. We can blame technology for this.

TYPE 1 [Gist-Content Question]

The professor states, "I'd like to cover how technology has changed how people consume food."

TYPE 2 [Understanding Organization Question]

The professor remarks, "Young people are often glued to computer games and TV shows, and many of them are making poor food choices. They're consuming convenience store food, frozen food, and other foods with low nutritional values. We can blame technology for this."

TYPE 3 [Connecting Content Question]

According to the lecture, technology has let people learn about nutritional information regarding the food they eat. They also have access to food blogs, giving them more recipes. And it lets people avoid criticism for certain choices. As for disadvantages, many young people are eating frozen food these days.

TYPE 4 [Speaker's Attitude Question]

The professor declares, "You see, people are much more conscious about the food they eat since others on social media pages are likely to make comments."

Summarizing

The professor states that modern technology has changed how people eat. He says that social media has made people more conscious about their food choices since others will comment about them on social media. He then notes that the Internet has changed eating habits. People can get many more recipes today than they could in the past. He also blames people being overweight on modern technology. He remarks that people play computer games and watch TV programs, so they do not cook. Instead, they eat food with poor nutritional value.

[TYPES 5–8]

TYPE 5 (A)   **TYPE 6** (C)

TYPE 7 (B)   **TYPE 8** (B)

Script 02-24

M Professor: Hi there. Are you waiting to see me? My office hours are almost finished, but I've still got some time to see you if you need something.

W Student: Oh, thank you, Professor. I don't want to impose, but I could use some advice on the short paper we're supposed to turn in next week.

M: No problem. Come on in and have a seat, please . . . Okay, so, uh, what do you need to know about the short paper?

W: Well, um, I was hoping to do it on butterflies and the four stages of their lives. Would, uh, would that be all right?

M: Hmm . . . Sorry, but I don't think so. Let me tell you why. Remember that this short paper is supposed to be about something connected with one of our lab assignments. As far as I can remember, we haven't done anything with butterflies this semester.

W: Oh, I see. I forgot that you had said that. [8]Then, um, do you have any ideas for me?

M: Well, we dissected shellfish in the lab last week.

Why don't you do your assignment on them?

W: Shellfish aren't really my thing. I didn't enjoy that lab at all.

M: Then, um, how about the first lab when we looked at some worms? I'm sure you could get a paper out of that.

W: Oh, yeah. That was a good lab. I totally loved it. I think that's what I'll write about. Thanks so much, sir. I appreciate your assistance.

TYPE 5 [Gist-Purpose Question]

In the professor's office, the student states, "Well, um, I was hoping to do it on butterflies and the four stages of their lives. Would, uh, would that be all right?" She is hoping to get approval for her chosen topic.

TYPE 6 [Detail Question]

The professor tells the student that the paper is "supposed to be about something connected with one of our lab assignments."

TYPE 7 [Making Inferences Question]

The professor is very helpful to the student. He also comes up with some paper topics for her. Thus, it can be inferred that he does not mind assisting his students.

TYPE 8 [Understanding Function Question]

When the student says, "Shellfish aren't really my thing," she is indicating her dislike for shellfish. So she is rejecting the topic that the professor has given her.

Summarizing

The student visits the professor to ask a question. She wants to know about the short paper due next week. The professor asks what she would like to know about it. She responds that her topic is on butterflies, but the professor says that is a bad choice. Her paper should be about something connected to a lab assignment. He suggests writing about shellfish, but she rejects his idea. Then, he mentions worms. The student states that she loved the lab on worms, so she will write about them.

Mastering **Topics** with Lectures | **B1** | p.68

| 1 ⓓ | 2 ⓓ | 3 ⓑ |

Script & Graphic Organizer 02-25

M Professor: In our previous class, we examined

the Italian Renaissance in the fifteenth and sixteenth centuries. Today, I'd like to cover the Northern European Renaissance. It took place later than the Italian Renaissance but was a direct result of the spreading influence of ideas coming from Italy. Oh, and when I say Northern European, I'm referring to France, the Netherlands, Great Britain, the German states, and Poland.

There were three major factors involved in the spreading of ideas in Northern Europe. They were the development of the printing press, the splitting of the Catholic Church, and the decline of feudalism. The printing press made books cheaper and more available and also helped spread ideas. The Reformation and the rise of Protestantism led to many people living more secular lives, which allowed new ideas to flourish. As the Catholic Church's influence waned, humanism gained importance. Remember that humanism is the idea that humans are of prime importance and that all humans have rights. Although not everyone embraced humanism, it took root during the Renaissance and has become quite influential, uh, even up to today.

The third factor, as I mentioned, was the decline of feudalism. For a millennium, feudalism had prevented much progress from being made in Northern Europe. However, thanks to the rise of independent towns and the use of money as a medium of exchange, the feudal system of lords and serfs began to decline. Suddenly, large numbers of freemen began demanding wages for their labor. As feudalism declined, governments in Northern Europe became more stable and centralized. Thus monarchies strengthened, which curbed the power of many nobles.

With stronger monarchies came more wealth and a desire to explore new aspects of life. In the sixteenth century, Northern European monarchs—particularly French kings—began to acquire a taste for Italian things. This led to the purchasing of Italian art and the hiring of Italian architects to design and build palaces and other buildings. Around the same time, in the early 1500s, many Northern European artists traveled to Italy. There, they were influenced by the works of Michelangelo, Raphael, and other notable artists. Furthermore, trade between Northern Europe and Italy increased. This too helped spread the ideas of the Italian Renaissance.

You should realize, however that not every Northern European country was equally influenced. On the European continent, for instance, the arts, architecture, and science were affected. As for Great Britain, the Renaissance came late, and its influence was mostly felt in literature. One need only look at the

Italian flavor of many of William Shakespeare's works to see proof of that. I refer, of course, to *Romeo and Juliet*, *The Twelfth Night*, and *The Merchant of Venice*.

Many of the people involved in the Northern Italian Renaissance were devoted to expanding man's knowledge of the world and to improving human progress. This led directly to the Age of Enlightenment, which took place in the seventeenth and eighteenth centuries. During that time, great scientific discoveries were made and theories promulgated. These all helped set the stage for our modern-day lives. In addition, many Northern Europeans got the urge to explore the world around them. This led to the building of large oceangoing ships which they sailed around the world.

The Northern European Renaissance

Causes of the Spread of Ideas:	Effects of the Spread of Ideas:
- The development of the printing press	- People began exploring new aspects of life
- The splitting of the Catholic Church	- Artists traveled to Italy
- The decline of feudalism	- Writers were influenced by Italy
	- The Age of Enlightenment occurred

1 [Gist-Purpose Question]

The professor states, "As the Catholic Church's influence waned, humanism gained importance. Remember that humanism is the idea that humans are of prime importance and that all humans have rights. Although not everyone embraced humanism, it took root during the Renaissance and has become quite influential, uh, even up to today." So he is describing how it became influential in the Renaissance.

2 [Connecting Content Question]

The professor says, "With stronger monarchies came more wealth and a desire to explore new aspects of life. In the sixteenth century, Northern European monarchs—particularly French kings—began to acquire a taste for Italian things. This led to the purchasing of Italian art and the hiring of Italian architects to design and build palaces and other buildings." Thus, both of them were responsible for helping spread various ideas of the Italian Renaissance.

3 [Understanding Organization Question]

The professor talks about how several of Shakespeare's famous plays, including *Romeo and Juliet*, have an Italian influence.

Summarizing

The professor mentions three main reasons that the Italian Renaissance spread to Northern Europe. First was the printing press. Second was the splitting of the Catholic Church and the rise of humanism. Third was the decline of feudalism. Monarchies also became stronger, so countries were unified. Monarchs such as French kings enjoyed Italian things, especially architecture. Northern European artists visited Italy to learn to paint. The literature in Northern Europe was also affected by Italy. For example, William Shakespeare's plays showed a strong Italian influence.

Mastering **Topics** with Lectures B2 p.69

1 C **2** B **3** B

Script & Graphic Organizer 02-26

W Professor: Most scholars believe humans reached the Americas by crossing a land bridge across the Bering Sea between what's now Alaska and northern Russia. The land bridge formed around twelve to eighteen thousand years ago during the last ice age. As the sea froze, the water level decreased, which exposed the seabed. At that time, people were still hunter-gatherers. Groups of people in northern Russia likely followed huge herds of animals across the land bridge and into the Americas. These people continued heading south throughout the continent. After only a thousand years, humans were living all across the Americas. They had even wandered, um, all the way down to the tip of South America.

M Student: Professor Burns, who were the first people to inhabit the Americas?

W: We call them the Clovis people. But not much is really known about them. The first evidence we have of them comes from an archaeological site near Clovis, New Mexico. That, by the way, is why we call the original inhabitants the Clovis people. Anyway, some of the artifacts found there were stone tools for cutting and stone-tipped weapons such as spears. Carbon-dating has shown these artifacts to be around 13,000 years old, making them among the oldest manmade objects found in the Americas. In addition, other examples of Clovis tools and weapons—especially spear points— have been found throughout North, Central, and South America. Based on this evidence, some archaeologists have concluded that the Clovis people were the first to arrive in the Americas and then spread out through both continents.

However, not everyone agrees with this theory. First, some scholars challenge the notion that the Clovis people spread throughout the Americas. Instead, they counter that other groups adapted Clovis ideas for tools and weapons. Thus, they claim it was the spreading of Clovis ideas, not the Clovis people, which brought Clovis-type spear points and tools to so many different sites. A second theory is that the Clovis people weren't the first to come to the Americas. Archaeologists excavating other sites have found manmade artifacts that have been carbon-dated to times earlier than Clovis artifacts. For instance, a site in Chile—near the bottom of South America—shows evidence of human habitations that differ from those of the Clovis people. The site has been dated to 13,000 years ago. If that's accurate, then the people who lived there must have entered the Americas much earlier. The reason is that they needed lots of time to make the journey from the northern land bridge to the land that far south. Personally, I disagree with the first theory but am undecided about the second.

The best argument that the members of one single group—the Clovis people—comprised the first Native Americans and were the ancestors of all other Native Americans is based on DNA evidence. If the Clovis people were really the first to reach the Americas and spread around, then all Native Americans should have similar genetic backgrounds. And guess what . . . In recent years, DNA testing of various Native American people has shown that they actually do share the same genetic background. Experts estimate that this genetic code arrived in the Americas about ten to fifteen thousand years ago. This, perhaps, is the strongest evidence that a single group of people was responsible for populating two entire continents.

The Clovis People

The Clovis People:	First Theory against the Clovis People:
- Crossed into the Americas over a land bridge in Alaska - Got their name from a place where their relics were found - Are thought to have been the first in the Americas - Came around 13,000 years ago	Did not spread through the Americas; only their ideas spread; is why so many Clovis artifacts are all over the Americas **Second Theory against the Clovis People:** Location of an old site in Chile that has habitations different from the Clovis people; may be from another tribe

1 [Gist-Content Question]

In her lecture, the professor mostly focuses on whether or not the Clovis people were the first to visit the Americas.

2 [Detail Question]

The professor declares, "The first evidence we have of them comes from an archaeological site near Clovis, New Mexico. That, by the way, is why we call the original inhabitants the Clovis people. Anyway, some of the artifacts found there were stone tools for cutting and stone-tipped weapons such as spears."

3 [Understanding Attitude Question]

The professor states that she disagrees with the theory when she declares, "Personally, I disagree with the first theory but am undecided about the second."

Summarizing

The first people came to America across a land bridge during the last ice age. They were hunter-gatherers following herds of animals. After a thousand years, humans had spread across both continents. The Clovis people were the first in the Americas. Some of their artifacts are from 13,000 years ago. Their artifacts have been found everywhere. Some archaeologists think only Clovis ideas, not people, spread. Others believe non-Clovis tribes settled parts of America. But scientific tests show that many Native Americans have similar DNA.

Mastering **Topics** with Lectures | **B3** | p.70

1 ⓒ   2 ⓑ   3 ⓒ

Script & Graphic Organizer 02-27

M Professor: Our next topic on childhood development is the preverbal memory abilities of infants. By preverbal, uh, I mean the time before infants can talk. The time when babies first begin to talk varies widely. As a baseline, most researchers use infants three months old and younger for their studies. I want to look at one researcher in particular. [3]Her name's Carolyn Rovee-Collier, and she's widely considered a leading expert on early infant behavior.

Rovee-Collier was one of the first researchers to believe infants can retain memories. **She did her initial work—which was brilliant—on this in the 1960s.** One day, her six-week-old baby son was sick. She observed that his mood improved when a toy mobile over his crib moved. Since Rovee-Collier was busy, she tied a soft belt around her son's ankle and attached it to a part of the mobile. When her son moved his foot, the mobile moved. This would make him happy, so he'd stop crying. Later, she discovered that her son was doing this regularly. She concluded that her son knew what he was doing and could remember that his actions made the mobile move.

Rovee-Collier believed that babies could learn to do something and do it again later based on their memories. This ability is called relational learning. It means that a person knows that certain actions will result in specific outcomes. For example, perhaps you press a button, and an electronic toy train starts moving. Then, you press another button, and the train stops. The next time you play with the train, you recall that one button starts it while another stops it. This shows you've remembered how something works and can associate an action with a result.

Rovee-Collier conducted countless experiments with many other children. Interestingly, she discovered that infants did not retain memories for long periods of time. For instance, she would expose infants to a task. Then, she'd wait, oh, a few days or weeks and show them the same task again. After a few days, most infants remembered the task. Yet for longer periods of time, there was little or no memory retention. Up to eight days was the average amount of time that they could remember something. Nevertheless, even after a two- or three-week period of not being exposed to the task, the infants could easily relearn it. They just had to be exposed to the task twenty-four hours before a full test was done. This proved to Rovee-Collier that the infants had retained the memories of those tasks. The infants just needed a, uh, slight push to remember.

Rovee-Collier believed she had successfully demonstrated that children younger than three months of age could make memories and had the skill of relational learning. However, not everyone accepted her ideas. In the 1960s, most of the American psychological establishment refused to believe her theories. The general idea of infants then was that they had no capacity to retain memories or to understand that their actions could lead to certain results. Rovee-Collier had to fight for years merely to get her papers published. It took even longer for her work to be accepted, as it is today.

Infant Behavior

Carolyn Rovee-Collier:	Her Experiment:	Relational Learning:	Result:
- Is a leading expert on early infant behavior - Conducted her initial work in the 1960s	- Tied a belt around her son - His movement moved a mobile - He remembered how to do this	- Is learning to do something and then remembering it - Babies did this during experiments	- Conducted many more experiments - Findings were rejected at first - Are accepted today though

1 [Detail Question]

Concerning relational learning, the professor says, "Rovee-Collier believed that babies could learn to do something and do it again later based on their memories. This ability is called relational learning. It means that a person knows that certain actions will result in specific outcomes."

2 [Making Inferences Question]

The professor states, "In the 1960s, most of the American psychological establishment refused to believe her theories. The general idea of infants then was that they had no capacity to retain memories or to understand that their actions could lead to certain results. Rovee-Collier had to fight for years merely to get her papers published." Thus, it can be inferred that she did not give up when people first rejected her theories.

3 [Understanding Function Question]

When the professor calls Rovee-Collier's work "brilliant," he is recognizing that it shows great understanding of infant behavior.

Summarizing

The professor mentions that Carolyn Rovee-Collier is a leader in the field of early infant behavior. He describes one of her experiments. Her infant son learned how to make a mobile move. He retained his memory of how to do that. Rovee-Collier thought babies had the ability of relational learning. She conducted more experiments on how long the infants could remember certain tasks. She discovered they could keep their memories for about eight days. At first, her work was rejected. But it was later accepted by psychologists.

1 Ⓐ   2 Ⓑ   3 Ⓐ

Script & Graphic Organizer 02-28

W Librarian: So, Joe, how are you enjoying your first day on the job at the library?

M Student: It seems all right so far, Mrs. Jones. But I think there's a lot that I need to learn about this job. I mean . . . I've only been working here for two hours, but I've already gotten several questions that I couldn't answer.

W: Is that so? Such as what?

M: Let me see . . . There was a paper jam in one of the copiers over there. Some student asked me if I could fix it, but, um, I had no idea. What am I supposed to do in that situation?

W: Hmm . . . We can often fix simple paper jams. I'll get someone to teach you how to do that. But if the copier breaks down, you need to inform a librarian. If we can't fix it, then we call the copier company. They'll send someone to fix it.

M: Okay, that's good to know. Thanks.

W: Any other questions?

M: Sure. I have lots. Okay, uh, what about when the computers aren't working well?

W: Which ones?

M: The ones that students use to search for books. You know, uh . . . Those computers over there. Someone asked me if I could fix the computer, but I didn't have a clue as to what to do. I felt really bad about that. I just told her that it was my first day here. She said it was okay and asked someone else for help. I really wish I could have helped her though.

W: Again, the best thing to do is to talk to a librarian. But be sure to watch what the librarian does to fix the computer. That way, you'll be able to solve the problems by yourself after you've been here for a month or two.

M: Sounds great. I'll be sure to do that. Thanks.

W: Anything else, Joe?

M: No, ma'am. Well, I'm sure there will be other things. But those are my only questions for now.

Service Encounter

Librarian's Question:	Student's Response:
Asks student how his first day of work is going	Has already gotten several questions that he cannot answer
Student's Problem:	Librarian's Solution:
Could not fix the copier or the computer	Contact a librarian and watch how the librarian fixes the problems

1 [Gist-Content Question]

The librarian asks the student, "So, Joe, how are you enjoying your first day on the job at the library?" Then, they proceed to discuss how his day is going.

2 [Understanding Attitude Question]

The librarian shows that she is concerned about the student by asking him how his day is going and by giving him advice on what to do when various problems arise.

3 [Understanding Organization Question]

While discussing the copier machine, the student mentions that he was unable to fix the problem with it.

Summarizing

The librarian asks the student how his <u>first day of work</u> is going. He says that he likes it, yet he has already gotten many difficult questions. There was <u>a paper jam</u>, but he could not fix it. The woman tells him to inform a librarian about that. There was also a problem <u>with a computer</u> that he could not solve. She again tells him to speak with a librarian. She mentions that he should watch how <u>others solve problems</u>. Then, he will be able to do the same in the future.

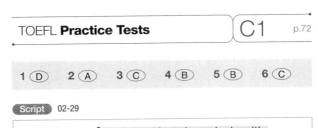

TOEFL **Practice Tests** | C1 | p.72

1 Ⓓ   2 Ⓐ   3 Ⓒ   4 Ⓑ   5 Ⓑ   6 Ⓒ

Script 02-29

M Professor: [5]Marine archaeology deals with artifacts found underwater. These artifacts are often found in shipwrecks or human settlements . . . **No, I didn't misspeak.** There are ancient human settlements underwater. They're the remains of places that were once on land but have been overtaken by the water. Many are in the Mediterranean area near

Greece, Egypt, Crete, and other places that have had human settlements for thousands of years. Typically, these areas are in shallow water, which makes excavating them somewhat easier. As for shipwrecks, well, they can be found just about anywhere—in shallow or deep water—in oceans, seas, bays, lakes, and rivers around the world.

The primary difficulty in marine archaeology is locating the site. For example, think about shipwrecks. The world's oceans and waterways are vast. So even the biggest ships that have sunk are but small dots on the ocean floor. Many ships sank during times when there were no radios, computerized navigation systems, or methods to judge a ship's precise location. You should also consider that many ships have been lost during bad weather, which can push a ship way off its intended course. Now you can start to understand how, uh, hard it must be to locate a sunken ship. Yes, Mary?

W Student: [6]Then how do marine archaeologists find sites or shipwrecks to excavate?

M: It's an involved process. First, they do their homework. Sound familiar? They might comb through archives looking for accounts of sunken ships from survivors. For wrecks in more modern times, insurance companies frequently have detailed records since ship owners and deceased passengers' families often make claims for losses. Then, the archaeologists try to pinpoint the sunken vessel's exact location. This is almost always impossible, but they can at least come up with a general idea of where the ship went down. After that, it's time to find the ship. Nowadays, many archaeologists use a device called a towed side-scanning sonar. It gets towed behind a research ship that follows precise paths across the area where the ship is believed to be. The device takes sonar images of the seafloor. Any unusual, uh, anomalies, shall we say, get investigated.

How do they investigate these anomalies? In shallow water, divers are used. But divers are limited in what they can do. For instance, they can only stay underwater for short periods of time, and they can't dive very deep. For deep shipwrecks, a robotic submersible or human-operated submersible may be used. A submersible is a, uh, a small submarine equipped with cameras and controls for picking things up off the seafloor. If the team is lucky, the submersible will identify a shipwreck site. As you can imagine, this is no simple task. It takes lots of money, time, and patience. Even the most famous shipwreck in history—the *Titanic*—remained hidden for decades due to its depth underwater and the inability of technology to go that far underwater. It wasn't until

the middle of the 1980s that the *Titanic* was finally located.

So a wreck gets found. What's next? Now come the tasks of identifying it, exploring it, and bringing up some of its artifacts. How do archaeologists identify it? Well . . . many ships have markings on them. These may be their names or identifying numbers. Iron- and steel-hulled ships may be shaped in ways that make them easy to identify. As for wooden ships, they may have disintegrated, so things like ship's bells, cannons, and other metal objects are used to identify the ship. The team must also explore the ship by using divers or, in many cases, submersibles that make video recordings.

The final task is to bring any artifacts that are found to the surface. Care must be taken to preserve these items. After being underwater for so long, exposure to air or sunlight could damage them. Many times, archaeologists place the artifacts in saltwater tanks when they're brought on board the research vessel. Doing this helps preserve them. Then, experts examine the items. Many are encrusted with rust or barnacles and other sea life. So the artifacts must be carefully cleaned before they can reveal their secrets. Now, I'd like to show you some slides from a recent shipwreck. I think you'll find them fascinating. Would someone hit the lights, please?

1 [Gist-Content Question]

Most of the professor's discussion is about how people engage in marine archaeology.

2 [Detail Question]

The professor comments, "Nowadays, many archaeologists use a device called a towed side-scanning sonar. It gets towed behind a research ship that follows precise paths across the area where the ship is believed to be. The device takes sonar images of the seafloor."

3 [Understanding Organization Question]

The professor discusses the process of finding shipwrecks by covering the steps in the order that they must be done.

4 [Making Inferences Question]

The professor says, "Now, I'd like to show you some slides from a recent shipwreck. I think you'll find them fascinating. Would someone hit the lights, please?" So he is going to show the class some pictures next.

5 [Understanding Function Question]

When the professor says, "No, I didn't misspeak," he is stressing to the students that they correctly heard what he said.

6 [Understanding Attitude Question]

When something is "an involved process," it is complicated. Thus, the professor means that finding a shipwreck site is complicated.

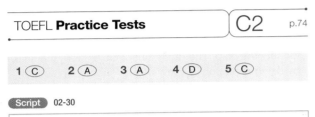

TOEFL Practice Tests **C2** p.74

1 Ⓒ   2 Ⓐ   3 Ⓐ   4 Ⓓ   5 Ⓒ

Script 02-30

M1 Student: Greetings, Professor Gray. You're having office hours now, aren't you?

M2 Professor: Indeed I am, Paul. Come on in and sit down, please.

M1: ⁴Thank you so much. I've, uh, I've got something I would really like to talk to you about. It concerns our big research paper that's due in three weeks.

M2: It's nice to know that you're already working on it. Most students wait until three or four days before it's due. Then, they stay up all night writing and writing. I must say that their papers are usually, er, quite disappointing.

M1: I don't plan to let you down like that, sir.

M2: Excellent, excellent. What's your topic?

M1: ⁵I'm going to be writing about the American labor movement in the late 1800s and the early 1900s.

M2: A good topic. What kind of angle are you going to take?

M1: I haven't decided yet. Currently, I'm just doing all of my research. I think that when I understand the topic a little better, I'll be able to, uh, you know, come up with an idea for my paper.

M2: That's probably the best thing you could do.

M1: So, uh, anyway, I was wondering . . . . I just checked these books out of the library. They're about the American labor movement but . . .

M2: But what?

M1: Well, the library has a lot of books on that topic. So I'm not sure if these are the best books or not. Would you, um, would you mind just looking at them and letting me know if I'm on the right track or not?

M2: Of course I don't mind. I'm always willing to help my most conscientious students. Let me see them.

M1: Great. Thanks. Here's one . . . and another . . . and the last two.

M2: Hmm . . . This is a good one here. So are these two . . . But . . . hmm . . . I'm not familiar with this author's work. It still might be a good book though. But, uh, Paul, I believe you're missing one important thing.

M1: I am? What is it?

M2: These are all secondary sources. You need to get a couple of books of primary sources. You know, such as speeches made by some of the leaders in the labor movement. Hold on a second . . . Here. This is a book from my collection. You can borrow it.

M1: Really? Wow. Thanks a lot.

M2: Just return it in good condition. And go back to the library to check out some others like it. Having primary sources should help you write a better paper. And if you need any more books, just let me know.

1 [Gist-Purpose Question]

The student mentions the books that he has checked out from the library, and then he asks the professor, "Would you, um, would you mind just looking at them and letting me know if I'm on the right track or not?"

2 [Detail Question]

The professor tells the student, "You need to get a couple of books of primary sources."

3 [Making Inferences Question]

The student notes that he is working on the paper that is due in three weeks. In response, the professor says, "It's nice to know that you're already working on it." The professor is clearly impressed with the student's study ethic.

4 [Understanding Function Question]

Telling the student that it is nice that he is working on the paper is a compliment.

5 [Understanding Attitude Question]

When the professor asks about the angle that the student is going to take on the paper, he is asking the student exactly what he is going to write about. The professor is trying to get more specific information on the student's paper.

Vocabulary Review p.77

1 Ⓐ   2 Ⓓ   3 Ⓓ   4 Ⓒ   5 Ⓐ
6 Ⓐ   7 Ⓒ   8 Ⓐ   9 Ⓑ   10 Ⓓ

11 Ⓐ   12 Ⓔ   13 Ⓓ   14 Ⓑ   15 Ⓒ

■▶ Chapter | 04 Social Sciences 2 • Conversations

Mastering **Question Types**
with Lectures & Conversations   A1   p.80

[TYPES 1–4]

TYPE❶ Ⓐ   TYPE❷ Ⓒ
TYPE❸ Ⓓ   TYPE❹ Ⓒ

Script 02-31

M Professor: I'm sure that many of you have read Homer's *Iliad*. For those of you who haven't, the *Iliad* tells part of the story of the Trojan War. Basically, the Greeks and the Trojans fought a ten-year war against each other. The Greeks ultimately won, and the city of Troy was sacked and burned. The *Iliad* only tells a short part of that story, but it's famous nonetheless.

Anyway, for centuries, most people assumed that Troy was a mythical city. The notion that there had actually been a war was regarded as . . . well, as ludicrous by most scholars. That is, uh, until Heinrich Schliemann went and found the city of Troy in 1873. ⁴This was arguably the greatest archaeological discovery in the world. **You have something to add to the discussion?**

W Student: Yes, sir. Um, about Schliemann . . . I mean, he wasn't a real archaeologist. And his field methods were simply awful. What do you think about that?

M: The man got results. Yes, his methods were . . . um, unorthodox. But he got results. Not only did he discover Troy, but he also excavated Mycenae in Greece. In doing so, he made a number of other invaluable discoveries that contributed to the advancement of human knowledge. I can't think of any other archaeologist—trained or not—who has done the same. In addition, Schliemann did more than all other archaeologists to increase the general public's interest in archaeology. For that, he deserves our respect and admiration.

What I find interesting is that people believed Troy was mythical for so long. Just by reading the *Iliad*, it should be obvious that Homer assumed his audience knew that a real war had been fought. That was actually how Schliemann found Troy. He read the *Iliad* and followed the clues that Homer had left. And voila . . . once he started digging, he unearthed the ancient city. In retrospect, anyone could have found Troy. I mean, Homer wasn't writing an historical document, but he still made it clear that he believed the Trojan War had really occurred.

TYPE❶ [Gist-Purpose Question]

The professor begins his lecture by talking briefly about the story of the *Iliad*. He is therefore providing the students with some background information.

TYPE❷ [Understanding Organization Question]

The professor talks about Heinrich Schliemann to describe how important his contributions to the field of archaeology were.

TYPE❸ [Connecting Content Question]

Concerning Schliemann, the professor states, "In addition, Schliemann did more than all other archaeologists to increase the general public's interest in archaeology." He is implying that archaeology became more popular after Schliemann made his discoveries.

TYPE❹ [Speaker's Attitude Question]

When the professor asks, "You have something to add to the discussion?" he is indicating that he sees that the student wants to say something. So he is giving her permission to ask her question.

Summarizing

The professor mentions that the *Iliad* tells part of the story of the Trojan War. He notes that people once thought that Troy was mythical until Heinrich Schliemann discovered its ruins in 1873. A student comments that Schliemann had awful field methods, but the professor remarks that Schliemann got results. His discoveries were very influential, and he increased the general public's interest in archaeology. The professor then states that it was by using the *Iliad* as a guide that Schliemann was able to find Troy.

[TYPES 5–8]

TYPE❺ Ⓐ   TYPE❻ Ⓐ, Ⓒ
TYPE❼ Ⓐ   TYPE❽ Ⓑ

Script 02-32

W Professor: Have you ever noticed how some people are excellent at perceiving others' emotional states? And, of course, you've probably noticed that some people don't recognize other people's emotions at all or simply ignore them, right? Why is that? Well, it has to do with emotional intelligence.

Emotional intelligence is something different from

what we think of as intelligence. You know, how smart a person is. But emotional intelligence is important, and psychologists have been devoting a considerable amount of time to it in the past few decades. So let's find out what it is.

Emotional intelligence refers to a person's ability to deal with emotions by being able to perceive them . . . to control them . . . and to evaluate and deal with them. Emotional intelligence has numerous applications in people's lives. Let's see . . . It can refer to a person's ability to listen to his or her own feelings as well as other people's feelings. That's what I was talking about when I said some people are, uh, in tune with other people's emotions while others have no clue about them. [8]In addition, emotional intelligence can refer to a person's ability to sort and evaluate feelings and then use that information in his or her thinking or actions. I should also mention that some psychologists believe we are born with emotional intelligence. Others believe it can be learned and developed. **It's the old nature versus nurture argument that we've discussed before.**

Psychologists have divided emotional intelligence into three . . . no, four . . . different categories. First is perceiving emotions in others. Second is using these emotions in the thinking process. Third is understanding the meanings of these emotions. And fourth is, um, it's managing these emotions.

The first category—the ability to perceive emotions—is the most basic. A person can perceive emotions in many ways. These include simply expressing one's emotional state as well as nonverbal reception. We often rely upon facial expressions, which are easily recognizable, to show our emotions. For instance, it's pretty easy to look at most people and tell if they are happy, sad, angry, afraid, nervous, or whatever.

TYPE 5 [Gist-Content Question]

The professor mostly discusses what emotional intelligence is and how it can be defined.

TYPE 6 [Detail Question]

The professor states, "We often rely upon facial expressions, which are easily recognizable, to show our emotions." She also says, "These include simply expressing one's emotional state as well as nonverbal reception."

TYPE 7 [Making Inferences Question]

The professor notes that there are four different categories of emotional intelligence and then names all

of them. She proceeds to discuss in detail the first one. So it is highly likely that she will discuss the second category next.

TYPE 8 [Understanding Function Question]

When the professor adds "that we've discussed before," she is reminding the students that they have already talked about the nature versus nurture argument, so they should know what she is referring to.

Summarizing

The professor mentions that emotional intelligence is different from regular intelligence. It refers to a person's ability to deal with emotions in various ways. Some psychologists believe people are born with emotional intelligence while others believe it can be learned and developed. There are four categories of emotional intelligence: perceiving emotions in others, using emotions in the thinking process, understanding the meanings of emotions, and managing emotions. The professor mentions that there are many ways to perceive emotions. These can be both verbal and nonverbal.

Mastering **Question Types**
with Lectures & Conversations

A2   p.82

[TYPES 1–4]

TYPE 1 C   **TYPE 2** D
TYPE 3 C   **TYPE 4** A

Script 02-33

W Professor: Running a business isn't easy. If any of a number of factors goes wrong, the business could fail. And one of the riskiest factors in running a business is making assumptions.

M Student: Assumptions? But shouldn't businesses always go with the facts? It seems like a business that relies on assumptions is guaranteed to fail.

W: Hmm . . . That's not always the case. Here, uh, let me give you an example, Stuart. Company A has a new product it has just developed. It thinks the product will become a bestseller. However, there's absolutely nothing on the market like it. The company goes ahead and decides to sell the product. Why? Because the decision makers there made an assumption that it would sell and not fail.

M: Okay, I see your point. I guess that, uh, in certain cases, making assumptions is unavoidable.

W: Correct. In fact, pretty much every business makes assumptions at some point. These could be explicit or implicit assumptions. They could also be spoken or unspoken assumptions. Sometimes they work out. Other times, uh, they don't. The problem is that many businesses are completely unaware that they are making assumptions. In order to be successful though, businesses should question everything and take nothing for granted.

One obvious instance when many companies make assumptions is while they are conducting business internationally. For instance, a business may assume that a product popular in the United States will be popular in, uh, Italy. Or a business may assume that practices followed in Japan are the same as those in, uh, say Brazil. This is particularly true with regard to respect for the law. In many developed countries, the rule of law is strictly followed. Yet businesspeople from these countries often assume that this is the case in other nations. That's far from the truth. And making assumptions like that can . . . kill your business. Let's look at the case study on page eighty-two in your text. It's a perfect example of how one business made many wrong assumptions while opening an overseas branch. I think you'll find it, uh, rather illuminating.

TYPE 1 [Gist-Content Question]

The professor mostly focuses on how risky making assumptions can be for businesses or businesspeople.

TYPE 2 [Understanding Organization Question]

The professor describes some examples of people making assumptions, and then she explains to the class what they mean.

TYPE 3 [Connecting Content Question]

The professor states, "In many developed countries, the rule of law is strictly followed. Yet businesspeople from these countries often assume that this is the case in other nations. That's far from the truth. And making assumptions like that can . . . kill your business." She clearly believes that assuming that the rule of law will be followed in a foreign country will make the company unsuccessful.

TYPE 4 [Speaker's Attitude Question]

The professor notes that many businesspeople from developed countries make erroneous assumptions when doing business in other nations.

Summarizing

The professor claims that it can be very risky for businesses to make assumptions. A student comments that making assumptions in business should guarantee

failure, but the professor shows how that might not happen. She claims that businesses must make assumptions when marketing new products. She mentions that businesses make explicit and implicit assumptions as well as spoken and unspoken assumptions. She uses an example of people conducting international business. She says that people often assume that the practices followed in their countries are the same in other nations.

[TYPES 5-8]

| TYPE 5 | D | TYPE 6 | B |
| TYPE 7 | D | TYPE 8 | A |

Script 02-34

W Student: Hello. I got a call from someone who said that I needed to come here. Is this the right place?

M Student Activities Center Employee: Um . . . I'm not sure. What did somebody call you about?

W: Oh, yeah, sorry. My name is Amy Winter, and I received a message that someone found my backpack. I left it in the campus center here yesterday, so I'm really happy it got turned in.

M: Ah, sure. We've got the backpack. The person should have told you to bring some kind of picture ID. Did you do that?

W: I did. Here's my driver's license.

M: Okay . . . It's right behind the counter here. Hold on a bit . . . And here you are.

W: Thank you so much.

M: ⁸You should probably check to make sure that everything is in there. Sometimes items get turned in, but, well, you know . . . **Various items sometimes just disappear . . .**

W: Hmm . . . It looks like everything is here. Wow, I had twenty dollars in my backpack, and it's still here. Is there any way I can thank the person who turned it in? I'd really like to express my appreciation.

M: Sorry. I'm not allowed to tell you the name of the person who gave it to us. But I can give the person a call to let him know you got your backpack. That's the best I can do.

TYPE 5 [Gist-Content Question]

In the conversation, the student and the employee mainly talk about the student's missing backpack.

TYPE 6 [Detail Question]

The man tells the student, "The person should have told you to bring some kind of picture ID. Did you do that?"

When the student asks for the name of the person who found her backpack, the man replies, "Sorry. I'm not allowed to tell you the name of the person who gave it to us. But I can give the person a call to let him know you got your backpack. That's the best I can do." So he implies that he wants to fulfill her request but cannot.

TYPE **8** [Understanding Function Question]

When the security guard states, "Various items sometimes just disappear," he is implying that even though the student's backpack has been returned, some of the items in it might be gone.

Summarizing

> The student states that a person called to tell her that her missing backpack had been turned in. The man says he has the backpack but needs to see some picture ID. The student shows the man her driver's license, and he gives her the backpack. He tells her to check for any missing possessions. The student remarks that even her money is still there. She wants to thank the person who turned in the backpack, but the man says he cannot give her the person's name.

Mastering **Topics** with Lectures | B1 | p.84

1 Ⓒ 2 Ⓑ, Ⓓ 3 Ⓐ

Script & Graphic Organizer 02-35

W1 Professor: When a company makes a new product, it needs to test the product before putting it on the market. So the company uses product testers. These are the invaluable people who try the product before it gets sold. Testers could be anyone. For instance, they could be various members of the public or professionals who do nothing but test new products.

Many product testers are regular people. Companies are constantly looking for people like, uh, you and me, to test new products. There are even websites where companies request volunteers to try their products. You can get paid to do product testing. A company will send you a product, tell you how to use it, and then ask you to complete a survey describing your experience with the product.

So what about professional product testers? There are two types. First, some companies specialize in testing products. They may focus on one product

or industry, such as, oh, children's toys, or they may test a variety of products. Sometimes, the companies are so well known that having their seal of approval indicates the product is of a very high standard. Second, there are professional testers who are, uh, well, I guess we could call them freelance product testers. For example, have any of you ever heard of beta testers?

M Student: They test new software for bugs and other problems, don't they?

W1: Yes, that's right. A beta tester simply takes a piece of computer software that's in its beta stage. That means it's not ready to go to the market yet. The beta tester uses the software and searches for problems. The beta tester might give an opinion of how user friendly the software is and whether the tester has any interest in using the software. Additionally, the tester might make other comments as well. That's one type of freelance product tester. There are, of course, others, but I don't see a need to go into them in detail.

Anyway, that's basically how product testing works. It relies upon product testers giving feedback— both positive and negative—to a company. This lets companies make changes and improvements to their products.

W2 Student: Professor Hammond, why do companies do product testing?

W1: First and foremost is safety. Companies don't want to sell unsafe products. That could result in injuries or deaths, which would cost a company a lot of money from lawsuits. Second, companies want to sell the best products so that people will buy theirs and not another company's. That's pretty much it.

Now, sometimes despite all of the testing done to make sure something is safe, there may still be problems. Even the most rigorously tested product may perform, uh, differently when it's mass-manufactured and then sold to the public. Every year, products that have been thoroughly tested fail to operate properly. They may even injure or kill some users. This leads to product recalls. A recalled product typically must be returned to the factory or to a repair shop. There, its problem can be fixed. You often hear about recalls concerning automobiles. There was one in the news recently I believe. Oh, and in some cases, dangerous products may simply be banned. This isn't common though. And it most frequently happens in the pharmaceutical industry. So now let me tell you how product testing is done with medicines.

Product Testers

Product Testers:	Beta Testers:
- Test products before they get put on the market	Test computer software in its beta stage; are freelance product testers
- Are companies that specialize in testing products	**Reasons for Testing:**
- Are freelance product testers	Provide positive and negative feedback; make sure that the product is safe

1 [Gist-Purpose Question]

After describing what beta testers do, the professor says, "That's one type of freelance product tester."

2 [Detail Question]

In response to a question on why company's do beta testing, the professor explains, "First and foremost is safety. Companies don't want to sell unsafe products. That could result in injuries or deaths, which would cost a company a lot of money from lawsuits. Second, companies want to sell the best products so that people will buy theirs and not another company's."

3 [Understanding Opinion Question]

While describing beta testers, the professor says, "These are the invaluable people who try the product before it gets sold." She believes that the work beta testers do is very important.

Summarizing

The professor discusses product testers. They are people who test new products. There are two types of product testers; some are companies that specialize in testing new products, and others are freelance product testers. The professor states that beta testers for computer software are freelancers. The testers give both positive and negative feedback to the company. This helps make the products safe, so people will not get hurt or killed when using them. It also detects any problems there may be with the products.

Mastering **Topics** with Lectures   **B2**   p.85

1 Ⓑ   **2** Ⓐ   **3** Ⓒ

`Script & Graphic Organizer` 02-36

M Professor: We often think of property as land or a house. But it's a bit more complex than that. To define property, first consider the relationships people have with things. These relationships may include the right to control and use the things, the right to sell or transfer them, and the right to reap the benefits of owning them. One philosopher who thought a lot about property was John Locke, an Englishman who lived in the seventeenth century. Locke is widely considered one of the most important philosophers in Western history. His theories on religion, property, and government heavily influenced a wide range of people. These include Voltaire, Rousseau, the Founding Fathers of the United States, and even Karl Marx.

Right now, I'd like to examine Locke's view of property. His main idea was based on what's called the labor theory of property. This is the notion that labor creates property and that those who do the labor should control the property. Locke thought this was a natural right. He believed that people owned their own bodies. Therefore, by applying their bodies to do labor to, uh, the land or something else, people acquired the right of ownership to whatever they produced. For example, Locke believed that a man who cleared some land of trees, plowed it, planted crops, and then harvested them was the owner of the results of his labor.

Locke placed limits on this property though. One's own labor was the first such limit. He thought a person could only do so much labor and accumulate so much property. He also believed an individual should only accumulate what he or she needed and should leave enough for others. [3]Finally, he thought that a person shouldn't take so much property that some of it would spoil from disuse. This, he proclaimed, was wasteful. **Essentially, Locke said not to fill your dinner plate with food if you're not planning on eating it all.** That's the closest analogy I can make.

Naturally, Locke had defenders and opponents. The Founding Fathers strongly supported his ideas on property. Yet some of the contradictions in his theories created some rather strong critics of his work. For instance, what would happen if the land being farmed was already owned by someone else? This was often the case in England in Locke's time. Locke claimed that those who had no land could labor on others' land to earn a living. Yet this contradicted his belief that those who do the work should be the property owners. Locke also contradicted his statement that labor is the best way to create property and wealth when he said that selling property for money was a better way to create wealth. Indeed, Locke supported the use of money over the barter system. He noted that money doesn't spoil or need constant labor to care for it. All in all, as you can likely see, Locke's theories on property were often conflicting. Here . . . Let me give you another example, and I think that you'll be able to see what I'm talking about.

John Locke and Property Rights

John Locke:	Labor Theory of Property:
- Was a seventeenth-century English philosopher - Was very important in Western history - Influenced many people, including the U.S. Founding Fathers	Labor creates property, so whoever does the labor should control the property Limits on the Theory: People should only do so much labor; should leave enough property for others

1 [Gist-Content Question]

Almost the entire lecture is about the thoughts of John Locke regarding property.

2 [Making Inferences Question]

At the end, the professor states, "All in all, as you can likely see, Locke's theories on property were often conflicting. Here . . . Let me give you another example, and I think that you'll be able to see what I'm talking about." He is probably going to continue talking about John Locke and property rights.

3 [Understanding Function Question]

The professor himself says that he is making an analogy.

Summarizing

One must think about the relationships people have with things when considering property. John Locke, an influential philosopher, thought about property rights. He based his ideas on the labor theory of property. He believed that labor creates property, so those who do the labor should control the property. He put limits on that though. He thought people should only do so much labor and should leave enough for others. The American Founding Fathers supported his work. But there were many contradictions in his work, which the professor discusses.

Mastering **Topics** with Lectures B3 p.86

1 Ⓒ   2 Ⓑ   3 Pan Am: ② Exxon: ③
The Makers of Tylenol: ①, ④

W Professor: Sometimes a company encounters serious trouble. When this occurs, it goes into what we call crisis management mode. So the firm takes certain steps to control the crisis before it gets out of hand. Some of these steps include dealing with the press, handling upset customers, and taking steps to prevent a similar situation from happening in the future.

M Student: What kinds of situations could cause a company to react that way?

W: Good question. One example is a product recall.

M: But those happen all the time.

W: True. In the auto industry, they happen virtually every year. And notice how well the companies handle the recalls. In general, I mean. Most auto companies have definitely mastered crisis management. However, disasters can also cause a company to go into crisis management mode. In 1988, for instance, a terrorist bomb destroyed a Pan Am airliner. Hundreds of people died. In 1989, an Exxon oil tanker ran aground in Alaska. This caused an enormous amount of damage to the environment. And, uh . . . in 1982, seven people in the Chicago area died when they took Tylenol that someone had laced with poison.

Those were all major problems. Now, uh, what can companies do when they occur? First, they often use public relations experts to handle TV and newspaper reporters. These experts do things like make it appear that the company is not at fault. Many large companies have public relations officials on staff to prepare reports and to handle the press. Their efforts are often vital to maintaining or restoring a company's image. After all, people can quickly lose faith in a company. Consider the three companies I just mentioned. The makers of Tylenol handled the media the best. They reacted quickly and kept the public informed at all times. Exxon did the worst. Its CEO ignored the media, and at first, the company did little to help the locals in Alaska who were affected by the oil spill.

Companies also need to deal with customers affected by the crisis. In the case of the Pan Am disaster, the airline did a poor job. It was sued by the families of the dead. The company stalled and tried to shift the blame to government agencies. It claimed the government should have warned the company about possible terrorist attacks. As for Exxon, it tried to shift the blame to one person: the captain of the tanker. Eventually, the company paid for the cleanup. It also compensated local fishermen for their losses. Tylenol's case was different. The company wasn't at fault, but it did its best to help the family members of those affected. It recalled all of its products across North America. Then, it destroyed them at a cost of over one hundred million dollars.

Lastly, a company needs to ensure that a similar incident won't take place in the future. Pan Am never got this chance. It went bankrupt in 1991. Yet airports worldwide improved their security measures. The Exxon disaster led to improved training for tanker crews while shipbuilding companies started making stronger tankers. Tylenol designed tamperproof pill bottles and spent millions ensuring the public its products were safe. Today, the Tylenol case is frequently cited as an effective response to a crisis and outstanding crisis management.

Crisis Management

Crisis Management Mode:	Public Relations:	Dealing with Customers:
- A company may encounter problems - Must take steps to control a crisis before it gets out of control - Are many ways to do this	- Can use public relations experts to handle media - Make it appear that the company is not at fault - Tylenol handled the media well - Exxon did poorly	- Pan Am handled customers poorly - Exxon tried to shift blame to the captain of the ship - Tylenol spent millions to handle its customers

1 [Detail Question]

Concerning public relations officials, the professor states, "First, they often use public relations experts to handle TV and newspaper reporters. These experts do things like make it appear that the company is not at fault. Many large companies have public relations officials on staff to prepare reports and to handle the press. Their efforts are often vital to maintaining or restoring a company's image."

2 [Understanding Organization Question]

Throughout the lecture, the professor describes some real crises from the past and then shows the students how each company responded to these crises.

3 [Connecting Content Question]

According to the lecture, Pan Am went bankrupt after the terrorist incident. As for Exxon, it tried to blame the captain of the tanker for the incident. And the makers of Tylenol both handled the media the best and spent millions trying to recover the image of the company.

Summarizing

The professor states that companies have many ways to overcome a crisis. One way is a product recall. She then says that disasters can make companies go into crisis management mode. She mentions the Pan Am terrorist bombing, the Exxon oil tanker running aground, and people dying after taking Tylenol. She notes that the makers of Tylenol handled public relations the best. Exxon and Pan Am both did poorly. She says that companies must make sure the same incident never happens again. Then she describes what happened to each company afterward.

Mastering **Topics** with Conversations B4 p.87

1 Ⓒ   2 Ⓐ   3 Ⓑ

Script & Graphic Organizer 02-38

M1 Professor: Good afternoon, Eric. What brings you to my office on this fine spring day? I imagined that you would be starting on your weekend by now.

M2 Student: Oh, no, sir. I've got a ton of work to do this weekend. So, uh, I guess I'll just be staying in my dorm and doing schoolwork tonight and tomorrow.

M1: You know . . . that's a good attitude to have. Too many young people these days place more importance on having fun than doing their studies. Anyway, uh, what can I do for you?

M2: I'm here to talk about the summer school class you're teaching.

M1: Ah, right. That should be a great class. I'm really looking forward to having you in it. We should learn so much during the summer.

M2: Actually, sir, I've got, um, some bad news about that class . . . I'm sorry, but I won't be able to take it.

M1: Goodness! Why ever not?

M2: Well, uh, I just found out that I got an internship to work for the city government. So, basically, I'm not going to have any time for the class.

M1: An internship? Well, I see that congratulations are in order.

M2: Thank you, sir. I was very pleased to get selected for the program. It should look good on my résumé when I apply to law schools next year. So I think I have to accept the offer.

M1: Of course you must. That makes the most sense. In that case, I suppose I completely understand why you won't be able to take my class.

M2: Thanks for saying that. I just wish . . . I just wish there were some way that I could stay enrolled in it.

M1: [3]In that case, here's something you should know . . . Not only will I be teaching that class during summer school, but I'll also be teaching it in the fall semester. So you can sign up for it then.

M2: Wow. Talk about a win-win situation. That's great news, Professor Wingard. Thanks for telling me that. I don't feel so bad anymore.

Office Hours

Student's Problem:	Professor's Response:
Cannot take the professor's summer school class	*Should do the internship to improve his résumé*
Professor's Comment:	**Solution:**
Will teach the same class during the fall semester	*Student can do the internship in the summer and take the class in the fall*

1 [Gist-Purpose Question]

The student goes to the professor's office to give him the news that he got an internship and will therefore not be able to take the professor's summer school class.

2 [Making Inferences Question]

The student states, "It should look good on my résumé when I apply to law schools next year." Students apply to graduate schools such as law schools during their senior years. Thus, it can be inferred that since the student will apply to law school next year, he is currently a junior.

3 [Understanding Function Question]

When the student calls the resolution that the professor suggests a "win-win situation," he is expressing his happiness with how everything has worked out.

Summarizing

The student visits the professor to discuss a summer school class. The professor says that he is looking forward to having the student in his class, but the student states that he cannot take it. He has a summer internship, so he will be too busy to enroll in the class. The professor then tells the student that he will teach the same class in the fall. So the student should be able to do the internship in the summer and take the professor's class in the fall semester.

1 Ⓓ 2 Ⓑ 3 Ⓐ 4 Ⓓ 5 Ⓓ 6 Ⓑ

Script 02-39

W Professor: For most of human history, people didn't use money. Instead, they relied on trading—or bartering—to get goods and services. Bartering can be a straightforward trade of one good for another. For example, I give you two apples in exchange for five potatoes. Bartering can also be a trade of a good for a service rendered. For example, a potato farmer hires three laborers to help him harvest his potatoes. In return, he gives them potatoes as payment.

The basis for bartering is need. Someone needs something that another person has. An agreement is reached, and goods or services—or both— are exchanged. This method hasn't changed in thousands of years. The method of exchange and the scope of bartering have, however, changed. Nowadays, bartering is done by individuals, large companies, and even governments. Trade exchanges have been established in many cities to help companies barter with other companies. At a trade exchange, a company can earn trading credits. It trades products to another company, which gives it trading credits. [6]These credits don't have to be used with the same company. They can be used with any other company.

M Student: That's not exactly bartering, is it? I thought bartering was the direct trading of one thing for another.

W: You're correct if we narrowly limit the definition of bartering. But with a modern trade exchange, the scope of bartering becomes wider and more flexible. Say that I have a computer chip-making company. I want to barter for silicon to use to make chips. But the silicon company doesn't want computer chips, and I don't have enough trade credits to get silicon. Sure, I could pay cash, but my company's cash flow is low because times are tough. Another company, which makes cars, wants to barter for computer chips. I give the chips to the car company, and it gives me some trade credits. I turn around and use those to get more silicon. Trading activity involving three companies or individuals is called triangular bartering by the way. When more than three are involved, it's called multilateral bartering. Thanks to trade exchanges, these types of bartering are becoming more common.

So large companies barter, and so do individuals. I'm sure some of you have firsthand experience bartering on the Internet, don't you? There are several bartering sites you can check out. The biggest issue on the Internet is trust. How do you know that the other person is someone who can be trusted? You don't, really, until you make the trade. Of course, most sites ban traders who make false claims about their goods and services. They also ban those who fail to complete the trades they agreed to. So Internet bartering is becoming more trustworthy.

In modern times, there are some other issues involved in bartering. One is taxation. Some people believe you don't owe taxes when you barter, but they're wrong. In the U.S., you must report the value of the items you bartered and pay taxes on them. This is relatively new though. It was in the late twentieth century that laws were enacted to force people to pay taxes on bartered goods and services. Other countries have similar laws as well. However, at the basic level, the government doesn't expect people to report bartering for tax purposes. So I don't think anyone expects you to report the computer games you and your friend exchanged and to pay taxes on them.

Another issue is called fair exchange. Basically, it concerns whether or not what you're receiving is a fair trade for your goods or services. Many barterers get less than the fair value that they deserve. Of course, it's their responsibility to know the value of their goods and services. Finally, bartering isn't an ideal way to store wealth. If you're bartering with food, the food might spoil. Thus your wealth won't keep for very long. However, money can be put in a bank and then be used later to purchase many things. As for bartering, to get something new, a person must want what you have to offer. Since this isn't always the case, many people have trouble surviving solely by bartering. For some things, they simply have to use money.

1 [Gist-Content Question]

During her lecture, the professor describes a number of different ways that people engage in bartering.

2 [Gist-Content Question]

The professor notes, "Nowadays, bartering is done by individuals, large companies, and even governments. Trade exchanges have been established in many cities to help companies barter with other companies." She also makes a point of calling it a "modern trade exchange." Thus, she is describing a modern-day form of bartering.

3 [Detail Question]

The professor mentions, "Trading activity involving three

companies or individuals is called triangular bartering by the way."

4 [Understanding Attitude Question]

The professor states, "Many barterers get less than the fair value that they deserve." She therefore believes that many barterers are not very good at it.

5 [Understanding Organization Question]

Concerning taxation, the professor explains, "One is taxation. Some people believe you don't owe taxes when you barter, but they're wrong. In the U.S., you must report the value of the items you bartered and pay taxes on them." She is attempting to correct a mistaken belief held by many people.

6 [Understanding Function Question]

When the student asks, "That's not exactly bartering, is it?" he is disagreeing with the professor in her analysis.

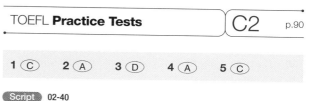

TOEFL **Practice Tests**   C2   p.90

1 ⓒ   2 Ⓐ   3 Ⓓ   4 Ⓐ   5 ⓒ

Script 02-40

W Student: I'm so sorry to bother you right now, but there's a problem with all of the printers here in the lab.

M Computer Laboratory Employee: A problem? What kind of problem is it?

W: Well, none of them is working right now. I tried all three of the printers, but there is something wrong with each of them. Do you think that you could take a look at them for me?

M: [5]Uh, sorry, but I'm not a computer technician. I don't have the slightest idea how to fix the printers. So I don't think that I can help you out at all.

W: You've got to be kidding me. You work in the computer lab, but you don't know anything about printers? You're serious?

M: Er, I know it sounds bad, but, uh, yeah. I just started this job last week. So, uh, I don't know much about anything here yet. Sorry.

W: Okay. That's fine. Do you think you can get one of the computer technicians that works here to look at the printer? I have to print a paper for a class that starts in an hour. I absolutely have to get this paper printed.

M: Um . . . To be honest, I'm the only one here

right now. You see, er, all three of our computer technicians are out of the office. They're students, you know. So, um, they're in class right now.

W: Do you know when they're going to return?

M: I think one of them said he'd be here at four. I don't know about the others. Sorry.

W: Four? That's too late for me. What am I supposed to do?

M: Uh, I don't really know. Maybe you could go to a friend's place and print your paper there.

W: All of my friends are at class now . . . Look. Are you sure that you can't check out the printers for me? I mean, I think that one of them is out of ink. Surely you can solve that problem for me, can't you?

M: Out of ink? You're not going to believe this, but . . .

W: But what . . . ? No, let me guess. You don't have any ink for the printers here.

M: Uh, right. We just ordered some this morning, but it's not due to arrive until tomorrow afternoon. Sorry again.

W: That's all right. It's not your fault, I guess. I'll just have to think of something to do.

M: Okay . . . If you don't mind my asking, what are you going to do?

W: I guess I'll go talk to my professor and explain the situation to him. And I'll come back here at four when the technician is supposed to be here. Hopefully, he'll be able to fix one of the printers.

M: That sounds great. I'm really sorry that I couldn't help you out. And good luck.

1 [Gist-Content Question]

The two speakers are mostly talking about the broken printers in the computer laboratory.

2 [Gist-Purpose Question]

The employee states, "You see, er, all three of our computer technicians are out of the office. They're students, you know. So, um, they're in class right now." So he is letting the student know why none of the three technicians is in the laboratory at the moment.

3 [Detail Question]

Concerning the ink for the printer, the employee mentions, "It's not due to arrive until tomorrow afternoon."

4 [Making Inferences Question]

Near the end of the conversation, the student says,

"I guess I'll go talk to my professor and explain the situation to him." She will probably visit her professor to speak with him and to explain her problem.

5 [Understanding Function Question]

When the student responds, "You've got to be kidding me," she is exclaiming that she does not believe what the student is saying. She does not understand how a person working in the computer laboratory cannot know how to fix a computer.

Vocabulary Review p.93

1 ⓓ	2 ⓓ	3 ⓐ	4 ⓒ	5 ⓐ
6 ⓒ	7 ⓒ	8 ⓐ	9 ⓑ	10 ⓓ
11 ⓓ	12 ⓐ	13 ⓔ	14 ⓑ	15 ⓒ

◼ Chapter | **05 Physical Sciences 1** • Conversations

Mastering **Question Types** with Lectures & Conversations ⟋ **A1** p.96

[TYPES 1–4]

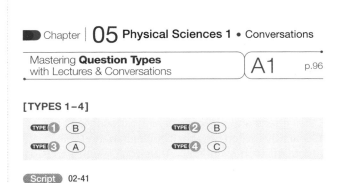

TYPE ① ⓑ **TYPE ② ⓑ**
TYPE ③ ⓐ **TYPE ④ ⓒ**

Script 02-41

M Professor: Before we start talking about how geysers form, I have a question . . . Have any of you ever seen an active geyser in person?

W Student: I have, Professor Johnson. I went to Yellowstone National Park for vacation two years ago. It was awesome to see them erupt.

M: Yes, I can imagine it was quite a sight. Has anyone else seen one in person . . . ? No . . . ? Oh well. That's too bad. Anyway, don't worry about it. I was just curious.

For a geyser to exist, there must be an adequate supply of surface water. This comes from rain and snow. It soaks into the ground and descends to the underground tunnels that comprise the, uh, the geyser's plumbing. In addition, the water must accumulate for a long period of time. How long? Well, scientists estimate that Yellowstone's numerous geysers discharge around seventy million gallons of water a day. That's a lot of water, huh? So it can take around 500 years or so for enough water to build up to enable a geyser to form.

What's next? Well, there has to be underground heat from molten rock. In other words, there should be a volcanic heat source. Third, again under the ground, there needs to be what's called a plumbing system. It functions as a, uh, pressure chamber. The plumbing system is basically a series of cavities or porous spaces just beneath the ground. And there needs to be a constriction at some point near the top. By the way, we categorize geysers according to the shapes of their plumbing systems. We'll discuss that in a bit though.

Fourth, there must be silica-rich rocks. These provide the, uh, the silica that seals the plumbing system. We call this material geyserite. It keeps the pressure in the geyser contained until it's time for the geyser to erupt. All four of these conditions are necessary for a geyser to exist. That explains why they're so rare throughout the world. Now, let's look at the different types of geysers. Open your books to page 287, please.

TYPE① [Gist-Content Question]

The majority of the professor's lecture is on the four conditions necessary for a geyser to exist.

TYPE② [Understanding Organization Question]

The professor explains, "Fourth, there must be silica-rich rocks. These provide the, uh, the silica that seals the plumbing system. We call this material geyserite. It keeps the pressure in the geyser contained until it's time for the geyser to erupt."

TYPE③ [Connecting Content Question]

The professor states, "So it can take around 500 years or so for enough water to build up to enable a geyser to form." In addition, when the water is heated, it is likely that a geyser will form under these conditions.

TYPE④ [Speaker's Attitude Question]

When responding to the professor's question on geysers, the student remarks, "It was awesome to see them erupt." She was clearly impressed by them.

Summarizing

The professor asks if anyone has seen a geyser, and one student mentions that she has. He then states the factors necessary for a geyser to form. First, surface water must go belowground and accumulate for around 500 years. Next, there must be heat from molten rocks. There must also be an underground plumbing system to act as a pressure chamber. And at the top, there must be a constriction for water to emerge from. Finally, geyserite—

a silica-rich rock—is necessary to contain the pressure in the geyser.

[TYPES 5–8]

TYPE⑤ Ⓑ   **TYPE⑥** Ⓓ
TYPE⑦ Ⓐ   **TYPE⑧** Ⓑ

Script 02-42

W Professor: Class is nearly over, so I'd like to take some time to tell you about one of history's most important chemists. I intend to do this at least once a week for the entire semester because it's vital for you to know the names of people who influenced this field.

The chemist I'd like to discuss is Antoine Lavoisier. As his name indicates, he was French. He was born in 1743 and sadly had the misfortune of living during the French Revolution. I say that because he was executed as a traitor in 1794. That unfortunate event deprived the world of a brilliant mind.

How brilliant? Well, let's see . . . Lavoisier came up with the Law of Conservation of Mass. It basically states that substances may change their state or form yet retain the same mass. So when there is a chemical reaction involving various substances, the total mass of the substances before the reaction and the total mass of the substances after the reaction is identical. This is one of the most important laws in both chemistry and physics. It's something I hope everybody remembers because it's vital to the field of chemistry.

[8]Lavoisier lived during a time when people believed in phlogiston. The phlogiston theory said that fire was comprised of an element called phlogiston. **Of course, nothing of the sort exists.** Lavoisier proved that by showing that the element oxygen has a critical role in the act of combustion.

Two more things, and then it's time to go. During Lavoisier's time, people thought water was an element. Lavoisier showed that water is a combination of hydrogen and oxygen. Finally, Lavoisier was the author of *Elementary Treatise of Chemistry*, the, uh, the first chemistry textbook. You should read it sometime. Not everything is accurate, but it will give you an idea of what people believed in the eighteenth century. I highly recommend it.

All right, uh, I think that's enough about Lavoisier's accomplishments. Please be sure to read the first ten pages of chapter two before we meet again. You'll need the information in those pages to understand my lecture.

TYPE 5 [Gist-Purpose Question]

The professor remarks, "This is one of the most important laws in both chemistry and physics. It's something I hope everybody remembers because it's vital to the field of chemistry."

TYPE 6 [Detail Question]

The professor says, "Finally, Lavoisier was the author of *Elementary Treatise of Chemistry*, the, uh, the first chemistry textbook."

TYPE 7 [Making Inferences Question]

First, the professor says, "Two more things, and then it's time to go." Then, at the end, she assigns the class homework, so she is probably going to dismiss the class for the day next.

TYPE 8 [Understanding Function Question]

When the professor says, "Of course, nothing of the sort exists," when talking about the phlogiston theory, she implies that the theory was incorrect.

Summarizing

The professor talks about Antoine Lavoisier. She says that he lived during the 1700s and was executed during the French Revolution. He was important to the field of chemistry for several reasons. He came up with the Law of Conservation of Mass, which states that substances can change their state or form but not their mass. He also proved the phlogiston theory was wrong and showed that water is a combination of hydrogen and oxygen. Finally, he wrote the first chemistry textbook, entitled *Elementary Treatise of Chemistry*.

Mastering **Question Types**
with Lectures & Conversations
A2   p.98

[TYPES 1–4]

TYPE 1 Ⓐ   TYPE 2 Ⓒ
TYPE 3 First Stage: [2], [3]   Second Stage: [1]
Third Stage: [4]
TYPE 4 Ⓐ

Script 02-43

M Professor: Okay, I know it's getting late in the day. ⁴But I need to discuss one more thing. And take notes, please, because you're having an exam next week. **You know what I'm saying, right . . . ?**

When we think of flares, we often think about fireworks that shoot in the air and suddenly burst into balls of light or, to be more correct, flaming particles. That's pretty close to what a solar flare is. Solar flares are found on the sun's surface. They're basically sudden, tremendous explosions that leap off the sun's surface. They're quite powerful, as they release energy that's equal to the power of millions— yes, millions—of hydrogen bombs. Temperatures in solar flares can be tens of millions of degrees Kelvin. That's hot. Really hot.

W Student: Professor Kennedy, are solar flares and sunspots the same thing?

M: No, but that's a good question. Solar flares typically occur near sunspots, but they're not the same. Solar flares happen when the sun releases some of the magnetic energy that's been building up in its atmosphere. This energy gets released in many forms. These include electromagnetic particles, such as gamma rays and X-rays . . . energetic particles, which include protons and electrons . . . and also mass flows.

There are three stages in a solar flare. Stage one . . . We call it the precursor stage. During this time, the release of magnetic energy is triggered. Stage two . . . This is the impulse stage. During it, the particles and the rays are accelerated to tremendous levels of energy. Then, they are emitted. Stage three . . . This is the decay stage. During it, there's a buildup and decay of soft X-rays. Each stage can have a duration as short as a few seconds to as long as an hour.

Solar flares can actually affect us here on the Earth. They can interrupt radio transmissions and cause problems for power grids. They can also cause problems for satellites orbiting the planet. There was a recent event I'd like to tell you about that involved solar flares, but we're out of time. We'll continue this discussion in our next class.

TYPE 1 [Gist-Content Question]

Most of the professor's lecture concerns solar flares.

TYPE 2 [Understanding Organization Question]

A student asks if solar flares and sunspots are the same, so the professor mentions sunspots to answer her question.

TYPE 3 [Connecting Content Question]

According to the lecture, the first stage in a solar flare is called the precursor stage and involves the release of magnetic energy. As for the second stage, particles and rays are accelerated during it. And during the third stage, soft X-rays begin to decay.

TYPE ④ [Speaker's Attitude Question]

First, the professor mentions that the students are having an exam. Then, he asks, "You know what I'm saying, right?" He tells the students that to indicate that the material he is going to discuss will be on the exam.

Summarizing

> The professor tells the students to listen closely since they have a midterm exam coming soon. He states that solar flares are similar to fireworks. They are sudden, tremendous explosions on the sun's surface. They contain the power of millions of hydrogen bombs. He notes that sunspots and solar flares are different from each other. He explains the three stages in a solar flare: the precursor, impulse, and decay stages. Solar flares can also affect the Earth by interrupting radio transmissions and causing power grid problems.

[TYPES 5–8]

TYPE ⑤ Ⓒ   **TYPE ⑥** Ⓑ
TYPE ⑦ Ⓑ   **TYPE ⑧** Ⓓ

Script 02-44

> **W Student:** Professor Gomez, do you have a few seconds? I need to ask you a quick question.
>
> **M Professor:** Sure, Amy. What can I help you with?
>
> **W:** Uh, actually, I'm looking for Professor Snyder. He hasn't been in his office for the last couple of days, and I absolutely have to speak with him.
>
> **M:** Well, uh, he's not going to be here until next week. He's at a conference that's out of the state.
>
> **W:** He's out of the state and won't be back until next week? Oh no! That's awful. Now what am I going to do?
>
> **M:** What exactly do you need to chat with him about?
>
> **W:** Well, you see . . . I'm planning to apply for the summer study-in-Spain program. Since he runs the program, I have to get the applications directly from him. ⁸ But the due date is this Friday, and you just said he won't be back until Monday.
>
> **M: Well, guess what . . . ?** Today's your lucky day, Amy . . . Here. You can have this.
>
> **W:** Wow. Thank you so much. Um, how is it that you just happen to have one of these forms lying around? Uh, if you don't mind my asking, that is.
>
> **M:** ⁷ I'm the deputy chair of the department, so I have all kinds of forms in my office. It's just your luck that I have the one you need. **It doesn't always work out that way.**

TYPE ⑤ [Gist-Purpose Question]

When the professor asks the student how he can help her, she responds, "Uh, actually, I'm looking for Professor Snyder."

TYPE ⑥ [Detail Question]

The student states, "Well, you see . . . I'm planning to apply for the summer study-in-Spain program. Since he runs the program, I have to get the applications directly from him."

TYPE ⑦ [Making Inferences Question]

When the professor says, "It doesn't always work out that way," he is implying to the student that he does not always have in his office the forms that some students want.

TYPE ⑧ [Understanding Function Question]

When a person says, "Guess what?" he or she is often about to surprise the person that he or she is speaking with. This is exactly what the professor is doing.

Summarizing

> The student tells the professor she is looking for Professor Snyder. The professor responds that Professor Snyder is out of the state at a conference and will not return until Monday. The student mentions that she needs to see Professor Snyder about the summer study-in-Spain program. She needs to complete an application form by Friday. The professor then gives the student a form that he has in his office. He explains that he is the deputy chair of the department. Therefore, he has many forms students need.

Mastering **Topics** with Lectures   **B1**   p.100

1 Ⓓ   2 Diesel: ①, ②, ④   Ethanol: ③   3 Ⓒ

Script & Graphic Organizer 02-45

> **M Professor:** Most cars run on gasoline. But quite a few vehicles run on diesel fuel these days. Some cars also use ethanol. What are the advantages— and disadvantages—of using diesel and ethanol instead of gasoline? And how do diesel and ethanol, uh, stack up against each other? Let's find out.
>
> Simply put, diesel fuel is any fuel that's used in a diesel engine. Diesel engines don't use spark plugs to ignite the fuel like gasoline-operated cars do. Instead, they operate on the compression of a fuel-

oxygen mixture. Most diesel fuel comes from oil, so it can be a fossil fuel such as gasoline. Other diesel fuels are made from organic products like soybeans or vegetable oils like canola oil. As for ethanol, it's made from organic matter. In America, most ethanol is produced from corn. In South America, particularly Brazil, people make ethanol from sugarcane.

There are two main advantages to using diesel fuel. First, it produces fewer carbon emissions than gasoline. Second, it's often lower in price than gasoline. The price can vary, however, depending on the region and the time of year. For instance, diesel made from oil is generally more expensive in winter because the demand for heating oil drives the price up. Another advantage of diesel is that it doesn't catch fire as easily as gasoline or burn as violently. For this reason, many military vehicles and both military and commercial ships have diesel engines.

W Student: What about the advantages of ethanol?

M: I was just about to get to that, Karen. Let me see . . . First, it produces less pollution per volume than regular gasoline. Of course, the process of making ethanol from organic matter produces some amount of pollution. In addition, depending on the organic matter used as well as the location, ethanol can be cheaper than gasoline. It basically depends on where the corn, sugarcane, or other material is harvested and how much it costs at the time. There are, however, ways to mitigate price increases in organic material. For example, in Brazil, most locally manufactured cars have engines that can use either gasoline or ethanol. That way, drivers don't have to worry about fluctuating fuel prices.

So which of the two is better . . . diesel or ethanol? Well . . . it mostly depends on the source of the diesel. Biodiesel, which is made from organic matter, produces about seventy percent less pollution than gasoline. But diesel made from fossil fuels doesn't come anywhere near that figure. In comparison, corn ethanol produces twenty-two percent less pollution than gasoline. And sugarcane ethanol produces fifty-six percent less pollution than gasoline. So biodiesel is the least harmful to the environment. ³It also takes less energy to make biodiesel than it does to make corn ethanol. But biodiesel is more expensive than fossil-fuel diesel, which makes it more attractive . . . **No. Excuse me . . . I mean less attractive to consumers.** Fossil-fuel diesel is also a known product since it's been available for more than a century. It's readily available, too. Ethanol and biodiesel are less well known, are not available everywhere, and do not work in all vehicles. For now, most of the world's vehicles run on gasoline or fossil-fuel diesel. This isn't likely to change in the near future.

Diesel and Ethanol

Diesel Fuel:	Ethanol:
- Used in diesel engines with no spark plugs	- Made from organic matter such as corn or sugarcane
- Produces fewer carbon emissions than gasoline and is cheaper	- Produces less pollution per volume than gasoline
- Biodiesel is the form of diesel the least harmful to the environment	- May be cheap depending upon the organic matter used

1 [Gist-Purpose Question]

Much of the lecture is a comparison of the advantages of ethanol with those of diesel.

2 [Connecting Content Question]

According to the lecture, diesel may be more expensive in winter, is used by many military ships, and does not need spark plugs to run an engine. As for ethanol, it can be made from both sugarcane and corn.

3 [Understanding Function Question]

When the professor says, "No. Excuse me," he is correcting a mistake that he just made while speaking.

Summarizing

The professor compares diesel fuel and ethanol with each other. Diesel is any fuel used in a diesel engine, which needs no spark plugs. It may often come from soybeans and canola oil. Ethanol is made from organic matter. Diesel is cleaner than gasoline and is often cheaper. Ethanol produces less pollution than gasoline and may be cheaper than it depending on where it is made. The material that diesel and ethanol are made of mostly determines which one is better than the other as a fuel source.

Mastering **Topics** with Lectures   B2   p.101

1 Ⓐ   2 Ⓒ   3 Ⓓ

Script & Graphic Organizer 02-46

W Professor: A volcano is created when magma, which is hot melted rock deep within the Earth, finds a weak spot in the crust and bursts through it. This usually happens on land, but it may happen under the water as well, particularly, uh, in the ocean. When magma appears above the ground, we call it lava. An erupting volcano can also spew rocks, hot ash, and various gases. [3]Volcanologists, that is, volcano scientists, have come up with seven main types of volcanoes. They are . . . stratovolcanoes, cinder cone volcanoes, shield volcanoes, lava dome volcanoes, supervolcanoes, submarine volcanoes, and subglacial volcanoes. **Those names are in your text, so you can check them out there.** Volcanoes typically differ in their sizes, shapes, and locations, the materials they eject, and the types of eruptions they have. Now, as I speak, take a look at the slides of volcanoes that I show up here on the screen.

First is the stratovolcano. We also call it a composite volcano. Look here . . . These volcanoes are very symmetrical, tall, and conical shaped. They're made of layers of ash and rocks that are then covered by lava, which cools. Over time, the process gets repeated, so stratovolcanoes have many layers. Mount Fuji in Japan, which you see . . . here . . . is a famous example of this type. Let's take a look at the cinder cone volcano next . . . It's often squat looking and very low. Most are fewer than 1,000 feet high. They're made of cinder-like rocks, which give the volcano its name. Most erupt a single time, and they form rather quickly. Some cinder cones are found next to larger volcanoes, and they're all connected to the same underground magma pool.

Next is the shield volcano. Take a look at it . . . Shield volcanoes formed the Hawaiian Islands. They're very broad and can be tens of miles wide. They may be high or low. It basically depends on their age and activity. The magma that comes to the surface through them has a low, uh, viscosity, so it can flow far. This helps give shield volcanoes their broad shapes. Okay, here's our next volcano . . . It's the lava dome volcano. Note its round shape . . . It's formed by magma with high viscosity. It doesn't flow far but instead builds up into a very round dome-like shape. Lava domes often form inside the craters of stratovolcanoes.

The fifth type is the supervolcano. These, fortunately, have only occurred occasionally in history. They're so massive that they cause great amounts of destruction when they erupt. Upon erupting, the volcano collapses on itself and leaves a ring, or caldera, of low ridges that's many miles wide. Yellowstone National Park in the U.S. sits atop one ancient supervolcano.

As I mentioned a minute ago, some volcanoes form underwater. These are submarine volcanoes. Here's a picture of one . . . When this happens, the lava cools very quickly. Over time, the cooling lava builds up and eventually breaks the surface. This forms a volcanic island, like Hawaii and Iceland. The last type

is the subglacial volcano, which can form under a glacier or icecap. Many of these formed during the last ice age. They're distinguished by their very flat tops, which were created because the rapidly cooling lava has nowhere to flow under the glacier or icecap.

Types of Volcanoes

Volcanoes and Their Characteristics:	*The Effects of Volcanoes:*
- *Seven types of volcanoes: stratovolcanoes, cinder cone, shield, lava dome, supervolcanoes, submarine, and subglacial volcanoes* - *Spew lava, rocks, hot ash, and gases from underground*	- *Can create high mountains* - *May form islands such as the Hawaiian Islands* - *May cause a great amount of destruction*

1　[Detail Question]

The professor states, "Shield volcanoes formed the Hawaiian Islands."

2　[Understanding Organization Question]

Throughout the lecture, the professor shows slides of the different types of volcanoes to the class while pointing out certain features that each one has.

3　[Understanding Attitude Question]

When the professor tells the students to check out the names of the volcanoes in their books, she is implying that she expects them to look at their books.

Summarizing

There are seven main types of volcanoes. Stratovolcanoes are symmetrical, tall, and conical shaped. Cinder cone volcanoes are low. Shield volcanoes formed the Hawaiian Islands. They can be many miles long. Lava dome volcanoes are round and form inside other volcanoes. Supervolcanoes cause extensive destruction. There was one in Yellowstone National Park in the U.S. Submarine volcanoes occur underwater. And subglacial volcanoes are found under glaciers or icecaps.

Mastering **Topics** with Lectures 　B3　 p.102

1 Ⓑ　　2 Ⓐ, Ⓒ　　3 Ⓒ

Script & Graphic Organizer　02-47

M1 Professor: The notion that life on the Earth may have originally come from space is gaining more credence these days. And, no, I don't mean that aliens colonized the Earth. I'm referring to very tiny life forms—uh, microbes—such as bacteria. There is mounting evidence that bacteria and other spores can survive journeys in space while attached to meteorites. This has caused some to believe that life on the Earth originated from outer space. Some experts additionally believe that life from the Earth could spread to other planets. This act is called seeding planets.

In the early twenty-first century, scientists discovered some new strains of bacteria high in the atmosphere. No one knows where these bacteria came from. Some people suggested that they were already on the Earth but were blown into the atmosphere. Perhaps a volcanic eruption did this. Supporters of this theory note that new types of bacteria are being discovered all the time. However, other scientists had a different idea. They theorized that a comet or meteoroid passing by or entering the Earth's atmosphere brought the bacteria from other worlds. Any reaction to that . . . ? Yes?

M2 Student: You can't be serious, can you?

M1: Listen to the evidence first, and then you can be the judge. Okay? So here's the question: How can bacterial spores—living organisms—survive a journey in space? Space is a harsh environment. It's intensely cold, it has no oxygen, and there's dangerous ultraviolet radiation from the sun, too. In addition, the bacteria would have to survive extreme heat upon entering the Earth's atmosphere. Well, some Swiss and German scientists set out to prove bacteria could travel long distances and survive. They examined some dust particles collected by Charles Darwin during his travels more than a century ago. They conducted experiments on the bacteria that had gotten attached to the spores. Here's what they learned: Those bacteria spores had traveled to other continents and had lived for at least two centuries.

Later, they devised some experiments that replicated the conditions of a meteoroid leaving its home world and coming to the Earth. They attached millions of bacteria spores to various materials and subjected the material to tests. Some tests were done under ultraviolet light like the sun's. Others were done using high-impact devices to crush the spores. Many spores survived these impact tests. Yet the ultraviolet light test results were different. In one test, millions of spores were brought into space on a Russian spacecraft. When released in space without being attached to anything, they all died. However, when mixed with red sandstone and similar material that had been collected from meteoroids from Mars, some spores survived exposure to ultraviolet light.

That's not a definitive study of course. The main reason is that the spores were exposed only for a short time. It would take a long, long amount of time for bacteria spores to reach another planet. I'm talking about tens of thousands . . . or even millions . . . of years. Still, the experiments offered the possibility that space spores could travel several light years and survive an impact on another world. Is that what happened on the Earth? Well, we may never know the answer to that question. But it's something that we could consider a definite possibility and that we should not simply dismiss as impossible.

Microbes in Outer Space

Microbes in Outer Space:	Theory:
- Bacteria and other tiny life forms - Can survive in outer space - Attach themselves to meteorites - Have been found high in the Earth's atmosphere	Life on the Earth may have come from outer space
	First Experiment: Examined bacteria collected by Darwin; had traveled far and were more than 2 centuries old
	Second Experiment: Bacteria in space that were attached to some materials survived ultraviolet light exposure

1 [Gist-Content Question]

The professor mostly discusses the possibility of bacteria surviving in outer space.

2 [Detail Question]

According to the professor, "In one test, millions of spores were brought into space on a Russian spacecraft. When released in space without being attached to anything, they all died. However, when mixed with red sandstone and similar material that had been collected from meteoroids from Mars, some spores survived exposure to ultraviolet light."

3 [Making Inferences Question]

The professor discusses the possibility of bacteria arriving on the Earth from other worlds. A student asks if he is joking, and he tells the student, "Listen to the evidence first." At the end of the lecture, the professor also says, "But it's something that we could consider a definite possibility and that we should not simply dismiss as impossible." Thus, it can be inferred that the professor believes that bacteria could have arrived on the Earth from elsewhere.

Some scientists are willing to accept that life on the Earth may have come from outer space. It could have arrived on the Earth by bacteria or other spores that were attached to meteorites. Scientists discovered new forms of bacteria high in the atmosphere. Some believed the bacteria were from other worlds. Swiss and German scientists working with bacteria collected by Charles Darwin learned that the bacteria had traveled to many places and had lived for two centuries. Another experiment proved it was possible for bacteria to survive in space.

Mastering **Topics** with Conversations — B4 — p.103

1 Ⓒ   2 Ⓓ   3 Ⓐ

Script & Graphic Organizer 02-48

W Student: Hi. This is the office I come to if I have a problem with my apartment, right?

M Housing Office Employee: Do you live in an apartment on campus?

W: Yes, sir, I do. I live in West Hall. I've got a suite with a couple of roommates, and we've got a huge problem. I should talk to you about it, shouldn't I?

M: Yes, I'm the person that you should speak with. What can I do for you today?

W: Okay . . . Our apartment in West Hall has a kitchen in it. Last night, we were using the oven when it, uh . . . it just suddenly stopped working. Something's wrong with it since it won't even turn on. Can you send someone out to fix it today?

M: Today? Sorry, but that simply isn't possible.

W: Why not? Aren't you supposed to help students when we have problems?

M: Of course. That's my job. But it's three o'clock on Friday afternoon. All of my repairmen are already busy doing different jobs. Then, they're going to go home for the weekend. Everyone has a full workload next Monday, too. So I think, uh . . . perhaps I'll be able to send a repairman over there next Tuesday. How does ten AM sound?

W: That's just not acceptable.

M: Excuse me?

W: I'm hosting a dinner party in my suite tomorrow. I absolutely must have my oven fixed by then. I insist that you send someone over to fix it.

M: Look, miss . . . I'd love to help you, but I can't. If you want, I can give you the telephone number of a repair company that can probably send a man over tonight. You'll have to pay for the repairs though.

W: Hmm . . . I guess I don't have much of a choice, do I?

M: Not really. Unless you want to wait. Here's his card. He's a friend of mine. He does good work, so he should be able to solve your problem. Tell him that I gave you his number, and you might get a special deal.

Service Encounter

Student's Problem:	Employee's Response:
Oven in her apartment is not working	Can send a repairman to fix it next Tuesday
Student's Reaction:	**Employee's Solution:**
Needs to have it fixed now because of her dinner party	Gives her a number to call another repairman to fix the oven

1 [Gist-Purpose Question]

The student visits the housing office because there is a problem with her oven and she wants to get it fixed.

2 [Understanding Attitude Question]

The student is very demanding as she insists that the man send someone to fix her oven immediately because of the party she is going to have.

3 [Making Inferences Question]

The man tells the student, "Tell him that I gave you his number, and you might get a special deal." He is implying that his friend might give the student a discount if she mentions his name.

The student visits the housing office to complain that the oven in her kitchen is not working. She wants a repairman to fix it today. The man says he cannot send anyone until next Tuesday because it is already Friday afternoon. On Monday, his workers will be busy as well. The student claims she is having a dinner party and must have her oven fixed. The man gives her the number of a repair company. So the student can call that and pay someone to fix her oven.

1 Ⓒ   2 Ⓐ   3 Ⓒ   4 Ⓑ   5 Known:

[2], [4]   Unknown: [1], [3]   6 Ⓓ

Script   02-49

M Professor: Let's look at the second-closest planet to the sun: Venus. Of all the planets, Venus is closest in size to Earth and nearest to Earth in distance. Ironically, we know less about Venus than the other planets because of the dense cloud cover that surrounds the entire planet.

Okay, a little background . . . Venus was named for the Roman goddess of love. It's clearly visible to the naked eye. It appears as a bright object in the evening and morning sky. I'm sure you've all seen it. Venus is about sixty-six million miles from the sun and around twenty-seven million miles from Earth. It's approximately eighty percent of Earth's mass and ninety percent of Earth's size. That's just about where the similarities end. Venus orbits the sun every 225 days. It has clockwise rotation on its axis. That's different from all of the other planets. Interestingly, it orbits the sun counterclockwise. Venus has a long day. The period between sunrise and sunset from one spot on Venus is fifty-eight Earth days. That means the planet makes one complete rotation every 116 Earth days. Imagine that.

Now, the planet itself . . . No human could survive there because of its atmospheric composition, atmospheric pressure, and temperature. As I just stated, Venus has a very dense cloud cover. Examinations of its atmosphere indicate that it's quite toxic. It's composed of ninety-six percent carbon dioxide, three and a half percent nitrogen, and smaller amounts of other elements or compounds. These include, uh, sulfur dioxide, argon, carbon monoxide, and helium. On top of that, Venus has a high atmospheric pressure. It's over ninety times that of Earth's at sea level. [6]Finally, the planet itself is extremely hot. It's actually the hottest planet in the solar system. **Yes, even hotter than Mercury.** It has surface temperatures that get up to 870 degrees Fahrenheit. Does anyone know why it's so hot?

W Student: Could it be because of the greenhouse effect?

M: Correct. The dense cloud cover on Venus traps the heat, much like a greenhouse does. This makes the planet hot. Even during nighttime on the part of the planet facing away from the sun, the planet remains hot. The heat there gets trapped and cannot easily escape the atmosphere.

W: What does the surface of the planet look like? Is there water on Venus like there is here on Earth?

M: We're not really sure about the surface. You see, since the 1960s, both the U.S. and the Russians have sent scientific probes to Venus. Some probes orbited the planet while others actually landed on it. We have a few color photographs from those missions. However, the probes that landed there didn't last long. Either the high pressure crushed them or the high temperature caused them to malfunction. Thus, they only sent back data for a few hours or even less before they stopped working.

As for your second question, no large—or even small—bodies of water have been found there. Some scientists thought the atmosphere might produce water with high acidic levels, but this hasn't been confirmed. Nor has it been disproved I should add. One result of this apparent lack of surface water is that there has been little erosion of the planet's surface. There's some evidence of wind, but this seems to have had little impact on the surface. In addition, radar mapping shows that the surface appears to consist of both lowlands and highlands. The highest mountains on Venus are around 18,000 feet high. That's a little more than half the height of Mount Everest. Venus also has many volcanic features. This indicates it either had or has an unstable surface. Approximately eighty-five percent of Venus's surface shows signs of volcanic activity in the past.

What does seem to be lacking are impact craters. You know, craters that are caused by meteors or asteroids crashing into a planet or moon. There are some craters on Venus that are as wide as twenty miles. But there are very few when compared to other bodies such as, uh, say, Earth's moon. This suggests that Venus's surface is quite young. Many objects may also not ever get a chance to strike the planet. The reasons are that they may be crushed by the high pressure or incinerated by the hot temperatures before they hit the ground.

1   [Gist-Content Question]

The professor mostly provides an overview of the planet Venus.

2   [Gist-Purpose Question]

The professor states, "Venus has a long day. The period between sunrise and sunset from one spot on Venus is fifty-eight Earth days. That means the planet makes one complete rotation every 116 Earth days. Imagine that." He is focused mostly on the length of a Venusian day.

3 [Detail Question]

The professor notes, "The dense cloud cover on Venus traps the heat, much like a greenhouse does. This makes the planet hot."

4 [Understanding Organization Question]

A student asks the professor about the surface of Venus. The professor then describes the surface of the planet according to what she asked.

5 [Connecting Content Question]

According to the lecture, the average surface temperature and the period of rotation of Venus are both known. The existence of water and the age of the planet's surface are not known.

6 [Understanding Function Question]

When the professor states, "Yes, even hotter than Mercury," he is implying that some people mistakenly believe that Mercury, not Venus, is the hottest planet in the solar system.

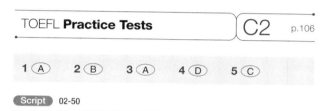

TOEFL **Practice Tests** C2 p.106

1 (A) 2 (B) 3 (A) 4 (D) 5 (C)

Script 02-50

W Professor: Walter, would you come in here for a moment? I'd like to have a word with you.

M Student: Uh, yeah. Sure. I-I-I'm not in any, uh, trouble or anything, am I?

W: Not at all, Walter. Not at all. I just want to talk to you about the paper you just turned in for my class.

M: Oh, are you talking about that one I wrote on the future of political systems?

W: Yes, that's exactly the one I mean. The one you submitted three days ago.

M: What about it? You didn't like it?

W: On the contrary, I loved it. I graded it last night, and I must say that I was impressed. Very impressed. You obviously put a lot of time and effort into that paper.

M: Thank you, Professor Schmidt. Yes, I worked on it for about two weeks to be honest. I probably tried harder on it than I usually do on my other assignments. You see, I love politics and consider it a hobby of mine.

W: Ah, that's right. I believe you're on the school's

student council, right?

M: Yes, ma'am, I am. I'm one the student senators. It's kind of fun. I was involved in student government when I was in high school as well.

W: Well, from what I read in your paper, you seem to have a good understanding of it. So, anyway, about your paper . . .

M: Yes?

W: I was thinking that you might consider submitting it to a professional journal.

M: Uh, what? You're not really serious, are you?

W: I most definitely am serious. You gave a very coherent explanation about the possible futures of various political systems. I must say that your ideas and theories were much better than a lot of the paid political pieces I read every day. You would, of course, have to expand your paper a bit. [4]You'd have to do some editing as well. But I could assist you with that if you wanted.

M: Uh, gee. I don't know what to say. It sounds like, uh, like a lot of work.

W: It would be. It would probably take you a couple of months to finish. But summer vacation is coming up soon. You could work on it then so that your classes wouldn't interfere. And it would be quite an accomplishment for an undergraduate to get published in a journal, you know.

M: Oh . . . Right. I hadn't thought of that. It would look good on my résumé, wouldn't it?

W: [5]It sure would. So what do you say?

M: Let me think about it. **But I'm leaning toward following your suggestion.**

1 [Gist-Purpose Question]

The professor wants to talk about the student's paper so that she can propose that he submit it to a professional journal.

2 [Detail Question]

The student says, "I'm one the student senators," so he is involved in student government.

3 [Understanding Attitude Question]

The professor notes that she loved the student's paper, so she believes that it was an outstanding piece of writing.

4 [Understanding Function Question]

When the student responds, "I don't know what to say," he is expressing his surprise since he was not expecting her to make that proposal.

5 [Making Inferences Question]

When the student states, "I'm leaning toward following your suggestion," he is implying that he is probably going to accept the professor's offer.

Vocabulary **Review**   p.109

1 (B)   2 (D)   3 (B)   4 (A)   5 (B)

6 (A)   7 (C)   8 (D)   9 (C)   10 (A)

11 (E)   12 (A)   13 (D)   14 (B)   15 (C)

Chapter | **06** Physical Sciences 2 • Conversations

Mastering **Question Types**
with Lectures & Conversations   A1   p.112

[TYPES 1–4]

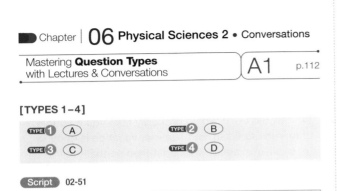

TYPE1 (A)   TYPE2 (B)

TYPE3 (C)   TYPE4 (D)

Script   02-51

M Professor: I'd like to cover methane. Does anyone know what it is?

W Student: [4]I do, Professor Taylor. Methane's a greenhouse gas.

M: Well done, Karen. But what do you mean by greenhouse gas?

W: Uh . . . I'm sorry, sir, but I'm at a loss for words.

M: Well, don't worry. I'll let you know what it is in a second. As Karen said, methane's a gas. It's odorless and lighter than air. It can be produced naturally or by man. Lots of it is produced by the decomposition of manure. In its concentrated form, methane is a potentially dangerous gas. Since its presence is hard to detect without special equipment, it can accumulate in areas that are not well ventilated. When large amounts of methane gather in one area, it displaces the oxygen in the air. This creates an oxygen-deficient atmosphere. This can lead to two problems. First, if the concentration of methane reaches five percent of the atmosphere, it can explode. Second, if people breathe an atmosphere comprised of just one percent methane, after a period of time, they can get sick and even die.

Karen identified methane as a greenhouse gas. I know that people often talk about greenhouse gases as if they were bad, but that's far from the case. First, greenhouse gases, such as, uh, carbon dioxide, water vapor, nitrous oxide, and, of course, methane, occur naturally. And it's a good thing they do because without them, the Earth would be too cold for life as we know it to survive. Without greenhouse gases, we estimate that the Earth's average temperature would be two degrees below zero Fahrenheit instead of its current fifty-seven degrees Fahrenheit. And for those of you who only know Celsius, two below zero Fahrenheit is about minus nineteen Celsius. And fifty-seven Fahrenheit is about fourteen Celsius.

W: How do greenhouse gases help the planet?

M: Basically, they allow sunlight to enter the Earth's atmosphere and to strike its surface. Some of this light reflects off the ground and heads back out as infrared radiation. However, greenhouse gases absorb lots of radiation. This traps heat in the atmosphere, which helps keep the planet warm.

TYPE1 [Gist-Content Question]

The professor mostly discusses the various effects of methane on the environment.

TYPE2 [Understanding Organization Question]

At the beginning of his discussion on greenhouse gases, the professor mentions, "Karen identified methane as a greenhouse gas. I know that people often talk about greenhouse gases as if they were bad, but that's far from the case." So he intends to describe how greenhouse gases benefit the planet.

TYPE3 [Connecting Content Question]

The professor states, "First, if the concentration of methane reaches five percent of the atmosphere, it can explode."

TYPE4 [Speaker's Attitude Question]

When the student says, "I'm at a loss for words," she means that she does not know what to say. Thus, she does not know the answer.

Summarizing

The professor describes methane as an odorless and lighter-than-air gas. He notes that it can be dangerous since it can explode when it is highly concentrated. Methane is also unsafe for humans to breathe. The professor then states that greenhouse gases such as methane, carbon dioxide, and water vapor benefit the planet. They keep the planet warm, which lets people survive. He explains that greenhouse gases prevent some of the sun's infrared radiation from leaving the atmosphere. This is what keeps the planet warm.

[TYPES 5–8]

TYPE 5 D **TYPE 6** C
TYPE 7 A **TYPE 8** C

Script 02-52

W Professor: [7]I'm sure you all know that the icicle-like and cone-like formations found in caves are stalactites and stalagmites. Professionals commonly refer to them as speleothems. **And, yes, before one of you asks, you need to know that term.** Anyway, stalactites and stalagmites are deposits of minerals that form in cave structures and line the insides of caves. Interestingly, they grow in pairs, so unless one has somehow broken off, you will always find one directly beneath the other. I should mention that it's not unusual for them to connect and thereby become a column.

Before I continue . . . I know everyone has trouble remembering which one is at the top and which one is at the bottom. When you get confused, just think of a stalactite holding tightly to the ceiling of a cave. That should make it easier to remember, right?

Stalactites and stalagmites don't form in all caves. They only grow in limestone caves. They are formed mostly of calcite, which we also know as calcium carbonate. How do they form? Okay . . . As rainwater falls to the ground and trickles into a limestone cave, it picks up carbon dioxide and various minerals from the limestone. Then, it forms something called calcium bicarbonate. Later, the water emerges from the cracks in the cave's roof. At that time, it comes into contact with the air in the cave. Then, some of the calcium bicarbonate changes into calcium carbonate. It's at that time that we can see calcite starting to form around the crack. As the water drips, the calcite grows in both length and width. After some time, it forms a stalactite. But don't wait around for one to form. They only grow about a quarter of an inch to an inch each century.

Oh, I almost forgot . . . Stalagmites. Some of the water dripping on the stalactites above falls to the caves' floors. Over time, the calcium carbonate in them forms stalagmites. This also explains why stalagmites have cone-like shapes and why they're directly beneath stalactites.

TYPE 5 [Gist-Content Question]

The professor focuses on stalactites and stalagmites, which are both formations that are found in caves.

TYPE 6 [Detail Question]

Concerning calcite, the professor says, "Stalactites and stalagmites don't form in all caves. They only grow in limestone caves. They are formed mostly of calcite, which we also know as calcium carbonate."

TYPE 7 [Making Inferences Question]

When the professor notes, "Before one of you asks, you need to know that term," she is implying that she has been asked this question before. That is how she knows to tell the students that the term is important.

TYPE 8 [Understanding Function Question]

The professor explains, "I know everyone has trouble remembering which one is at the top and which one is at the bottom. When you get confused, just think of a stalactite holding tightly to the ceiling of a cave. That should make it easier to remember, right?" So she is differentiating stalactites and stalagmites.

Summarizing

The professor tells the students that the formations found in some caves are called stalactites and stalagmites. She says they grow in pairs and may sometimes combine to create a column. She then mentions that stalagmites grow from the ceiling. Both formations appear in limestone caves. They are formed of calcite, or calcium carbonate. A combination of rainwater, carbon dioxide, and minerals creates them over many centuries. As for stalagmites, they form because of water dripping off stalactites. This is why stalagmites form underneath stalactites.

Mastering **Question Types**
with Lectures & Conversations

A2   p.114

[TYPES 1–4]

TYPE 1 B **TYPE 2** C
TYPE 3 Large Amounts of Permafrost: 1, 3
Small Amounts of Permafrost: 2, 4
TYPE 4 A

Script 02-53

W Professor: The scientific term for permanently frozen ground is permafrost. Any kind of soil, sediment, or rock that has been frozen for a minimum of two years is permafrost. By frozen, I mean that its temperature has continually remained at or below zero degrees Celsius.

Permafrost ranges in thickness from less than one meter deep to more than, uh, 1,000 meters in depth.

Some of it is just now forming while other areas have been permafrost for thousands of years. It's important to remember that we don't define permafrost by the amount of moisture it contains. Instead, it's defined solely by its temperature. Some permafrost has more than thirty percent ice while other areas have virtually none at all. In addition, some, um, permafrost may be covered by several meters of snow while other areas may have little or no snow. Interestingly, a landmass's proximity to large bodies of water tends to keep the ground's temperature from getting too low. So places like, say, Scandinavia and Iceland, have little permafrost despite their often incredibly cold temperatures.

There are several types of permafrost. For instance, there is warm permafrost, which has temperatures just below zero degrees Celsius. Warm permafrost can quickly thaw when the temperature rises. And then there is cold permafrost. [4]In cold permafrost, the ground temperatures may be between one and twelve degrees below zero. Please note that I'm using Celsius, not Fahrenheit. This cold permafrost can withstand considerable amounts of heat before it thaws. **An area with cold permafrost is not a place you want to be stranded. Believe me. I know.**

M Student: Where can we usually find permafrost?

W: Hmm . . . Well, as you would expect, it's usually found at high latitudes near the North and South poles. However, those aren't the only places where it exists. It can be found at high altitudes all around the world. In the Northern Hemisphere, just about one-third of the permafrost is found in Alaska, northern Canada, and the U.S. Rocky Mountains. The vast majority, however, is found in Siberia, Russia, and other northern lands in Asia and Europe. South of the equator, we can find most permafrost in Antarctica, the Antarctic Islands, and the Andes Mountains.

TYPE 1 [Gist-Content Question]

The professor mostly focuses on describing permafrost and its characteristics.

TYPE 2 [Understanding Organization Question]

When the professor describes some different types of permafrost, she gives the name and the temperatures at which each type exists.

TYPE 3 [Connecting Content Question]

According to the lecture, large amounts of permafrost are in Siberia and Antarctica. There are small amounts of permafrost in Scandinavia and Iceland.

TYPE 4 [Speaker's Attitude Question]

When the professor says, "Believe me. I know," she is indicating that she has been in an area that has cold permafrost before.

Summarizing

Permafrost is permanently frozen ground. It can be soil, sediment, or rock. Permafrost may be less than one meter deep or more than 1,000 meters deep. The amount of ice in it varies from thirty percent to almost zero. According to the professor, there are several different types of permafrost depending upon the temperature in the area. These include warm permafrost and cold permafrost. It mostly appears at high latitudes near the North and South poles. But there are many other places where there is permafrost.

[TYPES 5–8]

TYPE 5 D		**TYPE 6** B	
TYPE 7 A		**TYPE 8** C	

Script 02-54

M Student: Good morning. My name is Kyle Mercy, and I'm here on behalf of Professor Murdock. I need the key to the attic, please.

W Dean of Engineering's Office Employee: Hello. Professor Murdock needs to visit the attic?

M: Uh, not exactly. He instructed me to go to the attic to retrieve some equipment stored there. He needs it for a lab experiment he's conducting tomorrow.

W: [8]I see. Do you have a letter from him?

M: A letter?

W: The university stores sensitive documents for the school of engineering in the attic. We can't have unauthorized individuals just walking around up there. They could look at the documents and gain access to information they shouldn't be able to see.

M: Ah, okay. I get it now. Professor Murdock instructed me to tell you that he sent you an email. I guess he must have given me permission in the email.

W: Let me check . . . Hmm . . . Here it is . . . Okay, Mr. Mercy, it appears you are permitted to visit the attic. You need to wait about ten minutes though. I will be able to accompany you then.

M: Accompany me?

W: Of course. As I mentioned, we don't just let anyone up there. I need to see exactly what you're doing up there. Now let me complete typing this letter, please. Why don't you take a seat over there? I'll be ready to go upstairs soon.

TYPE 5 [Gist-Purpose Question]

At the beginning of the conversation, the student says, "I need the key to the attic, please."

TYPE 6 [Detail Question]

The student tells the woman, "He instructed me to go to the attic to retrieve some equipment stored there. He needs it for a lab experiment he's conducting tomorrow."

TYPE 7 [Making Inferences Question]

At the end of the conversation, the woman tells the student, "Now let me complete typing this letter, please."

TYPE 8 [Understanding Function Question]

When the woman asks, "Do you have a letter from him?" the student replies, "A letter?" He is clearly confused and does not know why the woman is requesting a letter.

Summarizing

The student visits the office of the dean of engineering and requests the key to the attic. He has to retrieve some equipment there for his professor. The woman asks for a letter and explains that access to the attic is controlled because sensitive documents are stored there. The student remarks that the professor sent the woman an email. The woman tells the student that she will accompany him to the attic in ten minutes. She needs to see what he is doing while he is up there.

Mastering **Topics** with Lectures B1 p.116

1 Ⓐ   2 Ⓒ   3 Ⓐ

Script & Graphic Organizer 02-55

W Professor: Now that we've covered continental drift, let's look at some, um, other ways that the Earth's features can change. Sometimes, these changes can be gradual. Other times, they can be quite dramatic, as with, say, floods and earthquakes. Glaciers may take many years—sometimes even centuries—to change the landscape. A flood, however, can alter a landscape in a matter of hours or days, and an earthquake can cause changes in just minutes or even seconds.

Glaciers are slow-moving sheets of ice found mainly in the Polar Regions and in mountain ranges high enough to have extremely cold temperatures. What happens is that, over time, a buildup of ice causes pressure in the glacier to grow. This makes the ice start moving through the force of gravity. Soon, it looks like a river of moving ice. Glaciers often move slowly. They usually move only a few meters per year. Typically, this movement is down the slope of a mountain or through a valley. As a glacier moves, it changes the land underneath it. How? Well, it can carve out lakes, widen valleys or make new ones, and push earth and large stones ahead of it. During the last ice age, huge sheets of ice moved down from the Arctic region. These altered the landscape of much of North America and Eurasia. Later, the ice sheets stopped advancing. They began melting and then retreated. Behind them, they left a very different land than what was there before. For instance, moving sheets of ice carved out the Great Lakes in North America.

Floods can also alter the landscape. Floodwaters can come from rivers or even the ocean. River floods are often caused by too much rainfall or snowmelt after winter. The amount of water is simply too much for the river banks. This flooding can be gradual or, um, dramatic and violent. When it's violent, the riverbanks are often washed away. Then, the fast-moving water can uproot trees and large stones and sometimes even cause mudslides. As the water recedes, it leaves behind large amounts of silt, which can alter the landscape further. On the other hand, ocean floods are different from river floods. Ocean floods usually occur during hurricanes or tropical storms. The force of the wind and the movement of the ocean are so strong that the ocean waters are carried far inland. The shapes of beaches and coastal cliffs can be altered, too.

M Student: [3]Professor, what about tidal waves?

W: First, it's better to call them tsunamis, not tidal waves. Nevertheless, yes, tsunamis can also shape the land. But they're quite rare and are primarily the direct results of underwater earthquakes. So I guess that's a good way to introduce earthquakes. When forces within the planet cause an earthquake, massive destruction can result over an area covering hundreds of miles. The land can literally shift positions by many meters. This can change the course of rivers, make cracks appear in the ground, and cause other changes, such as rockslides and the toppling of trees. However, most earthquakes are so weak that they don't alter the land at all. They just, uh, shake it a little. So those are some unusual ways that the land may change. Now, let's discuss the most common way it changes . . . through erosion.

Changes in the Earth's Features

Glaciers:	Floods:	Earthquakes:
- Are found near polar ranges and in mountain ranges - Are rivers of moving ice - Carve out lakes and valleys - Push earth and large stones ahead of them	- Come from rivers and oceans - Can be gradual or dramatic and violent - Leave behind silt and can change the landscape - May happen during hurricanes or tropical storms	- Shake the land - Can cause tsunamis - Can cause massive destruction over hundreds of miles - Change river courses, make cracks in the ground, cause rockslides, and topple trees

1 [Gist-Content Question]

At the beginning of the lecture, the professor states, "Now that we've covered continental drift, let's look at some, um, other ways that the Earth's features can change." Then, she proceeds to do that.

2 [Understanding Organization Question]

In talking about floods, the professor mostly describes the general effects that they have on the land.

3 [Understanding Function Question]

When the professor tells the student to call them "tsunamis" instead of "tidal waves," she is correcting the student.

Summarizing

The professor mentions that there are many ways the Earth's surface can change. One is by glaciers. Glaciers resemble rivers of moving ice. As they slowly move, they scrape the ground below them. This can create lakes, widen valleys, and make new ones. Floods can change the landscape quickly or gradually. They may occur by rivers or oceans. Tsunamis, which are caused by underwater earthquakes, sometimes shape the land. And earthquakes can cause massive amounts of destruction. But she also notes that most earthquakes are very weak.

1 Ⓒ   **2** Weather Fronts: ②, ③   Seasonal Weather Phenomena: ①, ④   **3** Ⓐ

Script & Graphic Organizer 02-56

M Professor: There are many types of precipitation. Of course, rain is the most common form. But what causes it? Let me give you a little background first. Then, I think you'll be better able to understand. Let me see . . . The sun's heat causes water on land and in the oceans and other bodies of water to evaporate. Thus it becomes water vapor. The water vapor rises into the atmosphere. As the temperature decreases higher in the atmosphere, the water vapor reverts back to liquid water. Then, these water droplets come together to form clouds.

After some time, these clouds simply have too much water in them. So they become oversaturated with water. As a result, they release some of their water. That's what causes rain. By the way, that water eventually evaporates and once again rises into the atmosphere. You should be aware that we refer to this as the water cycle. Anyway, this is a very simplified version of the water cycle. In fact, there are several ways that rain can be caused to fall once the air becomes saturated with water droplets. For instance, it can fall along weather fronts, on the windward sides of mountains, over superheated land due to the process of convection, and, uh, when seasonal weather phenomena, such as monsoons, occur.

One of the most common causes of rainfall is a weather front. Let me explain how this works. When cold and hot air meet, the hot air rises while the cold air sinks. Now, uh, something interesting about air is that warm air can contain more water vapor than cool air. Along a weather front, as warm air rises, it begins cooling off. Soon, it reaches the point where the cooler air temperature causes the air to be oversaturated with water. As a result, rain falls. Something similar happens when rain falls on the windward sides of mountains. In many places, the wind almost always blows in the same direction. For instance, winds in the Pacific Ocean off the North and South American coasts blow from west to east. As these winds move, they hit the mountain ranges on the west coasts of North and South America. The air goes up as it tries to get over the mountains. As it rises, it cools, so rain falls.

Rain caused by convection is normal in places with flat, open land that get lots of sunshine. The sun's rays heat the land, which warms the air. [3]As the air rises, condensation occurs, so those puffy clouds we often see on hot summer days then form. We call them cumulus clouds by the way. **Please remember that.** If it's hot enough and there's sufficient moisture in the air, thunderclouds may form. This can result in a thunderstorm. This brings us to the last major cause of rainfall: seasonal weather phenomena like monsoons. These are seasonal weather patterns that take place in various parts of the world. In Northeast Asia, monsoon rains fall in June and July. Monsoon rains are caused by bands of highly saturated air over the oceans that blow ashore, cool off, and then drop their rain. Monsoon rains dump so much water that they often cause floods. Still, their water is often crucial for farming.

The Causes of Rain

The Water Cycle:	The Causes of Rain:
- The sun heats water on land and in the oceans	- Weather fronts: cool air temperatures cause rain to fall
- Water evaporates and rises as water vapor	- Windward sides of mountains: rain falls as air tries to get over mountains
- When the temperature decreases, it becomes water	- Convection: the sun's rays heat land, condensation occurs, clouds form, and then rain falls
- Water droplets form clouds	
- Clouds become oversaturated with water, so they release the water as precipitation	- Monsoons: seasonal weather phenomena that drop lots of rain

1 [Gist-Purpose Question]

Prior to discussing the water cycle, the professor declares, "Let me give you a little background first. Then, I think you'll be able better to understand."

2 [Connecting Content Question]

According to the lecture, weather fronts are the most common reasons why rain falls and may occur on the windward sides of mountains. As for seasonal weather phenomena, they cause monsoons in Asia and can cause flooding as well.

3 [Understanding Attitude Question]

When the professor says, "Please remember that," he is implying that it is an important term which the students need to be aware of.

Summarizing

The professor explains the water cycle and how water evaporates, condenses, and falls to the ground as precipitation. He says there are many ways that rain

can fall. Weather fronts cause rain. Sometimes cool temperatures make the air oversaturated with water, so rain falls. Rain falls on the windward sides of mountains, too. Convection is another cause of rain. In hot weather, thunderstorms may often result. Finally, seasonal weather patterns such as monsoons can cause rain. They may cause flooding, but the rain is needed for farming.

Mastering **Topics** with Lectures **B3** p.118

1 Ⓒ   2 Ⓓ   3 Ⓐ

Script & Graphic Organizer 02-57

W Professor: Our planet is divided into layers. The top layer is the crust, the next is the mantle, and the third is the core. It's the core that I'd first like to discuss with you. So we'll start from the inside and move outward. [2]The first thing you need to know about the core is that it has two layers: the inner core and the outer core. The inner core is about 780 miles thick while the out core . . . **Oops.** I mean the outer core is around 1,370 miles thick. The outer core begins around 1,800 miles below the Earth's surface and extends to about 3,200 miles. Both the inner and outer cores consist primarily of iron and nickel. But they have trace amounts of other elements, too.

M Student: Professor Milton, how do we actually know this? I mean, uh, has anyone ever drilled, like, all the way to the center of the Earth?

W: No. No one's done that, Josh. But you raise a good point. How do we know this? Well, the statements on the composition of the core are based on a theory I believe is valid. Iron and nickel are two of the heaviest elements. So it's believed that, during our planet's formation, most of the iron and nickel sank to the Earth's center. Meanwhile, the lighter elements floated upward to the mantle and the crust. No one's ever visited the core or dug that deeply. [3]But the core's existence has been confirmed. How . . . ? Well, by seismic studies and calculations of the Earth's mass and density. **I can discuss this in more detail in a later class if you'd like me to.** Okay, everyone . . .?

Both the inner and outer cores are extremely hot. The outer core is believed to be around 7,000 to 9,000 degrees Fahrenheit. As a result of this intense heat, the outer core consists not of solid rock but of molten material. The inner core is even hotter. It's between 9,000 and 11,000 degrees Fahrenheit. But it's solid, not molten.

M: Why is that?

W: The pressure in the inner core is extremely high. This prevents the iron, nickel, and other elements from melting. Just in case you're wondering why the core is so hot . . . It's a result of the Earth's formation billions of years ago. Imagine how hot the Earth must have been back then if the core is still that hot now.

Together, the inner and outer cores are responsible for plate tectonics and magnetism. Plate tectonics refers to the Earth's crust being composed of plates. These plates have been moving and changing the shape of the planet's surface since its formation. Some scientists believe that the intense heat of the core makes it send out convection waves. These waves radiate to the surface and may be the reason why the plates move.

As for magnetism . . . Well, it's believed that the Earth's magnetism is created by the core. Because the Earth spins on its axis, the outer core revolves around the inner core, which remains stationary. This creates something called the dynamo effect. Basically, the interaction between the two cores creates the Earth's magnetic field. Now, let me explain what the importance of the magnetic field is before we move on to the mantle.

Earth's Inner and Outer Cores

Inner Core:	Outer Core:
- Is 780 miles thick	- Is 1,370 miles thick
- Is mostly iron and nickel	- Is mostly iron and nickel
- Is 9,000 to 11,000 degrees Fahrenheit	- Is 7,000 to 9,000 degrees Fahrenheit
- Is solid	- Is molten material
- Has high pressure	- Is responsible for plate tectonics and the planet's magnetism
- Is responsible for plate tectonics and the planet's magnetism	

1 [Detail Question]

The professor states, "Well, it's believed that the Earth's magnetism is created by the core."

2 [Understanding Function Question]

A person usually says, "Oops," after making a mistake. The professor gives the students the wrong number, so she says, "Oops," to indicate that she was wrong.

3 [Making Inferences Question]

When the professor tells the students, "I can discuss this in more detail in a later class if you'd like me to," she is indicating that she will not talk any more about that topic in her current lecture.

The professor notes that the Earth has both inner and outer cores. Each is mostly iron and nickel. This is known because of various theories about the Earth's formation and from seismic studies done on the cores. Both cores are very hot. The outer core is molten rock, but the inner core is solid despite being hotter than the outer core. The pressure in the inner core is very high. Both cores are responsible for plate tectonics and magnetism. The revolving of the cores creates the Earth's magnetism.

Mastering **Topics** with Lectures   B4   p.119

1 Ⓒ   **2** Ⓑ   **3** Ⓓ

Script & Graphic Organizer   02-58

W1 Student: Professor Anderson . . . May I have a moment of your time, please?

W2 Professor: Good morning, Julie. Um, are you all right? You look like something's bothering you.

W1: Well, actually, no, I'm not all right. I've got a big problem on my hands. I'd really like to talk to you about something.

W2: Of course. Of course. Please tell me what's troubling you.

W1: Thank you, ma'am. That's very kind of you . . . Okay, well, uh . . . I'll just be straight with you. I think I'm going to have to transfer to another school.

W2: Transfer? Well, I wasn't expecting you to say that. You know, it's none of my business, but . . . if your family is having money problems, there are lots of scholarships you can apply for. I'd be more than happy to write some recommendations for you. All you have to do is ask.

W1: No, no. It's not that. School's not cheap, but my family can afford it.

W2: Well, that's a relief. So, uh, what's the problem? It surely can't be your grades.

W1: [3]No, definitely not. It's just that . . . um, I've been thinking about my future . . . You see, I want to be a reporter when I graduate.

W2: Okay. So what does that have to do with transferring?

W1: Well, I was hoping to get a double major in journalism. But we don't have that major here. So I think it would be better if I transferred to a school with a Journalism Department.

W2: I see . . . Well, you are already a junior, so, you know, it might be hard to transfer so late.

W1: Then what could I do?

W2: Well, you could always stay here and graduate. Then, you could apply to a graduate program in journalism. There are several good ones around the country.

W1: Oh, right. I hadn't thought of that.

W2: Tell you what. Why don't you relax and think about this for a while? You don't want to make any rash decisions. After all, transferring schools is a big deal.

Office Hours

Student's Problem:	Professor's Response:
Wants to major in journalism, but the school has no Journalism Department	As a junior, the student would have a hard time transferring to another school
Professor's Suggestion:	Student's Response:
Stay at school and graduate and then attend a graduate program in journalism	Says that she had not thought of the idea that the professor suggested

1   [Gist-Content Question]

The student comes to the professor and tells her that she is considering transferring to another school, so that is what they mostly talk about.

2   [Detail Question]

The professor suggests, "Well, you could always stay here and graduate. Then, you could apply to a graduate program in journalism."

3   [Understanding Attitude Question]

When the professor asks, "What does that have to do with transferring?" she is indicating that she is confused by the student's statement about wanting to become a reporter after she graduates.

Summarizing

The student appears upset when she visits the professor. She says she has to transfer. The professor asks why and states that she can write some recommendations for scholarships if the student needs money. The student says it is not about money. She wants to be a journalist, but the school has no Journalism Department. The professor mentions that, as a junior, it would be hard for the student to transfer. She suggests that the student stay at school and then attend graduate school to study journalism.

1 Ⓑ   2 Ⓑ, Ⓒ   3 Ⓓ   4 Radio Waves: [1], [4]   Microwaves: [2], [3]   5 Ⓐ   6 Ⓑ

Script   02-59

W Professor: A wave is a disturbance that can move through space, has speed, and contains energy. All waves have certain characteristics. They include frequency, wavelength, speed, direction, amplitude, and intensity. Some common waves are created by sound and electromagnetic energy. Sound waves contain, well, er, sound, and we hear them when they cause vibrations in our ears. Electromagnetic energy contains a wide variety of elements that have waves. Some are radio waves, microwaves, infrared, ultraviolet, and visible light, and X-rays. Right now, I'd like to compare sound waves with radio waves and microwaves.

First, sound waves . . . All sound must have a source—something which causes the disturbance that creates the sound wave. Speaking is a good example. This is sound created by a human's vocal cords. Sound can also be created by mechanical means, such as a stereo, or by simple means, such as, uh, when one object strikes another. Having been created, sound waves travel outward from their source. Their movement and speed vary depending upon the medium they're traveling through. [5]Sound waves can move through all four states of matter: solids, liquids, gases, and plasma. However, they can't move through a vacuum. **So please remember that, despite Hollywood's best efforts to prove otherwise in numerous science-fiction movies, there's no sound in space.**

Some sounds are louder than others. The difference in sound loudness is referred to as amplitude. Why are some sounds perceived as louder than others? First, loudness is a measure of a sound's intensity. The source of the sound determines its intensity. For instance, a jet engine creates sounds louder than a, uh, person whispering. Loudness also depends on distance. The farther sound travels, the less intensity it has. Third, loudness is related to the medium the sound travels through. Let's see . . . Sound waves traveling through gas, such as the atmosphere, are louder than those passing through solids or liquids. Finally, sound waves can reflect off objects, which is why you can sometimes hear echoes.

Moving on to radio waves . . . Radio waves are part of the electromagnetic energy spectrum. They have the lowest frequency and the longest wavelength in that spectrum. In the electromagnetic energy spectrum, a long wavelength and low frequency mean less energy while a high frequency and short wavelength mean high energy, which is what X-rays have. Radio waves have many of the same characteristics as sound waves. They have speed, direction, and frequency and follow the other common principles of waves. They can reflect off objects and can pass through all mediums. However, unlike sound waves, radio waves can move through a vacuum. [6]This is why astronauts in space are able to talk with mission control back on the Earth.

M Student: Do radio waves have sound?

W: Hmm . . . That's a tricky question. We use radio waves for communication, but the human ear cannot hear them. We require mechanical devices, such as radios, to transform the radio waves into audible sound waves. That's the basic principle of radio communication. In addition, just like sound waves, long-wavelength radio waves lose intensity with distance. That's why you can't hear your favorite radio station when you move far from its source. Shorter radio waves, however, can reach greater distances by bouncing off the ionosphere. That's why long-range communication devices are called short-wave radios.

Okay, uh, let's quickly look at microwaves, which are also a part of the electromagnetic spectrum. They're right next to radio waves in frequency and wavelength. They're more powerful than radio waves but not as strong as X-rays. Microwaves are also used for communications and can travel longer distances than radio waves. For many years, microwaves were the main source of long-distance telecommunications. They also have more bandwidth than radio waves, so they have a greater capacity for communications. But unlike most sound and radio waves, microwaves can be dangerous to humans since they have the ability to cause changes in the objects they strike. This, incidentally, is the principle behind a microwave oven. The microwaves excite the water molecules in food. This causes them to vibrate, which heats the food. That's also why you shouldn't stand too close to a microwave oven or a microwave tower. Understand what I mean?

1 [Gist-Purpose Question]

About microwaves, the professor states, "Microwaves are also used for communications and can travel longer distances than radio waves. For many years, microwaves were the main source of long-distance telecommunications. They also have more bandwidth than radio waves, so they have a greater capacity for communications."

2 [Detail Question]

The professor comments, "A wave is a disturbance that can move through space, has speed, and contains energy."

3 [Understanding Organization Question]

The professor begins her lecture by describing the characteristics of waves. Then, she proceeds to describe some different types of waves.

4 [Connecting Content Question]

According to the lecture, radio waves have the longest wavelength on the electromagnetic energy spectrum and have a very low frequency. As for microwaves, they may harm people and are used in long-distance telecommunications.

5 [Understanding Function Question]

The professor states, "Despite Hollywood's best efforts to prove otherwise in numerous science-fiction movies, there's no sound in space." She is indicating that Hollywood movies do not show space realistically since they depict sound traveling in space.

6 [Understanding Attitude Question]

When the professor states, "That's a tricky question," she means that it is a hard question to give an answer to.

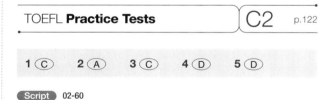

TOEFL **Practice Tests** C2 p.122

1 Ⓒ   2 Ⓐ   3 Ⓒ   4 Ⓓ   5 Ⓓ

Script 02-60

W Student: Good afternoon, sir. Is your name Scott Johnson?

M Financial Aid Department Employee: Yes, I'm Scott Johnson. How may I help you today, Miss . . .

W: Jenkins. Julie Jenkins.

M: Ah, yes, Miss Jenkins. You called me yesterday with a problem, didn't you?

W: Yes, that was me. Do you have some time to talk to me now, Mr. Johnson? I have class in about thirty minutes, and it's on the other side of campus. So if I could take up about, uh, two or three minutes of your time, that would be great. Then, I can get going to my class.

M: Sure. I'm just doing some paperwork now, so I've got time to chat.

W: Great. So, uh, what about my problem? What do you think I should do about it?

M: I'm sorry, Miss Jenkins, but would you mind explaining it to me again? I deal with lots of students every day. They all have unique issues. So, uh, I don't want to confuse yours with someone else's. You would definitely wind up getting bad advice. And neither of us wants that.

W: Yeah, that makes sense. Okay, so, um, where should I start?

M: From the beginning is usually the best place.

W: I suppose you're right. All right. The beginning . . . Last week, I got a letter from this office. It informed me that my application for a scholarship had been rejected.

M: Do you have the letter with you?

W: No, I don't. I left it in my dorm room. I didn't expect that you'd ask me for it. Sorry.

M: That's all right. I'm sure there's a copy on the computer system somewhere. I can look it up later.

W: ⁵Great. Anyway, so, uh, basically, I need five hundred more dollars right now. **If I don't get the money by next week, I'll have to drop out of school.**

M: I see.

W: So is there, uh, you know, anything that this office can do for me? A grant? A loan? A work-study opportunity? Anything?

M: We could probably arrange for an emergency loan for you. You'd have to apply for it though. Do you have the forms?

W: No, I don't, but I'd love to see them. This is my last year, and I really don't want to drop out of school.

M: I totally understand where you're coming from. Why don't you fill out these forms right here by, say . . . tomorrow? You can come back here and drop them off with me. And I'll do my best to get you a loan for the amount you need.

1 [Gist-Purpose Question]

The student tells the man that she needs more money to pay for her tuition, so she is in his office to find out what kind of financial assistance she can get.

2 [Detail Question]

The man tells the student, "We could probably arrange for an emergency loan for you. You'd have to apply for it though."

3 [Detail Question]

The man instructs the student, "Why don't you fill out these forms right here by, say . . . tomorrow? You can come back here and drop them off with me."

4 [Making Inferences Question]

The student mentions, "This is my last year," so she implies that she is a senior.

5 [Understanding Function Question]

When the student mentions that she needs the money by next week, she is implying that her tuition is due next week.

Review   p.125

1	Ⓒ	2	Ⓐ	3	Ⓑ	4	Ⓒ	5	Ⓐ
6	Ⓓ	7	Ⓑ	8	Ⓐ	9	Ⓐ	10	Ⓓ
11	Ⓒ	12	Ⓔ	13	Ⓑ	14	Ⓐ	15	Ⓓ

■▶ Chapter | **07** Arts 1 • Conversations

Mastering **Question Types**
with Lectures & Conversations   **A1**   p.128

[TYPES 1–4]

TYPE❶ Ⓐ   TYPE❷ Ⓓ
TYPE❸ Oil Paints: ①, ②, ④   Watercolors: ③
TYPE❹ Ⓓ

Script 02-61

M Professor: The vast majority of painters rely either on watercolors or oil paints to paint with. These two paints have some differences though.

Historically speaking, both types of paints have, uh, been around for centuries. Watercolors, however, are much, much older than oil paints.

W Student: How old are watercolors, Professor Daniels?

M: Well, let me put it this way . . . Primitive men used watercolors to create cave paintings thousands of years ago. That's how old they are. Still, watercolors in their modern form were not created—or perfected I should say—until many years later. This happened during the eighteenth and nineteenth centuries in Great Britain. As for oil paints, well . . . There's a text from Greece that mentions them being used in the fifth century. And some form of oil paint was used in Japan in the eighth century. However, oil paints as we know them today were invented in the fifteenth century by Jan van Eyck.

Okay, but let me get back to their differences now . . . Basically, there's one major difference. It's the transparency of the paints. The pigments in oil paints are, uh, they're opaque. But it's the o-o-opposite case for watercolors. The result is that painters using each medium must employ, uh, different styles. For instance, an artist using oil paints can simply paint one opaque color over another until he gets the desired result. Watercolor artists, however, are unable to do this.

Oil painters can generally achieve the results they want. If they make an error, all they have to do is paint over it with another color. No one will know the difference in the end. [4]Watercolors, on the other hand, are much more unpredictable. Watercolor artists simply can't paint over their mistakes. **Thus, they often have to improvise when something unexpected happens while they are painting.**

There are some other basic differences. Let me see . . . Ah, with oil paints, a color can be made lighter by mixing it with white paints. With watercolors, the paint can be lightened by adding, logically enough, water.

TYPE 1 [Gist-Content Question]

The professor focuses on discussing how watercolors and oil paints are different from one another.

TYPE 2 [Understanding Organization Question]

The professor says, "However, oil paints as we know them today were invented in the fifteenth century by Jan van Eyck."

TYPE 3 [Connecting Content Question]

According to the lecture, oil paints were used in Japan in the eighth century, make use of opaque pigments, and are easy to make corrections with. As for watercolors, primitive men were the first to use them.

TYPE 4 [Speaker's Attitude Question]

The professor notes that watercolor artists have to improvise whenever they make mistakes. This means that an artist must change the painting in some manner whenever he or she makes an error while painting.

Summarizing

The professor notes that watercolors were first utilized by primitive men. As for oil paints, they were used many

centuries ago by the Greeks and Japanese, but modern oil paints were invented by Jan van Eyck in the fifteenth century. Oil paints are opaque while watercolors are not. This affects how the artists must make their paintings. Oil painters can eventually get their desired results, but watercolor painters have to be careful about making mistakes. So they may have to improvise while making their paintings.

[TYPES 5–8]

| TYPE 5 | C | TYPE 6 | B |
| TYPE 7 | D | TYPE 8 | A |

Script 02-62

M1 Professor: Let's move on to an American original and one of the artists from the American Gilded Age whose works I love. That was the period from 1870 to 1900. It happened after the American Civil War ended. It was mostly a time of prosperity in the country. As for the world of art, American art became more prominent then.

Look at this portrait . . . Can anyone tell me its name . . . ?

W Student: That's *Whistler's Mother*.

M1: Well done, Katie. Do you know the name of the artist?

W: Er . . . Sorry. I have no idea.

M1: Jason? Your hand is up.

M2 Student: [8]I'm pretty sure Whistler painted it. But I don't know his first name.

W: Whistler painted his own mother? **No kidding.**

M1: Yes, he did. His name was James Abbott McNeill Whistler. He painted *Whistler's Mother* in 1871. A model never appeared for her appointment, so Whistler asked his mother to pose instead. She agreed, and he painted a truly amazing portrait. It has come to symbolize motherhood around the world.

Now, how about a bit about Whistler himself? He was from Lowell, Massachusetts, but moved to St. Petersburg, Russia, with his family as a youth. There, his parents recognized his talent for art and enrolled him in private lessons. In his teens, Whistler decided to become a professional artist, but he didn't become famous for many years.

The first work he exhibited was *La Mere Gerard* in 1858. Here it is . . . In the 1860s, he started painting night scenes, uh, often set in harbors. He preferred using blue and light green colors. See here . . . here . . . and here . . .

He's also noted for the influence Japanese art had on him. In the 1850s, Whistler first saw Japanese art and was captivated by it. He appreciated the monochromatic colors, uh, like these here . . . the cropped figures . . . and the economical way that the Japanese painted figures . . . Whistler's etchings, particularly those he made in Venice, clearly show the influence that Japanese art had on him. Here are a couple of other paintings . . .

TYPE 5 [Gist-Content Question]

During his lecture, the professor mostly focuses on the styles that Whistler used.

TYPE 6 [Detail Question]

The professor remarks, "Now, how about a bit about Whistler himself? He was from Lowell, Massachusetts, but moved to St. Petersburg, Russia, with his family as a youth. There, his parents recognized his talent for art and enrolled him in private lessons."

TYPE 7 [Making Inferences Question]

At the end of the lecture, the professor says, "Here are a couple of other paintings." So he is likely going to show some more of Whistler's works next.

TYPE 8 [Understanding Function Question]

When the student says, "No kidding," she is expressing her surprise that Whistler was the artist who painted *Whistler's Mother*.

Summarizing

The professor shows a painting, and a student identifies it as *Whistler's Mother*. The professor says that it was painted by James Abbott McNeill Whistler, an artist from the American Gilded Age. Whistler started taking art lessons in St. Petersburg, Russia, and decided to become a professional artist. His first exhibited work was *La Mere Gerard*. He often used blue and light green colors. He was influenced by Japanese art due to the monochromatic colors, cropped figures, and economical way the Japanese painted. His etchings clearly show this influence.

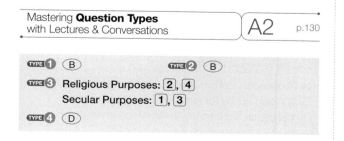

Mastering **Question Types**
with Lectures & Conversations

A2 p.130

TYPE 1 (B)   **TYPE 2** (B)

TYPE 3 Religious Purposes: [2], [4]
        Secular Purposes: [1], [3]

TYPE 4 (D)

Script 02-63

W1 Professor: I'd like to go over the role of music in ancient times. As you should know, music is pretty much as old as humanity. From the earliest times in human history, music has played a key role in virtually all of the world's civilizations. Many biomusicologists . . . er, those would be people who study the effects of music on people . . . uh, they believe that the human brain is, hmm . . . wired for music I guess we could say.

The first musical instruments ever made were probably simple whistles. These would have been used both for music and also as a form of communication. After whistles, various other wind instruments plus, um, stringed instruments, likely followed. Of these, most experts believe the flute was the first to be made. Some of these early instruments have even been found. They're such enchanting relics.

But it is likely that human vocals also played a major role in music. How major? Well, let's go back around, oh, around 5,000 years in the past. At this time, music was mostly played for people's enjoyment. Yet it was also used in various ceremonies.

W2 Student: Ceremonies? Such as what?

W1: Mostly religious ones. For instance, the earliest known songs in Western culture are the biblical psalms. People not only sang them but also used them in religious rites. In addition, a simple reading of the Bible reveals numerous passages that refer to the uses and benefits of music. According to the Bible, music can be used for either good or evil. When perverted, it can be used for evil purposes. However, when properly employed, it can uplift a person's thoughts, inspire that individual, and, uh, elevate the soul. I must say that I agree.

But music wasn't just used in religious life. It had a role in secular society, too. In ancient Egypt, most festivals incorporated music. These songs were for members of every social class. Manual laborers also worked to the rhythms and sounds of songs. And, uh, street dancers often made music and performed. Dance troupes did the same.

TYPE 1 [Gist-Content Question]

Almost the entire lecture is about the roles that music played during ancient times.

TYPE 2 [Understanding Organization Question]

When discussing the Bible, the professor focuses on what is written in the Bible about music.

 **[Connecting Content Question]**

According to the lecture, music was utilized for rites and inspired people when it was used for religious purposes. As for music's secular purposes, it was sung by manual laborers and was performed for street dancers.

 [Speaker's Attitude Question]

When describing the first musical instruments, the professor exclaims, "Some of these early instruments have even been found. They're such enchanting relics." So it appears that she appreciates them.

Summarizing

> The professor comments that biomusicologists believe the human brain is wired for music. Vocals were important to ancient music. Music was used in many early religious ceremonies. Biblical psalms are the earliest known songs in Western culture. They were used in religious rites. The Bible notes that music can be used for both good and evil. For good, it can inspire people and elevate their souls. Ancient music also had a role in secular society, such as being used by manual laborers and street dancers.

[TYPES 5–8]

TYPE 5 Ⓒ   TYPE 6 Ⓐ

TYPE 7 Ⓒ   TYPE 8 Ⓐ

Script 02-64

> **W Professor:** Good morning, Larry. What brings you here so early in the morning?
>
> **M Student:** Professor Gardner, I'm so glad you're in your office. I have a big request to make of you.
>
> **W:** Oh? What's so important that has you here at eight thirty in the morning, Larry?
>
> **M:** Oh, excuse me. Yeah, it is early, huh? Anyway, you know that upcoming music recital? The one that happens in three weeks?
>
> **W:** Yes. What about it?
>
> **M:** I want to participate in it, so I need to try out for it. We were supposed to sign up for a time, but, er . . . I never got around to doing that. And the audition starts this afternoon at one thirty.
>
> **W:** Yes, that's correct. I know since I'll be one of the judges today. So what do you want me to do for you, Larry?
>
> **M:** Um . . . Is there, like, um, any possible way that I can still try out for the recital? I know I didn't register for a time, but . . . Uh, can I be the last to sing at the audition or something?

> **W:** Sure. I think that's possible. But you have to be there by one thirty. If anyone doesn't show up, you can try out in that person's spot. If everyone shows up, you can go last. [8]But don't be late, or you're going to lose this opportunity. Okay?
>
> **M:** You can count on me, Professor. Thanks for giving me a second chance. **I won't let you down.**

 [Gist-Purpose Question]

The student goes to the professor to get her permission to attend the audition that will take place later that afternoon.

 [Detail Question]

The professor tells the student, "But you have to be there by one thirty," when she gives him permission to attend the audition.

 [Making Inferences Question]

Since the musical recital is not class related and the professor is involved with it, it can be inferred that she assists with extracurricular activities at the school.

 [Understanding Function Question]

When a person says, "I won't let you down," that individual is promising to do whatever he or she just said. So the student is letting the professor know that he will definitely attend the audition.

Summarizing

> The student visits the professor to talk about an audition for an upcoming music recital. He never signed up for a tryout time, and the auditions begin at one thirty. The professor says she is a judge at the tryouts. The student asks to be permitted to audition. The professor tells him to show up at one thirty. If any student misses the tryouts, he can take that student's spot. Otherwise, he can try out last. The student thanks the professor for giving him a second chance.

Mastering **Topics** with Lectures   B1   p.132

1 Ⓓ   2 Fact: ②, ③   Not a Fact: ①, ④   3 Ⓒ

Script & Graphic Organizer 02-65

> **M Professor:** Let's continue our examination of East Asian art by looking at Chinese ceramics. By ceramics, I mean anything which is made of earthen materials such as clay and is fired at high

temperatures. So pottery is one example of a ceramic. Nowadays, Chinese ceramics are among the most highly prized and sought-after works of art. The main reasons for this are their craftsmanship, beauty, and age. The Chinese have the world's longest-lasting ceramics industry. It goes back roughly 18,000 years.

Why did the Chinese—and for that matter, most ancient people—make ceramics? Primarily for their usefulness. Simple pieces of pottery could be used as vessels for holding anything from water to grain. All classes of people could afford it, which made it practical. Of course, some ceramics were shaped into beautiful art objects for members of the upper class. Eventually, the Chinese developed porcelain, a high-quality form of porcelain, er, I mean, ceramics, valued by the royal family, nobility, and wealthy members of society.

³Today, experts categorize Chinese ceramics in three distinct ways. They are by the temperature they were fired at, the locations of the materials used to make them, and the era during which they were made. **Do I need to repeat that . . . ?** No . . . ? All right, let's look at heat first. Some ceramics are high fired, uh, made at high temperatures, while others are low fired, or made at lower temperatures. Based on the temperature and the type of materials used, there are three main types of ceramics: earthenware, stoneware, and porcelain. Earthenware is fired at lower temperatures than the other two types. It's also more porous. Stoneware and porcelain are fired at higher temperatures, but stoneware isn't very porous.

The region of China from which the ceramic comes is also important. As I mentioned, all ceramics come from clay. But there are many types of clay. For instance, clay with large amounts of kaolin is used to make porcelain. Kaolin, just so you know, is a whitish substance that can be mined. China's geography is roughly divided by the area between the Yellow and Yangtze rivers. They split the country into northern and southern divisions. Thus, art historians define Chinese ceramics as being either northern Chinese or southern Chinese.

Finally, Chinese ceramics have distinct characteristics depending on when they were made. Over the centuries, Chinese ceramics have changed and evolved as new methods of making them and designing their outsides were used. Even the earliest known samples—from thousands of years ago— have paintings or etchings on them. Of course, the type of design or picture has changed over time.

Let me give you some examples of how ceramics have changed over time. At first, most Chinese ceramics were low-fired earthenware. Later,

craftsmen discovered methods for creating higher temperatures, so they began making stoneware. Then, during the ninth century, a method for making pure white porcelain was discovered. And speaking of color, it may sometimes be an indicator of where a Chinese ceramic comes from. A ceramic's color often depends on the material used. Thus, the color can help pinpoint a geographic location in China where a ceramic was made since that region may have a certain type of clay or other pottery-making material.

Chinese Ceramics

Characteristics:	Firing Temperatures:
- Are highly prized and sought-after works of art - Have great craftsmanship, beauty, and age - First used to hold things - Used by all classes of people - Developed porcelain for the upper classes to use	Can make earthenware, stoneware, and porcelain depending on the firing temperature
	Region: Can be divided into northern Chinese and southern Chinese depending on the type of clay used
	Period Made: The methods of making ceramics and the designs used have changed over time

1 [Gist-Content Question]

The professor spends most of the lecture discussing the various ways in which Chinese ceramics may be categorized.

2 [Detail Question]

According to the lecture, it is a fact that the Chinese ceramics industry is the oldest in the world and that Chinese ceramics can be divided into ceramics from two separate regions. It is not a fact that ceramics were used only by the upper classes and that the first pots were fired at high temperatures.

3 [Understanding Function Question]

When the professor asks if he should repeat the information, he is implying that the material was hard, so the students might not have been able to write everything down.

Summarizing

The professor notes that China has the world's longest-lasting ceramics industry. The Chinese mostly made ceramics to serve as vessels to hold things. There are three ways to divide Chinese ceramics: by the temperatures they are fired at, by the locations of the materials used to make them, and by the era when they were made. Depending on the heat used, earthenware, stoneware, and porcelain can be made. Chinese ceramics are often either northern Chinese or southern Chinese. And the designs used on them have changed over time.

Mastering **Topics** with Lectures   B2   p.133

1 Ⓐ   2 West Africa: ①, ③, ④   Jamaica: ②
3 Ⓐ

`Script & Graphic Organizer` 02-66

W Professor: Hip-hop is a musical genre that has its roots in inner-city African-American culture. It began in the Bronx in New York City in the early 1970s. From there, it gained popularity in America during the 1980s and has since spread across the world. At first, hip-hop was a genre performed and enjoyed solely by African-Americans. Today, however, it's performed and listened to by people of all races. And it's no longer just a musical genre. Instead, it has become, uh, a culture. How? ³Well, hip-hop has its own clothing styles, its own forms of dancing, and even its own language to go along with its rapping lyrics and musical beats.

M Student: Are hip-hop and rap the same or different? **A part of me says yes, but another part says no.**

W: Hmm . . . Why don't you let me explain a little more, and then you'll be able to decide for yourself? Hip-hop is a musical style that incorporates rapping—or speaking—in either prose or verses as opposed to singing the lyrics. The music is often borrowed from other songs but may sometimes be original. It's typically played through a music system by a DJ. Record scratching is a common aspect of hip-hop performances, too. And there are often percussion breaks in the music during which the rapper performs. So to return to your question, what do you think now?

M: I'd say that they belong to the same genre.

W: I agree . . . Hip-hop is primarily an African-American genre, yet it also has influences from Africa and Jamaica. In Western Africa, where most American slaves came from in the past, many storytellers used singsong chants. They brought this style of music to America with them. Think about the field calls and responses slaves used while working on the plantations. Nowadays, many African-Americans have these, uh, verbal sparring contests

in which each person tries to outdo the other. They often insult their opponents in amusing, almost singsong, ways. These contests are descendants of Western African music. In addition, in the early 1970s, many Jamaicans in the Bronx used sound systems to provide music for live performances. Poor Jamaican immigrants often couldn't afford musical instruments to create background music. This style was picked up by African-Americans, and now it's a part of hip-hop.

During the seventies, street parties and corner rapping contests became popular forms of entertainment in New York City. Then, in 1979, the first hip-hop record was made. The music quickly spread across the country. By the late 1980s, hip-hop was becoming mainstream. It wasn't just ethnic music but was something that people from all backgrounds were enjoying.

By the 1990s, hip-hop had become a part of world culture and had spread, um, almost everywhere. At the same time, the innocent, playful lyrics of early hip-hop started changing. Suddenly, the lyrics were about poverty and the oppression of the lower classes. Hip-hop began diversifying, and new genres emerged. The most dominant was called gangsta rap. Its songs were about the violent street life of the inner city. Its lyrics were often about committing crimes, treating women harshly, and killing the police. Needless to say, there was a backlash against those lyrics and the messages they conveyed. Now, let's listen to a few early hip-hop tunes. Here's one of my favorites.

Hip-Hop Music

Origins:	Influences:
- *Began in the Bronx in New York City in 1970s*	*Singsong chants and calls and responses of African storytellers and slaves; use of sound systems instead of live music by Jamaicans*
- *Spread across America and the world later*	
- *Was first enjoyed by African-Americans*	**Relationship with Rap Music:**
- *Is enjoyed by people of all races today*	*DJ plays music for both; both use record scratching; both have percussion breaks for the performers to use*
- *Has become its own culture*	

1 [Understanding Organization Question]

The professor says, "Hip-hop began diversifying, and new genres emerged. The most dominant was called gangsta rap."

2 [Connecting Content Question]

According to the lecture, storytellers using singsong

voices, slaves making field calls, and people having verbal sparring contests were West African influences. As for Jamaican influences, people used sounds systems instead of live music.

3 [Understanding Attitude Question]

When the student says, "A part of me says yes, but another part says no," he is indicating that he is undecided about the answer to the question he just asked.

Summarizing

The professor states that hip-hop began in New York City in the 1970s and then spread across America and the world. It was initially an African-American genre, but people of all races enjoy it now. Hip-hop and rap are two similar genres. Singsong chants and field calls and responses from African slaves were one influence on hip-hop. Jamaicans using sound systems instead of live performances was another. One new genre of hip-hop is gangsta rap. But there was a backlash against it because of the nature of its lyrics.

Mastering **Topics** with Lectures   B3   p.134

1 Ⓒ   **2** Ⓑ   **3** Ⓐ

Script & Graphic Organizer 02-67

M Professor: When you write stories, you need to develop your characters. You need to make people that are realistic. The key to developing believable yet interesting characters is to create a backstory and complete psychological profile for them. Once you have a full picture of a person, you can have that individual act in believable ways.

How can you do this? Create an in-depth portrait of that person. This should include, uh, this person's background, career, family, interests, and goals. After you've developed this information, you should determine how each trait affects the character. For instance, how does she interact with her family members? What skill sets have past jobs given her? What knowledge does she have because of her hobbies and interests?

You should also determine the person's major character traits. Is the character lazy? A hard worker? A liar? Confident? Anxious? Optimistic? Aggressive? Does the person tend to let other people's needs come before hers? These characteristics will help you develop a more detailed psychological profile for

the character. For example, how does the character respond to different situations? What emotional responses does the character have to different experiences? What motivates her—pride, ego, fear? Determining this information is critical so that the character responds to situations in a believable and consistent manner. This development is also important if you want to make a person change her character during the story. Allowing readers to understand the person's tendencies helps ensure that any type of character growth will be more realistic.

Make sure to develop the character's physical traits, too. Hair color, eye color, and body type are important. But don't focus solely on them. You should also describe characteristics such as how the person dresses and how the person physically carries herself. Does the character have any particular mannerisms? All of these qualities will help readers create a mental image of that person.

Now, here's a key point . . . When you're writing about the person, don't tell the readers what the character is like. Instead, express these characteristics by noting how the person acts and reacts to situations. For instance, showing a person taking credit for another's work is more effective than simply saying that the person is deceitful. Dialogue can help bring a character to life, too. For example, the tone a person takes in a certain situation can say a lot about what that person is really like. How other characters respond to or speak about the person can be another successful way to show what she is like. Having a colleague say she is grateful for all the times when the character helped her through difficult situations is more effective than saying the person is a team player.

Ultimately, developing a realistic three-dimensional character is crucial to making sure that readers are invested not just in your characters but also in what happens to them. Having said that, let's practice what I just taught you. It's time for a writing exercise. Please get out your pens and notebooks.

Character Development

In-Depth Portrait:	Major Character Traits:	Physical Traits:	Writing about the Person:
- Describe background, career, family, interests, and goals - Show how traits affect character	- Can develop a psychological profile - Show how character responds	- Show what character looks like - Describe mannerisms - Let readers create mental picture of the character	- Don't tell readers what character is like - Describe actions and use dialogue

1 [Gist-Purpose Question]

The professor states, "Determining this information is critical so that the character responds to situations in a believable and consistent manner."

2 [Understanding Organization Question]

During his lecture, the professor describes some ways that writers can develop their characters, and he goes into detail on each point that he mentions.

3 [Making Inferences Question]

At the end of the lecture, the professor comments, "It's time for a writing exercise. Please get out your pens and notebooks." He is going to give the students a writing assignment now.

Summarizing

The professor mentions that writers must develop the characters in their stories to make them realistic. First, they can create in-depth portraits of the characters. These can include a character's background, career, family, interests, and goals. Next are the person's major character traits. These make a character's responses both believable and consistent. Physical traits should be developed, too. When writing, the author should not tell the readers what a character is like. Instead, the character's actions as well as dialogue can show readers what that person is like.

Mastering **Topics** with Conversations B4 p.135

1 Ⓒ   2 Ⓑ   3 Ⓓ

Script & Graphic Organizer 02-68

W Student: Hello, sir. I've got a big problem, and I really hope you can help me solve it.

M Computer Services Office Employee: I'll do my best for you. What kind of problem do you have?

W: I've been trying to log in to my school account, but I can't. Instead of letting me log in, I get this message. The message reads "access denied." I've tried to log in to my account on three different computers, but the same message keeps, uh, popping up. I'm not sure what's going on.

M: Okay. Why don't you give me your name? Then I'll see if I can figure out what the problem is.

W: Sure thing. My name is Janet Lincoln. That's L-I-N-C-O-L-N. Uh, you know, like the president.

M: No problem. Hold on a moment . . . And one more moment, please . . . Aha. I've got the problem figured out.

W: You do? That was fast. What is it?

M: Well, it seems as though you have an overdue library book. It's been late for, hmm . . . a little more than two months now. Since you owe such a large fine, your computer access has been suspended. All you need to do is pay the fine on the book. Then, we can let you back into the computer system.

W: A library book? That's odd. What's the title of the book?

M: The title? I'm sorry, but I can't tell. It's not that I don't want to. The computer just doesn't show that information. Uh, out of curiosity, why do you say that's odd?

W: I haven't checked out any library books all semester.

M: Hmm . . . Give me your school ID number, please.

W: Sure. It's 345-213-9000.

M: Okay . . . Now I see the problem. There are apparently two students named Janet Lincoln on this campus. I bet you didn't know that, did you? The other one has the overdue book. You don't have any problems. If you can be patient for a minute, I can turn your computer access back on. Mistakes like this can sometimes happen. It's a good thing that you came here to this office today.

Service Encounter

Student's Problem:	Man's Response:
Gets an "access denied" message when she tries to log in to her student account	Has an overdue library book with a large fine that she must pay in order to get access to her account

Student's Observation:	Man's Discovery:
Has not checked out any library books all semester	Are two Janet Lincolns at school, and the other one has the overdue book

1 [Gist-Purpose Question]

The student tells the man, "Well, I've been trying to log in to my school account, but I can't. Instead of letting me log in, I get this message. The message reads 'access denied.'"

2 [Detail Question]

The man discovers that there are two students on campus named Janet Lincoln. The other student has the overdue library book. So the two students' accounts have been mixed up with one another.

3 [Understanding Function Question]

The man wants the student's ID number so that he can guarantee that he is looking at the correct computer file. He is confirming her identify with that number.

Summarizing

The student visits the computer services office with a problem. When she tries to log in to her account, she gets an "access denied" message. The man tells her that she has an overdue library book that she owes a fine on. The student claims she has not checked out a book that semester. The man gets her ID number and learns the school has two students named Janet Lincoln. The other one has the overdue book. The man tells the student he will fix the problem with her account.

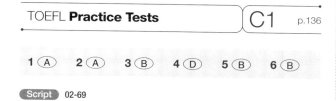

TOEFL Practice Tests **C1** p.136

1 (A) 2 (A) 3 (B) 4 (D) 5 (B) 6 (B)

Script 02-69

M Professor: That's enough about Renaissance art. So let's move on to the architecture of that period. We'll start with Italy since Italian architecture, just like Italian art, greatly influenced the rest of Europe.

In the early fifteenth century, a series of events occurred that helped advance the Italian Renaissance. First, there was a period of political and religious stability. Second, the northern Italian city-states of Florence, Genoa, Pisa, Milan, and Venice became extremely wealthy and powerful. Just so you know, I mentioned Florence first because the architectural movement of the Italian Renaissance began there. All of these city-states were run by influential families that enjoyed art and wanted new buildings designed and erected. Third, the Roman Catholic Church began to commission great buildings. This eventually included the Basilica of St. Peter's in Vatican City. Finally, the ideas of ancient Rome and Greece began to spread throughout the literature and art of the age.

Let me provide you with a little background now. During the late fourteenth and early fifteenth centuries, Gothic architecture dominated. This style originated in France in the twelfth century and lasted to the sixteenth. Cathedrals and castles were often done in the Gothic style. Common design features were pointed arches and flying buttresses, which were used to support high walls. Gothic cathedrals had high walls and tall spires. Many Gothic cathedrals were among the tallest buildings in the world up until the 1800s. Impressive, huh? Gothic artists also cared little about order or proportion.

Now, um, how do Gothic and Renaissance architecture differ? The major way is in how the architects viewed the designs of the buildings. I should mention that the Italians never really embraced Gothic architecture. It was more of a Northern European style. In fact, Italy had fewer Gothic buildings than any other Western European country. On the contrary, Italian architects historically designed buildings like their Roman ancestors had. Unlike Gothic architects, they often based their designs on precision and order. This was much like the Romans and the ancient Greeks had done. So you could say that the Italian architects weren't breaking away from the Gothic style since they had never really embraced it in the first place. It's more correct, I suppose, to say that they developed their own style based on Roman architecture.

Roman architecture stressed mathematical precision. Everything in a Roman building was purposely designed and planned. Proportion was important, and the building itself had to be aesthetically pleasing. From the Romans, Italian Renaissance architects learned about symmetry. For example, the facade, or front, of an Italian Renaissance building had to be symmetrical on both sides. Most Italian Renaissance buildings were shaped like squares and had additions that were symmetrical and in proportion. Gothic buildings, meanwhile, were narrower, higher, and more rectangular. Italian Renaissance architects also imitated the Roman usage of columns, domes, and semicircular arches and vaults. The walls and the ceilings in the buildings' interiors were typically decorated with frescoes. Many of the interior and exterior details were actually copied directly from Roman examples.

Okay, let's take a look at some slides . . . Perhaps the best place to observe the Gothic and Renaissance styles together is in Florence, Italy, at the Basilica di Santa Maria del Fiore, commonly called the Florence Cathedral. See it here . . . and here . . . It uses both Gothic and Renaissance styles. The reason for this is that it was constructed over a period of 140 years starting in 1296. The main building's shape is a Latin cross, which is typical of Gothic cathedrals. See it here . . . After a century, the cathedral was complete except for its dome. The original plan called for a Roman-style dome with no external support from flying buttresses. But, uh, no one could figure out how to build such a dome since the Roman art of dome-making had been lost.

That's when Filippo Brunelleschi, one of the most famous early Renaissance artists, arrived. He had visited Rome, where he examined some domes there. And he'd read some ancient Roman texts on architecture. He won a commission to complete the cathedral's dome, which he did in 1436. Take a look . . . Can anyone tell me what kind of style he used?

1 [Gist-Content Question]

The professor describes both Renaissance and Gothic architecture in his lecture.

2 [Gist-Purpose Question]

The professor asks the students, "Now, um, how do Gothic and Renaissance architecture differ?" Then, he describes the differences between them.

3 [Detail Question]

The professor says, "Gothic cathedrals had high walls and tall spires."

4 [Understanding Function Question]

About Florence Cathedral, the professor remarks, "It uses both Gothic and Renaissance styles." He then comments on both styles used in the cathedral.

5 [Connecting Content Question]

The professor first notes that Gothic cathedrals had very high walls. He then mentions that Florence Cathedral was built in the Gothic style. So it can be inferred that Florence Cathedral is a very high building.

6 [Making Inferences Question]

At the end of the lecture, the professor says, "Take a look . . . Can anyone tell me what kind of style he used?" He will most likely wait for a student to answer his question.

1 Ⓓ   2 Ⓒ   3 Ⓑ   4 Ⓓ   5 Ⓐ

Script 02-70

W Student: Professor Hertz, do you have some time to talk to me right now?

M Professor: Oh, hi, Cindy. I wasn't expecting to see you here today. Actually, uh, I was getting ready to attend a staff meeting. And then I've got another appointment right after that. Do you think I can speak with you tomorrow?

W: Well, uh, to be honest, this is really, really important. If you don't mind, could you just give me a couple of minutes? That's all the time that I need.

M: Really important, huh? Well, staff meetings are pretty boring anyway. So, what's going on that you need to chat about?

W: It's about some information that I read in our textbook. I think that it's . . . uh, it's wrong.

M: Wrong? How so?

W: Take a look at page eighty-two in the book, please. Here . . . I brought my copy along with me. It's in the section about Julius Caesar. Check out the dates . . .

M: Hmm . . . My goodness! You're absolutely right, Cindy. How on earth did these errors get published?

W: I don't know, sir.

M: Well, this is a brand-new edition. I'm going to have to make a phone call to the publisher and let the people there know that they've printed some wrong material. They should be ashamed of themselves for making these mistakes.

W: I totally understand, sir. But, uh, what about the class?

M: Class . . . ? Oh, right. I'll be sure to tell everyone in the class about the mistakes in the book. I guarantee that I won't forget about that. Out of curiosity, Cindy . . . How did you know that these dates were wrong?

W: I was doing some online research about Caesar. I found a timeline about his life on one website. [5]But when I started going through the book, I realized that the dates on the timeline and the ones in the book didn't match. So, uh, I did some more research, and . . .

M: And that's when you realized the book was wrong. Well done, Cindy. **You're a regular historical detective.**

W: Thank you, sir. I appreciate your saying that very much.

M: Now . . . guess what I'm going to do for you?

W: I don't know, sir. I give up.

M: I'm giving you a bonus point on your final grade. And I'm going to let the class know that you were the one who found the mistakes. What do you think of that?

W: I'm very pleased, sir. I'll take the bonus point, but you don't have to tell the class it was me. I'd actually prefer to remain anonymous if you don't mind.

M: Okay. That's fine. I understand. Now, if you'll excuse me, I really ought to get going.

1 [Gist-Purpose Question]

The student wants to talk to the professor because she needs to show him some mistakes in their textbook.

2 [Understanding Attitude Question]

The professor says, "I'm going to have to make a phone call to the publisher and let the people there know that they've printed some wrong material. They should be ashamed of themselves for making these mistakes." He is clearly upset by the mistakes in the book.

3 [Understanding Organization Question]

When the student mentions Julius Caesar, she brings up the fact that the mistakes in the book concern his life.

4 [Making Inferences Question]

At the end of the conversation, the professor tells the student, "I really ought to get going." At the beginning of the conversation, when the student asks to speak with him, he says, "Actually, uh, I was getting ready to attend a staff meeting." So he is most likely going to attend the staff meeting.

5 [Understanding Function Question]

When the professor calls the student "a regular historical detective," he is giving her a compliment.

Vocabulary Review

p.141

1	D	2	D	3	B	4	C	5	C
6	A	7	D	8	B	9	C	10	A
11	D	12	E	13	B	14	A	15	C

Chapter | **08 Arts 2** • Conversations

Mastering **Question Types**
with Lectures & Conversations

A1 p.144

[TYPES 1–4]

TYPE **1** B   TYPE **2** C

TYPE **3** Cause: 2, 4   Effect: 1, 3

TYPE **4** A

Script 02-71

W Professor: In the years after World War I, society changed dramatically. There was quite a bit of, uh, upheaval in society in the United States. This was true for people in all classes and ethnic groups. One of these societal changes was called the Harlem Renaissance. You may have also heard people call it the New Negro Movement or the Black Movement.

The Harlem Renaissance began, oh, approximately in 1918, which was when World War I ended. It lasted for more than a decade until the Great Depression. Basically, here is what started the movement. Many African-Americans in the rural South were experiencing depressed economic situations. In search of opportunities, some migrated northward. They moved to cities such as Chicago, Washington, D.C., and New York City. This, uh, influx of new people sparked the Harlem Renaissance.

What was the Harlem Renaissance? It was . . . hmm . . . It was really the reawakening of the cultural spirit of African-Americans. It was mostly a literary movement, but the Harlem Renaissance also affected both art and music. Still, the writers from this period are better known than other types of artists. Among the writers of this time were Langston Hughes and Claude McKay. Both were poets. Yet there were also many novelists, short-story writers, and even journalists who were prominent during this period.

What united the writers of the Harlem Renaissance? Two things really. This was a social movement, so many writers focused on how blacks— uh, African-Americans that is—were discriminated against in the U.S. The second focus was that many writers were attempting to create a more unified culture among African-Americans. And, importantly, they wanted this culture to be a positive force, not a negative one. These writers expressed their pride in being black. They also explored themes in their writing that were important to the black community at the time. You should have noticed that aspect in your reading assignment for today's class. So let's look at a couple of my favorite poems by Langston Hughes right now. You'll see just how impressive a writer he really was.

TYPE 1 [Gist-Content Question]

The professor's lecture mostly focuses on the effects of the Harlem Renaissance on African-American culture.

TYPE 2 [Understanding Organization Question]

When discussing the causes of the Harlem Renaissance, the professor describes the situation—particularly the economic one—in the entire United States at the time that the movement began.

TYPE 3 [Connecting Content Question]

According to the lecture, African-Americans leaving the rural South and parts of the country's economy becoming depressed were causes of the Harlem Renaissance. As for its effects, African-Americans became proud of being black, and they attempted to become more unified.

TYPE 4 [Speaker's Attitude Question]

About Langston Hughes, the professor comments, "So let's look at a couple of my favorite poems by Langston Hughes right now. You'll see just how impressive a writer he really was." By calling him impressive and mentioning that some of his poems are favorites of hers, she is indicating that she likes his writing.

Summarizing

The Harlem Renaissance began in 1918 after World War I and lasted until the Great Depression. It started because Southern African-Americans began moving north to look for economic opportunities. The Harlem Renaissance was the reawakening of the cultural spirit of African-Americans. It affected literature, art, and music. Langston Hughes and Claude McKay were two notable poets from this time. The writers focused on how African-Americans were discriminated against. They also tried to create a more unified culture around African-Americans. They wanted this to be a positive force.

[TYPES 5-8]

TYPE 5 Ⓑ   **TYPE 6** Ⓐ

TYPE 7 Ⓐ   **TYPE 8** Ⓑ

Script 02-72

W1 Professor: Ellen, would you turn off the projector, please . . . ? Thanks so much. **8**Okay, class, I think this is the perfect time to talk about montage. Can someone tell me what it is?

W2 Student: Montage is when you take various scenes and then put them together to form an

entirely new one.

W1: I couldn't have said that any better myself. Yes, montage is the process—or technique—of putting together selected pieces of film in order to form a continuous whole. It's also the term used to describe the end result of that process.

Montage is a fairly old technique. It was first used in the 1910s by Soviet filmmakers during the height of the Russian Revolution. The filmmakers used montage since they had a specific purpose in mind: They wanted to incite their audiences. They wanted to enrage them. This, of course, was done for the purpose of the revolution. By using montage properly, filmmakers can show on screen exactly what many writers can convey on paper. Here's an example. Sergei Eisenstein directed the movie *Strike* in 1925. Near the end of the film, the strikers in the movie are violently cut down with weapons. During the massacre, Eisenstein added some shots of cattle being slaughtered. The message was that the masses were being slaughtered just like animals. That was an effective example of montage.

So . . . in the film clip we just saw, who can tell me which scene shows an outstanding example of montage?

M Student: The shower scene. It's got to be that.

W1: Absolutely. In the movie *Psycho*, Alfred Hitchcock never actually shows the woman being murdered. Did you notice that . . . ? Instead, he shows the killer's knife and the woman in the shower. However, you, the audience, immediately realize what's happening. But you don't actually see it occur. Hitchcock was a master of montage. He often used it to create suspense in many of his films. In the next clip, let's check out a few more examples of montage. Ellen, could you hit the lights again, please?

TYPE 5 [Gist-Content Question]

During her lecture, the professor mostly focuses on past uses of montage in films.

TYPE 6 [Detail Question]

The professor says, "Sergei Eisenstein directed the movie *Strike* in 1925. Near the end of the film, the strikers in the movie are violently cut down with weapons. During the massacre, Eisenstein added some shots of cattle being slaughtered."

TYPE 7 [Making Inferences Question]

At the end of the lecture, the professor states, "In the next clip, let's check out a few more examples of montage. Ellen, could you hit the lights again, please?" She is going to show the students some more scenes from films.

TYPE 8 [Understanding Function Question]

When the professor remarks, "I couldn't have said that any better myself," she is indicating that she is in complete agreement with the student's definition of montage.

Summarizing

The professor defines montage as the putting together of different scenes to form a new one. He says that Russian filmmakers began using it in the 1910s for political purposes. They were trying to enrage their audiences. Sergei Eisenstein used montage effectively in *Strike* in 1925. It showed scenes of strikers and cattle being killed simultaneously. He then mentions that another famous montage is from *Psycho*. It is the scene where the woman is murdered. The professor says that Alfred Hitchcock often used montage to create suspense.

Mastering **Question Types**
with Lectures & Conversations

A2   p.146

[TYPES 1–4]

TYPE 1 (A)   TYPE 2 (A)
TYPE 3 (C)   TYPE 4 (B)

Script 02-73

W Professor: ⁴All right, everyone. Who can tell me what kind of instrument we just heard? **Peter, why don't you take a shot?**

M Student: It sounded like a, uh, a synthesizer to me.

W: Indeed it was. You have good ears. Now, tell me . . . What is a musical synthesizer?

M: It's an electric keyboard that makes all those cool different sounds.

W: Yeah, I suppose that's one way of putting it. Peter's right, class. A musical synthesizer is an electronic instrument that can produce a wide variety of sounds. At the mere touch of a button, it can produce thousands of sounds, notes, and frequencies.

As for its name, well . . . The synthesizer's name comes from what it does: It synthesizes sound. This means that it electronically takes parts—sound waves in this case—and puts them together to

make something new. Keeping my explanation really simple, synthesizers produce a variety of sound waves which are then combined either to make complex sounds or to, uh, to mimic the sounds produced by various musical instruments. Just so you know, the newest synthesizers are called digital synthesizers. The reason is that they've been programmed by a computer either to generate or manipulate sounds at the flick of a switch or by using, um, something called a preset. In addition, please remember that synthesizers are not always keyboards. Even though most people believe that, it's not true. There are both guitar synthesizers and saxophone-style synthesizers.

The first person to use a synthesizer in modern-day music was Wendy Carlos. This was in 1968. After her, other musicians recognized its potential. The use of the synthesizer rapidly spread. Today, many musicians—especially those who frequently perform on stage—utilize synthesizers. So, um, no longer does a musician need a full orchestra or band playing numerous instruments. A synthesizer can do the trick instead. It can also make songs performed live sound very similar to the way they sounded during the studio recording. This is another appeal of synthesizers since many musicians sound, er, quite different when live and in the studio.

TYPE 1 [Gist-Content Question]

The professor mostly spends her time describing what musical synthesizers are able to do.

TYPE 2 [Understanding Organization Question]

The professor tells the students, "In addition, please remember that synthesizers are not always keyboards. Even though most people believe that, it's not true. There are both guitar synthesizers and saxophone-style synthesizers."

TYPE 3 [Connecting Content Question]

The professor states, "They can also make songs performed live sound very similar to the way they sounded during the studio recording."

TYPE 4 [Speaker's Attitude Question]

When someone asks, "Why don't you take a shot?" it means that the person should try to answer the question. So the professor is asking the student to give her an answer.

Summarizing

A student identifies the music the class heard as coming from a synthesizer. A synthesizer is a musical instrument that can produce a wide variety of sounds. It can make complex sounds produced from a variety of musical instruments. But they are not always keyboards. Nowadays, there are both guitar synthesizers and saxophone-style synthesizers. Wendy Carlos was the first person to use the synthesizer for modern-day music. Now, many musicians use it since they do not need a full orchestra or band to accompany them when they perform.

[TYPES 5–8]

TYPE 5 C		TYPE 6 A	
TYPE 7 B		TYPE 8 A	

Script 02-74

M Gymnasium Employee: Good morning. How may I be of assistance?

W Student: Hello. Is it possible to reserve rooms in the gymnasium here?

M: It depends. You're a full-time student here, right?

W: That's correct.

M: Good. Only full-time students, faculty, and staff can make reservations. What kind of room do you need? I mean, you're not talking about reserving a squash court, right?

W: That's correct. I'm competing in a dance contest in a couple of months. So I need to practice my routine as often as I can. I heard the gym has some rooms with mirrors on all of the walls as well as padded floors. I'd love to use something like that.

M: You're in luck. We have three of those rooms, and one of them is currently available. ⁸Would you like to use it now?

W: Actually, I've got to attend a class in ten minutes. **But I plan to come back at, uh . . . five thirty this evening.** Oh, one more question . . . Can I make several reservations at one time? I mean, uh, I'd like to reserve a room four times a week.

M: Sure. That's possible. But one thing . . . If you miss a reservation, all other reservations you made will automatically be canceled. And yes, you can have the room at five thirty. I just need to see your ID to make the booking.

W: Here you go. Thanks so much for your help. I appreciate it.

TYPE 5 [Gist-Purpose Question]

The student asks, "Is it possible to reserve rooms in the gymnasium here?"

TYPE 6 [Detail Question]

The student tells the man, "I'm competing in a dance contest in a couple of months."

TYPE 7 [Making Inferences Question]

When the man states, "Only full-time students, faculty, and staff can make reservations," he implies that faculty members can use the facilities at the gym.

TYPE 8 [Understanding Function Question]

When the student tells the man, "But I plan to come back at, uh . . . five thirty this evening," she is implying that she wants to book a room for that time.

Summarizing

The student visits the gymnasium and asks the man about booking a room. Because she is a full-time student, she can do that. She is competing in a dance contest and wants a room with mirrors and padded floors to practice in. There is a room available now, but she plans to return in the evening. She asks about making multiple bookings, and the man responds that she can do that. She then gives the man her ID card in order to book a room for this evening.

Mastering **Topics** with Lectures **B1** p.148

1 B	2 D	3 A

Script & Graphic Organizer 02-75

M Professor: Another American architect was Albert Kahn. Interestingly, he's more famous as a designer of industrial buildings than anything else. But he designed quite a few different types of buildings. Kahn was born in Germany in the 1860s and immigrated to Detroit, Michigan, with his family when he was eleven. His family experienced some, ah, financial problems, so Kahn had to leave school to start working. He never finished school or attended a university. This lack of a formal education often made Kahn feel like he had to work harder than other architects to prove himself. Lucky for him, he got a job as an errand boy at an architectural firm in Detroit. He had always been talented at drawing, so he eventually became a draftsman before becoming renowned as an architect.

Much of Kahn's work is found in Detroit and other parts of Michigan. In fact, he's often called the builder or architect of Detroit. He worked with many of the top industrialists of the time, including Henry Ford. Kahn eventually became famous for specializing in industrial factories. He was a practical designer who used simple designs and basic materials, such as steel, glass, and concrete, for his projects. This helped him win several commissions since industrialists knew he wouldn't overspend or give them something they didn't want or need. Kahn also developed a reputation for completing his work on time and for being easy to work with. Unlike other artists, Kahn lacked a distinctive style. He used whatever style was needed to get a particular job done. He did, however, often make use of new building methods, including using steel rods to reinforce concrete.

One of Kahn's largest industrial projects was the River Rouge Ford Automobile Manufacturing Plant, which he designed in 1917 and which was completed in . . . uh, 1928, I believe. There's a picture of it in your books on page ninety-two. Check it out. At the time, it was the world's largest manufacturing facility. By the 1930s, Kahn had become so famous that he was receiving commissions to design factories in foreign countries. His largest project abroad was in the Soviet Union, uh, you know, Russia. In the 1930s alone, Kahn's firm designed over 500 factories for the Soviets.

W Student: Pardon me, but weren't America and the Soviet Union enemies at that time? Why was he working for the enemy?

M: Actually, the U.S. and the Soviet Union had a fairly good relationship until around 1946. So, Kahn wasn't consorting with the enemy or anything. In fact, he played a big part in the Allies winning World War II. How? Well, his factories in the U.S. and the Soviet Union produced most of the tanks, planes, and other war machines that helped defeat Germany and the other Axis powers. In fact, the last building he ever designed was a bomber-making factory in Detroit.

³**Now, uh, where was I . . . ?** Oh, yes. So anyway, Kahn was a great designer of industrial factories, but those weren't the only buildings he designed. Until he died in 1942, he worked on many other projects. Among the best known are several buildings on the University of Michigan campus. He also designed many buildings in downtown Detroit. The Fisher Building, done in the Art Deco style, is widely considered the best of these.

Albert Kahn

His Life:	His Work:
- Immigrated to Detroit in the 1860s	- Designed many industrial buildings
- Lacked a formal education	- Used simple designs and basic materials
- Worked as an errand boy at an architectural firm	- Did work on time and was easy to get along with
- Worked as a draftsman before becoming an architect	- Lacked a distinctive style
	- Often got commissions from abroad

1 [Gist-Content Question]

The professor mostly focuses on the kind of work that Albert Kahn did.

2 [Detail Question]

About Kahn's style, the professor remarks, "He was a practical designer who used simple designs and basic materials, such as steel, glass, and concrete, for his projects."

3 [Understanding Function Question]

When a person says, "Where was I?" the person means that he has temporarily forgotten what he was saying.

Summarizing

Albert Kahn was a famous designer of industrial buildings. He lacked a formal education but worked at an architectural firm as a boy, which started him in architecture. Many of Kahn's works are in Michigan, particularly Detroit. He used simple designs and basic materials and did not overspend. He had no distinctive style but did what was needed to finish a job. Kahn often got work from abroad, including from the Soviet Union. Many of his buildings were used to manufacture war material during World War II.

Mastering **Topics** with Lectures
B2 p.149

1 ⓓ   2 ⓐ   3 ⓒ

Script & Graphic Organizer 02-76

W Professor: Our next project is to work on collages. First, I want to describe what they are. Then, we're going to make some of our own. Yes, Greg? Question?

M Student: Yes, ma'am. Are we going to get a grade

on this project?

W: Yes, you are, so please pay close attention . . . Okay, so, uh, what's a collage? Anyone . . . ? No . . . ? [3]Okay, a collage is an art form that uses many items to make a single work of art. These items can be common things, like, uh, pieces of string, colored paper, ribbons, buttons, photos, newspaper clippings . . . **Well, you get the point.** Anyway, these items are all glued or attached to a larger piece of paper, cardboard, canvas, or some other kind of surface. I'm sure most of you have made a collage at some point in your lives. Perhaps back in elementary school.

How about the history of collages? Well, their exact origin is unknown, but they . . . Excuse me. I'm sorry. Uh, they seem to have originated in China at the time when paper was invented. That was around 200 B.C. Years later, Japanese poets glued pieces of paper and fabric together to make surfaces upon which they could write poems. These were collages as well. In medieval Europe, people made collages in handmade books. And many times, noble families in Europe used pieces of cut paper and fabric to decorate their coats of arms. So as you can see, collages were widespread. By the late 1800s, making collages had become a common hobby, so people stopped considering them art. Around this time, scrapbooks and photo albums became people's favorite places to make them. Some people tried elevating collage-making to an art form, but this didn't happen until the twentieth century.

M: What changed people's minds?

W: Pablo Picasso . . . Yes, Picasso was the first major artist to use collages as an art form. Around 1912, he made a work that used oil paint, oil cloth, paper, and a piece of rope to create a three-dimensional image. This was his first collage. Later, Picasso and a French artist, Georges Braque, experimented with collages as part of their work with Cubism. Picasso and Braque are also credited with coining the term "collage." It comes from the French word *coller*, which means "glue" in English. They were trying to create a new style of painting by making collages of paper, fabric, and even wood on canvas. They thought it made their work more realistic. Around 1916, the Dada art movement experimented with collages. The Dadaists often tried to shock the contemporary art world. Some of them believed the use of real objects in a collage on canvas would, uh, manage to do that.

At first, the art world was shocked. But, gradually, the collage began to be accepted as a serious art form. Well-known artists such as, uh, Henri Matisse, Jasper Johns, Ellsworth Kelly, and David Hockney worked with collages either to prepare to make paintings or to use in actual works of art. Hockney is especially known for using photographs in collages. Okay, I think that's enough background. Let's make some collages for ourselves.

Collages

What They Are:	Who Used Them:	Modern Times:
- Art forms that use many items to make a single work of art	- Originated in China	- First used as art by Pablo Picasso in 1912
- Use common items and glue or attach them to paper, cardboard, or canvas	- Were made by Japanese poets	- Worked with Georges Braque
	- Medieval Europeans made handmade books of them	- Made by Dadaists
	- Decorated noble families' coats of arms	- Have been accepted as serious art nowadays

1 [Understanding Attitude Question]

Throughout the lecture, it is clear that the professor believes that collages are something that should be considered art.

2 [Understanding Organization Question]

Concerning Picasso, the professor notes, "Yes, Picasso was the first major artist to use collages as an art form." So Picasso helped legitimize collages as an art form.

3 [Making Inferences Question]

The professor makes a long list of items that can be used in collages. Then, she pauses and comments, "Well, you get the point." She is implying that there are more items that can be used in collages, but she is not going to tell the students any more of them.

Summarizing

The professor describes collages as an art form that uses many things to make a single work of art. Artists glue or attach things to paper, cardboard, or canvas. Collages were used in China, Japan, and medieval Europe. In the 1800s, collage-making became a hobby for many people. In 1912, Pablo Picasso began using the collage. He worked on them together with Georges Braque. Artists in the Dada movement used collages as well. The collage later came to be accepted as a serious art form.

1 Ⓒ   **2** Ⓒ   **3** Paracas Art: ③, ④
Nazca Art: ①, ②

Script & Graphic Organizer 02-77

M Professor: There was a lot of unique art in pre-Columbian American cultures. Just so you know, by pre-Columbian, we mean the time before Christopher Columbus arrived in the Americas. Let's say, uh, before 1500. In the area covered by modern-day Peru, there were two main groups of people who lived there before the Incas. They were the Paracas and the Nazca. The Paracas culture was older. It flourished in a small area of Peru from, oh, around 1100 B.C. to 200 B.C. The Nazca culture came later. It lasted from around 100 to 800 A.D. By the way, we don't know their real names. The names of both cultures come from the geographical regions where remains of their civilizations have been found.

Little is known about the Paracas since only a few of their sites have been found. They lived in southern Peru near the coast in a very arid land. So the artifacts that have been found have been well preserved. The Paracas buried their dead in desert tombs and wrapped the corpses in heavy textiles—like blankets—in a style similar to Egyptian mummies. Many of these textiles are well preserved and are some of the finest extant Paracas artworks. They're woven and have colorful, elaborate patterns. They obviously took great skill and a lot of time to weave. You should have noticed the pictures of these textiles in your text while doing your reading last night. Archaeologists have also found many pieces of Paracas pottery. Much of it has distinctive cat-like shapes. This shows the influence of the Chavin, a nearby civilization that, uh, worshipped cats. However, there are several differences in the style of pottery that each tribe made. That's how we know to differentiate between the two.

The Nazca lived in southern Peru and arose after the Paracas declined. They too excelled at making textiles and pottery that were very stylized. One difference between the two is that Nazca pots often had double spouts whereas Paracas pottery had a single spout for pouring. The Nazca also colored their pottery before firing it. This gave it a glazed look and better preserved the color. Many surviving examples of Nazca pottery are painted with mythical symbols from their culture or with battle scenes. As for textiles, the Nazca utilized many of the same methods the Paracas did. Thus their textiles are quite similar in that they're complex, colorful, and highly stylized. Since the Nazca also wrapped their dead in textiles and buried them in the desert, we have several examples of Nazca textiles to examine today.

You've probably all heard of the Nazca lines, right? You know, those are the elaborate lines they drew to form various shapes in the desert. How did they make them though? The Nazca created the images by removing the darker top layer of desert rock and soil to reveal the lighter-colored earth below. The extremely arid desert has kept the images from eroding, so the pictures have lasted for more than a thousand years. Many of the lines form the shapes of animals. Some images are similar to those that appear on Nazca pottery. For whatever reason, the Paracas never created any lines. No one knows the purpose of the Nazca lines, but there are several theories as to why they created such extensive works of art.

Paracas and Nazca Art

Paracas Art:	Nazca Art:
- Are many woven, colorful, and elaborate blankets	- Made pots with double spouts
- Are often well preserved	- Colored their pottery before firing it
- Made pottery with cat-like shapes	- Painted mythical symbols on their pottery
- Made pots with single spouts	- Made textiles like those of the Paracas
	- Made elaborate lines of various shapes in the desert

1 [Gist-Purpose Question]

The professor states, "They lived in southern Peru near the coast in a very arid land. So the artifacts that have been found have been well preserved. The Paracas buried their dead in desert tombs and wrapped the corpses in heavy textiles—like blankets—in a style similar to Egyptian mummies. Many of these textiles are well preserved and are some of the finest extant Paracas artworks."

2 [Detail Question]

About the Nazca lines, the professor says, "You know, those are the elaborate lines they drew to form various shapes in the desert."

3 [Connecting Content Question]

According to the lecture, the Paracas made single spouts on their pottery, and they also put cat-like shapes on their pottery. As for the Nazca, they colored their pottery and then fired it, and they made double spouts on their pottery.

In pre-Columbian times in the area in modern-day Peru, there were two main groups of people: the Paracas and the Nazca. Much Paracas art is well preserved. Many artworks are colorful and elaborate textiles. Much of their pottery has cat-like shapes on it. The Nazca also made textiles and pottery. Their pots had double spouts, but the Paracas' pots had single spouts. The Nazca's textiles resembled those of the Paracas. The Nazca also made lines in the desert that show various shapes. No one knows their purpose.

Mastering **Topics** with Conversations B4 p.151

1 (B)   2 (C)   3 (A)

Script & Graphic Organizer 02-78

M Professor: Hello there. I believe that you're waiting for me, aren't you? Thanks for your patience. It seems that lots of students want to talk to me today.

W Student: Thanks, sir. I'm glad that you still have some time to speak with me.

M: Oh, you don't need to thank me for doing my job . . . So what do you need?

W: Well, sir, I happened to miss today's lecture. I'm terribly sorry about that, but I had a doctor's appointment. I've got a note here from my doctor if you'd like to see it.

M: No, no. That's perfectly all right. I don't take attendance, so it's no problem anyway.

W: Oh, right. So, uh, anyway . . . One of my friends said that there were a few handouts in class, so I was hoping that I could pick them up from you.

M: Sure. I've got them right here. Here you are . . . And you'd better be sure to get some notes from your friend. Today's lecture is going to be very important to our midterm exam . . . uh, if you know what I mean.

W: ³Right. I'll be sure to do that. Oh, and, sir . . . One more question if I may.

M: I'm all ears.

W: Great. My friend also said that you assigned a paper in class. However, he was, um, kind of unclear on what we're supposed to write about. Would you mind telling me what the paper is about?

M: Not at all. Okay, you need to choose one of the topics that we've studied in class over the past two weeks. And then you have to write a short paper on it. That's all there is to it.

W: How short is short? Er, I mean, about how many pages should that be?

M: Good question. I suppose different professors have different definitions of what short means. As for me, a short paper is somewhere between four and five pages. I think that is long enough for you to get your point across. But it's not so long that it becomes a research paper.

W: Excellent. Thanks so much for clearing that up. And thanks for the handouts as well.

Office Hours

Student's Problem:	Professor's Response:
Missed class so shows the professor her doctor's note	Is not concerned about the note since he does not take attendance
Student's Question:	Professor's Response:
Wants to know about the paper the professor assigned	Write a four- or five-page paper on a topic covered in class during the past two weeks

1 [Gist-Purpose Question]

The student goes to the professor to ask him a couple of questions. She wants to know about the handouts in class, and she asks about the paper he assigned as well.

2 [Making Inferences Question]

The professor indicates that many students have been speaking with him today, and he also tells the student that he does not mind her visiting him at all. So it can be inferred that he likes speaking with his students.

3 [Understanding Function Question]

The student says she has one more question, and the professor responds, "I'm all ears." This expression means that a person is willing to hear what another one has to say. So the professor wants the student to ask her question.

The professor asks the student if she is waiting to talk to him, and she says yes. The student apologizes for missing class and offers to show the professor her doctor's note. Then, she asks the professor for the handouts he gave the class. The student wants to know more about the paper the professor assigned. The professor tells her that they must write about a topic that was covered in class during the past two weeks. And the paper should be about four or five pages long.

TOEFL Practice Tests

C1 p.152

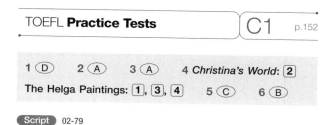

1 D   2 A   3 A   4 *Christina's World*: 2
The Helga Paintings: 1, 3, 4   5 C   6 B

Script 02-79

W Professor: Andrew Wyeth was born in 1917 and died in 2009. He mainly lived in Pennsylvania and Maine. [5]Much of his work is, incidentally, based on the landscapes and people in those two states. Wyeth is known mostly as a realist. **So for you non-art history majors in this class, that means that he, uh, basically painted whatever he saw exactly as he saw it.**

Wyeth learned how to draw and paint from his father, a well-known illustrator, when he was young. By the time he was twenty, Wyeth had held his first exhibition. He didn't make extensive use of colors in his paintings. In fact, his works often used simple shades of gray, yellow, green, and brown. Many of his paintings appear dull in color, which makes them seem somewhat common. However, at the same time, these colors give his works a more realistic appearance.

One of Wyeth's most famous paintings, which was done in the realist style, is a painting called *Christina's World*. It's up here on the screen . . . Notice how it shows a young woman lying down in a field and looking at a farmhouse in the distance . . . In actuality, she's not lying down. She's crawling toward the house. She was a real woman—a neighbor of Wyeth's in Maine. Her name was Christina Olsen, and she was paralyzed from the waist down. That's why she's crawling, not walking, in the painting. Wyeth was inspired to paint this scene after seeing Christina crawling across a field one day. By entitling his painting *Christina's World*, Wyeth tried to show others what life would be like as a paralyzed person such as Christina.

Some of you are probably aware of Wyeth because of the series of paintings that he did of his neighbor, Helga Testorf. During the 1970s and 1980s, Wyeth painted over 240 pictures with Helga as the central figure. This collection is generally referred to as the Helga paintings. Okay, uh, so Wyeth wasn't very creative when it came to naming his paintings. Oh,

he also painted the entire collection in secret. Neither Wyeth's wife nor Helga's husband knew that she was posing for Wyeth.

M Student: Were the two of them, uh, you know, romantically involved?

W: I suppose that would make the story more interesting . . . But . . . Alas, there's no evidence they ever had an affair. Wyeth simply felt that secrecy was necessary since he had a particular vision in mind for these paintings. He believed he wouldn't be able to finish the series if people were looking at the Helga paintings and criticizing them. It took him fourteen years before he felt the series was complete. Many of the Helga paintings show her outdoors in common scenes as a part of the landscape. Look at the screen again . . . Here, you can see Helga leaning against a tree on a summer day. Note her golden-reddish hair. It often stands out in the paintings. She's also unsmiling and seems passive. Most of the paintings show her like this. As time passed, though, Helga became more comfortable posing for Wyeth. She sometimes even fell asleep in various poses while he was painting. [6]Wyeth also painted some nudes as Helga's body itself became the landscape Wyeth was searching for.

It was in 1985 that the entire Helga collection was first shown in public. **It made quite a splash.** I remember being amazed when I first saw the pictures. Anyway, I'm not sure what the reactions of Wyeth's and Helga's families were when the secret was revealed. However, it seemed to have had no bearing on the friendship between the two families. After all, Helga worked as a caregiver for the elderly, and she was Wyeth's caregiver until he died.

Wyeth has both admirers and detractors in the art world. Despite having his detractors, he is generally regarded as one of the greatest American artists of the twentieth century. One frequent criticism of his work is that it was too, uh, common, in an era when abstract painting was in favor. In addition, uh, some critics have even called his works illustrations, not paintings, since the subjects were so commonplace and his colors so dull. Wyeth personally despised criticism of his works. That's one reason why the Helga paintings remained unseen until he had finished them.

1 [Gist-Content Question]

During her lecture, the professor both discusses Andrew Wyeth's life and focuses on some of his more famous paintings.

2 [Detail Question]

The professor notes, "One frequent criticism of his work is that it was too, uh, common, in an era when abstract painting was in favor." So some critics felt his work was not special at all.

3 [Understanding Organization Question]

During her lecture, the professor mostly discusses the most famous paintings that Wyeth made.

4 [Connecting Content Question]

According to the lecture, *Christina's World* features a woman with a disability. As for the Helga paintings, they contain some nudity, show a woman with red hair, and took a long time to complete.

5 [Understanding Function Question]

When the professor indicates that Wyeth "basically painted whatever he saw exactly as he saw it," she is describing him as a realist. Thus, it can be inferred that Wyeth did not use the abstract style of painting.

6 [Understanding Attitude Question]

When some makes "a splash," there is a lot of publicity concerning it. That is what the professor means regarding the Helga paintings.

TOEFL **Practice Tests**   C2   p.154

1 Ⓒ   2 Suggestion: ②, ③   Not a Suggestion:
①, ④   3 Ⓐ   4 Ⓓ   5 Ⓑ

Script 02-80

W Student: Hello. I need to talk to someone about my housing during summer school.

M Housing Office Employee: Ah, sure. You can talk to me about that. What exactly do you need to know?

W: Well, my name is Molly Summers. I have a room in West Hall for the entire summer. But you know, there's a lot of construction going on outside of West Hall these days.

M: That's right. The school is currently renovating Barnum Hall, so it must be pretty noisy up there. Oh, right. Let me guess . . . You want to change dorms?

W: Yes, I do. It would be great if I could move somewhere else. Is it possible to do that?

M: It sure is. We've got lots of dorm rooms available right now. You can have your choice of rooms in East

Hall, Anderson Hall, Bush Hall, or, uh . . . There's one more . . . Ah, right. Pierson Hall. I always forget about that one.

W: Wow. I never realized that so many dorms were open this summer.

M: Yeah. We have several summer programs going on this year, so we have to open a lot of dorms. So, uh, anyway . . .

W: Ah, right. The dorm. Hmm . . . I'd totally love to get a room in Anderson Hall. That's on the other side of campus. And I don't think there's any construction going on there.

M: Yes, I believe you're correct about that. So do you have a roommate already picked out? Or would you like for us to choose your roommate for you?

W: Roommate? Uh, I was hoping for a single.

M: Sorry, but there aren't any singles left on campus.

W: Really? But I've got one in West Hall.

M: You must have signed up for that one a long time ago. Singles get snapped up very quickly during the summer session. So, uh, all that we have left for you are doubles and triples.

W: I definitely don't want a triple.

M: What's wrong with a double?

W: First, I've got to do a lot of studying this summer. The classes I'm taking are extremely important to my major. So I don't want to risk getting a roommate that parties a lot and has lots of friends over. And I don't want to disturb her either since I'll be staying up late studying.

M: Well, you could keep your single in West Hall and just study at the library. Then, the noise won't bother you too much. Or you could get a place off campus.

W: Oh, that would be too expensive. Hmm . . . I'm going to have to give this some serious thought. If I decide to change rooms, I'll come back.

M: Sounds great. Good luck with your decision.

---

1 [Gist-Purpose Question]

The student says, "It would be great if I could move somewhere else."

2 [Detail Question]

During the conversation, the man suggests that the student study at the library and live off campus during the summer. He does not suggest that she select a triple or ask her roommate not to invite students into her room.

3 [Understanding Function Question]

The man asks, "What's wrong with a double?" He wants to know why the student is opposed to living in a dormitory room with a roommate.

4 [Understanding Attitude Question]

The man states, "We have several summer programs going on this year, so we have to open a lot of dorms." He implies that the number of summer programs is more than usual.

5 [Making Inferences Question]

The student mentions that she is going to be studying a lot. She also states that she does not want a roommate that "parties a lot and has lots of friends over." She implies that she has no interest in socializing during the summer.

Vocabulary Review

p.157

1	A	2	B	3	D	4	C	5	D
6	B	7	A	8	A	9	D	10	B
11	D	12	B	13	E	14	A	15	C

Experiencing the TOEFL iBT Actual Tests

Actual Test | **01**   Listening **Set A**   p.160

| 1 Ⓐ | 2 Ⓒ | 3 Ⓒ | 4 Ⓑ, Ⓒ | 5 Ⓐ |

6 Ⓓ   7 Ⓐ   8 Toothed Whales: ③, ④
Baleen Whales: ①, ②   9 Ⓐ   10 Ⓒ   11 Ⓒ

12 Ⓐ   13 Ⓒ   14 Ⓑ   15 Ⓓ   16 Ⓐ
17 Ⓒ

[Questions 1-5]

Script 03-03

M Student: Professor Chambers, did you see the news? This is so exciting.

W Professor: What news are you talking about, Peter?

M: The news about the colonial outpost that was unearthed by the construction crew working right outside the city. It looks like it's going to be an amazing find. I don't think anything like this has been found locally in a long time.

W: Ah, yes, I'm aware of it.

M: What's going to happen to the site? I mean, uh, the construction crew has to stop working until archaeologists can examine it, right? It would be terrible if they're permitted to keep working. That could destroy the entire site. From what I have read, the site dates back to around 8,000 years ago. It's also supposed to have quite a few artifacts.

W: You don't have to worry too much, Peter. There are laws about this sort of thing.

M: There are? So the construction crew has to stop? They can't do any more work, right?

W: That's correct.

M: Great. Then what happens next?

W: First, the government is notified and made aware of the discovery. That has already happened. Then, a team of archaeologists is sent to the site to investigate it. If it's a minor site, then the ruins can be excavated somewhat quickly. By quickly, I mean several days to a couple of weeks. After that, construction can resume at the site.

M: But this is supposed to be a major site.

W: Right. In that case, extensive digging may take

place. And if any human remains are found, the bones are exhumed and often taken to a museum or research center to study. When something like that occurs, the construction work could be halted for months.

M: I never knew any of that. I'm glad there are laws in place to prevent people simply from destroying important sites from the past.

W: Would you like to know something interesting?

M: Sure.

W: I'm going to be a member of the team that's visiting the site tomorrow.

M: No way.

W: I've done this kind of thing several times before. In fact, I was the first person that the state archaeologist, Dr. Preston Schultz, called. He wants me to take a look at the site since pre-Columbian cultures native to this area of the country are my particular specialty. ⁵So I'll be leading the group that's going. By the way . . . what are you doing tomorrow?

M: Are you serious?

W: Totally.

M: Count me in. I'm considering pursuing a graduate degree in pre-Columbian archaeology. This would be great hands-on experience. What time are we leaving, and what do I need to bring with me?

W: We're going to leave from here at 6:30 in the morning. Wear comfortable clothes and bring lots of water and snacks. It's going to be hot, and we'll likely be at the dig site all day long. I'll be responsible for bringing the tools such as shovels, trowels, and buckets. Please don't forget to bring a notebook and your digital camera. I know you have a good one. We're going to take lots and lots of pictures, and they need to be of the highest quality. I'll bring everything else that we need.

M: Sounds great. I'll see you outside Henderson Hall tomorrow morning. Thank you so much, Professor Chambers.

1 [Gist-Purpose Question]

The student visits the professor to tell her the news about a recent discovery and to discuss it with her.

2 [Detail Question]

The student states, "From what I have read, the site dates back to around 8,000 years ago."

3 [Making Inferences Question]

The student says, "I'm glad there are laws in place to prevent people simply from destroying important sites from the past." So it can be inferred that the student is concerned about protecting the site.

4 [Detail Question]

The professor tells the student, "Wear comfortable clothes and bring lots of water and snacks," and, "Please don't forget to bring a notebook and your digital camera."

5 [Making Inferences Question]

When the professor asks the student, "What are you doing tomorrow?" she is implying that she would like him to accompany her to the site.

[Questions 6-11]

Script 03-04

M Professor: All right. That's enough about sharks. Let's turn our attention to another marine life form: the whale. Some of you may believe that whales are fish. But, uh, well, you'd be wrong about that. Whales are mammals. They have lungs, not gills like fish have. In order to breathe, a whale must break the water's surface to get air. Every whale has a hole on the top part of its body. It's usually located near the head. This hole is called, appropriately enough, a blowhole. It's the blowhole through which the whale breathes. Here's how . . . When a whale surfaces, it first clears the water out of the blowhole by expelling the air remaining in its lungs. This causes a water spout to come out of its blowhole. That's why sailors on whaling ships used to say, "There she blows." They meant that they had seen a spout of water from a surfacing whale.

W Student: Professor Nelson, I have a question. Are dolphins a species of whale? I mean, they also have blowholes and are mammals that live in the ocean, right?

M: Well, that's an interesting question, Tina. And it takes us into what I was planning to talk about next: the classification of whales. ¹⁰To begin with, there is a bit of confusion over whether dolphins and their close cousins—porpoises—are really whales or not. All whales belong to the order *Cetacea*. **That's C-E-T-A-C-E-A in case you need the spelling.** Dolphins and porpoises both belong to the same order, but they're considered a, uh, a subclass of whales. We often call them toothed whales. However, sperm whales, killer whales, and a few other whales also belong to the same subclass. And no one would deny that a sperm whale is a whale. So according to the classification system, yes, we can say that dolphins are a type of whale. But for general usage, most people, including some scientists, consider dolphins and porpoises to be separate from whales.

Besides toothed whales, there's another subclass of whales. These are whales that lack teeth. They're called baleen whales because the insides of their mouths have large rows of stiff growths called . . . yeah, you guessed it: baleens. Baleens are, uh . . . they're sort of like the bristles on a stiff brush or the teeth of a comb. Most of the very large whales— except the sperm whale of course—belong to the baleen subclass of whales. That includes the blue whale, which is the largest of all whales, as well as the humpback and right whales. Take a look at the screen now, and you can see some of these whales. Here's a humpback whale . . . Notice the rows of baleens in its mouth.

W: [11]Um, sorry to interrupt again, sir, but I have another question if you don't mind.

M: Not at all. What is it?

W: Thanks. Uh, how do baleen whales get their food?

M: You're full of good questions today, Tina. The baleens act like a sieve. Basically, the whale dives through a mass of plankton or krill. They're both tiny marine life forms. The whale scoops a lot of water in its mouth. Then, it filters the water through the baleens. In the process, the plankton and the krill get trapped in its mouth, so it can, uh, eat them. As for toothed whales, they eat much larger things. Let's see . . . Sperm whales are famous for eating giant squid. In the past, when sperm whales were hunted, whalers frequently found the hard, beak-like mouths of giant squids in the stomachs of sperm whales. In addition, many people have observed sperm whales with ring-like marks on their bodies. They were likely caused by the suction cups of the giant squids' tentacles. There must surely have been many epic battles beneath the ocean's surface. Oh, and killer whales eat seals and other large marine species while dolphins eat various types of fish.

Let's cover whale reproduction now. Female whales are called cows while the males are called bulls. The bulls all sing songs to try to attract a cow. A cow typically chooses the bull with the best song . . . Okay, I see some of you laughing, but you shouldn't. That's what they do. It's their nature. Anyway, bulls sometimes even fight over a cow. They fight by butting heads with one another. A typical cow gives birth every two to four years. Only one baby gets born at a time. The baby whale is born tail first and near the surface so that it can quickly get some air. The cows also nourish their young with milk, just like all mammals do. Toothed whales may

nurse their babies for two to three years. However, baleen whale babies nurse for only four to eleven months. Of course, this varies from species to species. Any questions . . . ? No . . . ? All right, let's move on to those whale songs some of you were snickering about a second ago.

6 [Gist-Purpose Question]

During his lecture, the professor mostly talks about the subclasses of whales and their various characteristics.

7 [Detail Question]

The professor states, "Sperm whales are famous for eating giant squid. In the past, when sperm whales were hunted, whalers frequently found the hard, beaklike mouths of giant squids in the stomachs of sperm whales."

8 [Connecting Content Question]

According to the professor, both dolphins and porpoises are toothed whales. He also mentions, "Oh, and killer whales eat seals and other large marine species while dolphins eat various types of fish." Concerning baleen whales, he states that they eat plankton, and he says, "Most of the very large whales—except the sperm whale of course—belong to the baleen subclass of whales. That includes the blue whale, which is the largest of all whales, as well as the humpback and right whales."

9 [Making Inferences Question]

At the end, the professor states, "All right, let's move on to those whale songs some of you were snickering about a second ago." This indicates that he is planning to continue his lecture by talking about something else.

10 [Understanding Function Question]

The professor spells the word because he believes that it is difficult for the students to spell it. He implies this by stating, ". . . in case you need the spelling."

11 [Understanding Attitude Question]

When the professor responds, "You're full of good questions today, Tina," he is indicating that he is happy with the questions that the student is asking. He is giving her a compliment.

[Questions 12-17]

`Script` 03-05

M Professor: It's time to talk about light and how it's used in art. Would someone hit the lights, please . . . ? Thank you. Okay, look up at the screen, please . . . This slide shows a ball illuminated by light that is hitting it from the upper-left side. But don't just pay attention to the illuminated part of the ball. Notice how the parts of the ball that are out of the light appear to be various shades of gray, not black, as some of you might think. What is the reason for this . . . ? Anyone . . . ? Okay. Well, this happens because the light that hits the ball is both reflected and refracted. Oh, please notice the dark shadow cast by the ball that appears on the ground away from the light, too.

Okay. Tom, would you turn the lights back on, please . . . ? Thanks again. Did everyone see the contrast between light and dark . . . ? Good . . . This method of taking a two-dimensional object and using light and shade to create the illusion of a three-dimensional object is called chiaroscuro. Yeah, that's a long word, so let me spell it for you. It's C-H-I-A-R-O-S-C-U-R-O. Everyone got that . . . ? Now, what does it mean? Hmm . . . it either comes from an Italian term meaning "light-dark" or a French one meaning "clear-obscure." Considering these two contradictory terms, I'm sure none of you would be surprised to know that there is no precise definition for chiaroscuro. Basically, as I just pointed out, we use the term to describe the contrast of light and dark in a painting or other artwork.

You may think that using chiaroscuro is rather, uh, simple to do, but you'd be surprised by how many artists have difficulty reproducing colored objects as three-dimensional solids. The reason is that the brain, uh, over-processes what the eyes see. Your eyes eliminate the various hues created by both reflected and refracted light hitting an object, so you will only see the actual color of the object. What you miss is everything else that gives the painting both depth and perspective.

Art historians know that chiaroscuro was first used in Athens in the fifth century. Yet it was the Renaissance artist Leonardo da Vinci who really, uh, pioneered the technique. Later, Caravaggio further developed its use. Finally, Rembrandt perfected it. Other artists, of course, have used chiaroscuro with very much success, but those three men were instrumental to its development.

We also credit Leonardo with pioneering another technique concerning light. That's sfumato. Ah, another new word. It's spelled S-F-U-M-A-T-O. What's this? Well, at the place in a painting where light and dark meet, there's often a sharp line or contour created. However, using sfumato, uh . . . it softens the transition from light to dark. Hold on a second, and I'll show you an example. I've got one more term for you.

That term is tenebrism. That's T-E-N-E-B-R-I-S-M. Caravaggio developed it. Tenebrism is the use of extreme contrasts between dark and light colors.

For instance, there might be a dark—almost pitch-black background—yet the characters in the painting are extremely bright. Nowadays, some people are convinced that Caravaggio was actually mad . . . er, I mean insane to some extent . . . and believe that this was how he actually saw the world. As a general rule, artists use tenebrism for dramatic effect since the darkness is purely negative. On the other hand, a shadow created by chiaroscuro is a more positive form.

[17] **All right. It's time to look at some slides again. Tom, do you mind . . . ?** Thanks a lot. I'm sure all of you recognize this painting. It's Leonardo's *Mona Lisa,* arguably the most famous painting in the world. It also presents us with an outstanding example of sfumato. Look carefully around both her lips and her eyes. Here . . . Do you see that shading? That's how sfumato works. And notice the outline of her body with the background. Right here . . . This is chiaroscuro.

Now, here's Rembrandt's *The Night Watch*. It's a personal favorite of mine. Notice how he muted the background. Because of that, the point of the greatest illumination is on a central figure. Here . . . See . . . ? This is kind of how, uh, stage lighting works for plays and other performances. Stage lighting—putting a spotlight on someone—directs the audience's attention to one place. Rembrandt essentially did the same thing here. In addition, you'll notice that the harmony of light and shadow creates both senses of pattern and movement in the painting.

Here's another Rembrandt I like . . . This is called *Self Portrait as St. Paul*. You can see that the light puts the focus on his face. However, even though it's, uh, well lit, there are still shadows on his face. This is an example of chiaroscuro. Because of its effects on the cheeks here . . . the mouth here . . . and especially the eyes here . . . St. Paul looks as if he's thinking about something. Don't you agree? And that, students, is why Rembrandt is known as the master of light and shadows.

12 [Gist-Purpose Question]

At the beginning of the lecture, the professor declares, "It's time to talk about light and how it's used in art." He then proceeds to discuss chiaroscuro, sfumato, and tenebrism, which are all concerned with light and dark.

13 [Detail Question]

According to the professor, Tenebrism is "the use of extreme contrasts between dark and light colors."

14 [Understanding Function Question]

While discussing the *Mona Lisa,* the professor points

out how Leonardo da Vinci used both sfumato and chiaroscuro in the painting.

15 [Understanding Organization Question]

During the lecture, the professor first explains the concepts of chiaroscuro, sfumato, and tenebrism. Then, he shows the students some slides of paintings and points out how these concepts are used in the paintings.

16 [Making Inferences Question]

While showing the class some paintings, the professor first says, "Now, here's Rembrandt's *The Night Watch*. It's a personal favorite of mine." Then, he says, "Here's another Rembrandt I like." He also refers to Rembrandt as "the master of light and shadows." The professor is implying that Rembrandt is one of his favorite artists.

17 [Understanding Attitude Question]

During the lecture, the professor asks the student to turn the lights off and on. Then, he tells the class he wants to look at some more slides. When he asks, "Tom, do you mind?" he is asking the student to turn off the lights again.

Listening **Set B**   p.171

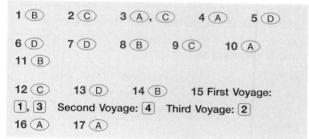

1 Ⓑ   2 Ⓒ   3 Ⓐ, Ⓒ   4 Ⓐ   5 Ⓓ

6 Ⓓ   7 Ⓓ   8 Ⓑ   9 Ⓒ   10 Ⓐ

11 Ⓑ

12 Ⓒ   13 Ⓓ   14 Ⓑ   15 First Voyage:

[1], [3]   Second Voyage: [4]   Third Voyage: [2]

16 Ⓐ   17 Ⓐ

[Questions 1-5]

`Script` 03-07

W Student: Good morning, sir. I'm here about the job that was advertised in the student newspaper.

M University Museum Employee: Ah, that's great to hear. You're the first student to respond to the advertisement.

W: Are you serious? But the ad was placed, uh, what . . . three days ago, right? I can't believe no one has responded to it yet. I guess that the student paper must not have a big circulation.

M: Could be. But it's still early. So perhaps some other people will come and apply. But for your sake, you'd better hope that too many people don't, you

know.

W: Yeah, that's a good point. A really good point now that I think about it.

M: So which job are you here to apply for? There were three of them that were listed in the ad.

W: [5]Oh, that's right. I totally forgot about that. I'm here to apply for the job in the curator's office.

M: Ambitious, aren't you?

W: Uh, yeah, I guess . . . Well, um, I've always been interested in museums you see. We've got a couple of them in my hometown, so, uh . . . I guess that's where I spent most of my free time. Like, oh, during vacations and on weekends. It's always been my dream to work in a museum. I know that sounds strange to most people, but, well, that's the kind of person that I am.

M: Well, you sure sound like you enjoy being in museums a lot. That's pretty unique for most students at this school. Anyway, what are you? A junior? A senior?

W: Er . . . Actually, um . . . I'm only a sophomore, so . . .

M: I'm very sorry, but the job is not open to sophomores. Only third- and fourth-year students are allowed to apply. I really regret to say that, Miss . . . Uh, what's your name anyway?

W: Amy Jackson.

M: Amy Jackson? H-h-hold on a minute . . . I've got a note here about you.

W: You do? That can't be good.

M: On the contrary . . . Just a second . . .

W: Sure.

M: Well, Miss Jackson. It seems that you have friends in high places. I have a note from your advisor Dr. Lucas in the Archaeology Department. Apparently, he thinks very highly of you. He also . . . strongly encourages us to waive the requirement that you be a junior or senior for this position.

W: That's great. So . . .

M: Yeah, sure. You can apply for the position. I'll attach this note to the form. That way, Dr. Carter—he's the curator by the way—will be able to see it.

W: Thank you so much, sir.

M: Hey, slow down. You don't have the job yet. But between you and me . . . Last year's assistant to the curator was simply awful. He didn't care about museums at all. When Dr. Carter learns how much you love museums, well . . .

W: So I've got a chance then, right?

M: Yes, I think that you do. I'm assuming, of course, that your grades are good. Students with bad grades are unqualified. Oh, and the work hours have to fit your schedule as well.

W: I guess we'll find out sometime soon, won't we? Do you have an application form for me to fill out, please?

1 [Gist-Purpose Question]

The student goes to the museum to apply for a job. For most of the conversation, she and the employee discuss the job opening that she is interested in.

2 [Gist-Purpose Question]

At the beginning of the conversation, the student tells the employee, "Good morning, sir. I'm here about the job that was advertised in the student newspaper."

3 [Detail Question]

First, the employee tells the student, "Only third- and fourth-year students are allowed to apply." Then, he states, "I'm assuming, of course, that your grades are good. Students with bad grades are unqualified."

4 [Making Inferences Question]

The employee states, "Well, Miss Jackson, it seems that you have friends in high places. I have a note from your advisor Dr. Lucas in the Archaeology Department. Apparently, he thinks very highly of you. He also . . . strongly encourages us to waive the requirement that you be a junior or senior for this position." By writing the letter recommending her, the student's advisor is showing that he likes her very much.

5 [Understanding Function Question]

The employee responds that the student is ambitious when she mentions that she wants the job in the curator's office. By stating that she is ambitious, the employee is implying that the position is a high-level one.

[Questions 6-11]

`Script` 03-08

W Professor: The idea that life exists on other planets has been a major feature of science fiction for decades. In reality, however, so far, no life has been found on any other planets in our solar system. But . . . is it possible that life may exist on planets outside of our solar system on what astronomers call exoplanets? So far, more than 5,000 exoplanets have been discovered. And astronomers are locating

more and more of them virtually every week. Yet no evidence of life on them has been detected. And to be honest, this may never happen. The reason is that there are several problems in finding exoplanets in the first place. And detecting signs of life on them is an even harder proposal.

The biggest problem is the distance involved. The nearest exoplanet discovered thus far is, um . . . 4.2 light years away from Earth. Most of the exoplanets astronomers have found are within 400 light years of Earth. That may not sound like much, but the distances involved are enormous. In addition, this area extending 400 light years is just a tiny patch of our own galaxy, the Milky Way.

The second problem with searching for exoplanets is the detection methods astronomers use. The methods currently utilized have mostly only been able to find enormous exoplanets. Some are up to 7,000 times bigger than Earth. As a comparison, Jupiter, the largest planet in our solar system, is only 318 times the size of Earth. Now you see how big these exoplanets are, huh? [11]Some exoplanets are so large that many astronomers believe they may be failed stars. We call them brown dwarfs. **Anyway, the problem with these exoplanets is that they're likely made of gas, just like Jupiter and Saturn are.** Therefore, they probably lack life forms. Okay, uh, they lack life as we know it. By that, I mean carbon-based life. So far, astronomers have found around a couple of hundred rocky planets, but many of them are still larger than Earth. They could—in theory—support carbon-based life, but there's no way of checking on that now.

M Student: I'm curious, Professor Milton. Why are the methods that astronomers are using now unsuccessful at, uh, finding smaller Earth-like planets?

W: Well . . . aside from distance and size, the third biggest problem is the glare from stars. Exoplanets orbit stars just like Earth orbits the sun. But stars are bright, so that makes it difficult to see things near them. Sometimes, however, astronomers get lucky. An exoplanet will travel in front of the star as observed from Earth. This is called a transit. When a transit occurs, the star's brightness dims. But this is a long process. The reason is that astronomers must wait for this to happen at least three times to confirm that it's an actual exoplanet that's causing the star to dim. After all, sunspots can also cause a star to dim.

Fortunately, astronomers are starting to use special telescopes designed to block a star's brightness. By doing this, they can see what is around a star. Several exoplanets have even been found thanks to these telescopes. Oh, here's something else: Some exoplanets are so enormous that the force of their gravity causes their stars to move slightly. When this happens, astronomers can measure this movement against background stars. And the distance the star moves can even help astronomers figure out how big an exoplanet is and how much gravitational pull it has. Yes? Another question?

M: Yes, ma'am. Are there any other methods that are being used to find exoplanets?

W: Yes, there is another. Astronomers can make use of something called the Doppler wobble, or Doppler shift, to do this. A star may wobble slightly when a small exoplanet orbits it. Again, gravity causes this to occur. But this is a much smaller wobble than that caused by massive exoplanets, so it's not easily noticed. But by examining the light from a star, astronomers can determine if there are any exoplanets orbiting it. You see, uh, when a star moves closer to Earth, its light spectrum shifts toward blue. When a star moves away from Earth, its light spectrum shifts toward red. Upon detecting this movement or, uh, wobble, an astronomer can know that the star has at least one exoplanet orbiting it. Many times, it's actually impossible to see the exoplanet because the star is too bright and the exoplanet is too small. As a matter of fact, very few exoplanets have been seen and photographed. But we still know that they are there.

As a result of these issues, finding small Earthlike exoplanets is difficult. And astronomers lack the resources, er, you know, money and telescopes, to examine every star visible from Earth. So there are surely many more exoplanets just waiting to be discovered. As for life on other planets . . . Well, that's a long shot. You see, Earth is located in what is known as the habitable zone. Let me discuss that right now, and then you'll see why finding extraterrestrial life on other planets is going to be so hard.

6 [Gist-Purpose Question]

Throughout the lecture, the professor focuses mostly on the different ways that astronomers try to find exoplanets.

7 [Gist-Content Question]

The professor explains that transit occurs when a planet passes in front of the star that it orbits as seen from Earth. She states that astronomers can use transits to identify exoplanets.

8 [Detail Question]

While discussing the Doppler wobble, the professor mentions, "But this is a much smaller wobble than

that caused by massive exoplanets, so it's not easily noticed." This indicates how difficult it is for astronomers to see any changes in a star's movement.

9 [Understanding Organization Question]

The professor discusses several different methods that astronomers use to find exoplanets, and she provides details on all of them.

10 [Making Inferences Question]

At the end, the professor states, "You see, Earth is located in what is known as the habitable zone. Let me discuss that right now, and then you'll see why finding extraterrestrial life on other planets is going to be so hard." She will likely discuss the habitual zone next.

11 [Understanding Function Question]

The professor notes that "some exoplanets are so large." She then states that many of them are made of gas, "just like Jupiter and Saturn are." She therefore implies that Saturn is a large planet.

[Questions 12-17]

`Script` 03-09

M Professor: As you should remember, after Christopher Columbus discovered the New World in 1492, the Europeans began colonizing parts of it. This is what began the Age of Exploration, or as some historians refer to it, the First Age of Exploration. By the end of the 1600s, most of North and South America had been claimed by Spain, Portugal, England, France, and the Netherlands. The Europeans had established colonies in parts of Asia and Africa. And Dutch explorers had sighted Australia and New Zealand during that time. But for the most part, the First Age of Exploration was concentrated in the Americas. It was in the 1700s that the Second Age of Exploration began. By the start of the 1900s, the Europeans had explored, well . . . let's see . . . the vastness of the Pacific Ocean and the deepest and darkest parts of Africa. They had claimed large parts of Asia. They had explored the Arctic regions, too.

The most famous explorer of the Second Age of Exploration was Captain James Cook of England. Cook was a naval officer, so he did his explorations in the service of England, not for personal gain or glory. He did, uh, gain much of both though. His specialties were navigation and mapmaking. In these areas, Cook was perhaps surpassed by no one during his time. His maps of Newfoundland, Australia, New Zealand, and many Pacific islands were superb. They served as the basis for other maps for several decades afterward.

As an explorer, Cook gained fame for three long

voyages—mainly in the Pacific Ocean—that he took. The first took place between 1768 and 1771. Yeah, long time, huh? The purpose of the voyage was to reach Tahiti. There, an astronomer on board his ship was scheduled to observe Venus as it neared the sun. Cook and his men traveled on the *H.M.S. Endeavour.* They reached Tahiti in time for the astronomer to make his observations. **[17]** Then, they sailed to New Zealand and Australia. There, Cook became the first person to make maps of New Zealand and the east coast of Australia.

W Student: I'm sorry, Professor Arthur, but I thought you said that the Dutch reached those places first.

M: Ah, yes, Dutch explorers sighted New Zealand and Australia first during the 1600s. However, only one, Abel Tasman, did any exploring of the area. I should also mention that there is some speculation that the Portuguese discovered Australia first, but that's a controversy which hasn't been settled yet. Anyway, by Cook's time—the late 1700s—neither New Zealand nor Australia had been fully explored. The Dutch never even attempted to colonize either land. Some people even doubted that they actually existed. So part of Cook's orders on his first voyage were to find those two lands and to map them. You know, Cook himself doubted that they were real places. But the Polynesians on Tahiti confirmed that they were real. They advised Cook on how to reach them with no problems. Nevertheless, *Endeavour* encountered problems and almost sank off the Australian coast. After making repairs, Cook returned home to England in July 1771.

Cook's second voyage lasted from 1772 to 1775. This time, he took two ships with him. The main purpose of this voyage was to search for a large southern continent that many scientists believed existed. Cook believed the continent was Australia, but the scientific community thought there was another land. I'm talking, of course, about Antarctica. Cook's ships extensively explored the southern oceans. They came close to, but did not sight, Antarctica. Still, Cook discovered many Pacific islands. Among them was Easter Island, which has those famous stone statues. I'm sure you all have seen them. Oh, and when Cook returned to England in 1775, scientists of the time generally began to agree that Australia was the great southern continent.

Cook's third voyage lasted from 1776 to 1779. During this trip, Cook attempted to find a waterway between the North Pacific Ocean and the North Atlantic Ocean. This was called the Northwest Passage. Many explorers had searched for it throughout the numerous islands and ice fields

of northern North America. None of them was successful though. Cook's idea was to look for a passage from the Pacific side. His two ships left England, traveled around Africa, crossed the Indian Ocean, and then went north. They discovered the Hawaiian Islands. Then, they moved along the coast of North America. They went up into the Bering Sea between Russia and Alaska. Along the way, Cook, as usual, made extensive maps of everywhere he went.

Unfortunately, bad weather and ice in the Bering Sea made it impossible to continue their mission. Cook and his men then returned to Hawaii. Tragically, on February 14, 1779, a dispute with the native Hawaiians turned ugly. Cook was killed during the battle. This brought an end to the life of one of history's greatest explorers.

12 [Gist-Purpose Question]

The professor spends most of the lecture talking about the three main voyages that James Cook went on.

13 [Detail Question]

When discussing the First Age of Exploration, the professor mentions, "The Europeans had established colonies in parts of Asia and Africa."

14 [Understanding Organization Question]

The professor first goes over Captain Cook's first voyage, and then he covers the second and third voyages. Thus, he discusses them in chronological order.

15 [Connecting Content Question]

According to the professor, on Captain Cook's first voyage, he mapped parts of the east coast of Australia and took a scientist to Tahiti. On the second voyage, he and his crew attempted to find Antarctica. And on the third voyage, he and his crew tried to find the Northwest Passage in North America.

16 [Detail Question]

The professor says, "Cook and his men then returned to Hawaii. Tragically, on February 14, 1779, a dispute with the native Hawaiians turned ugly. Cook was killed during the battle."

17 [Understanding Function Question]

When the student asks her question, she is showing that she is confused. The professor previously mentioned that the Dutch had reached New Zealand and Australia, but he then mentions that Captain Cook was the first person to map these lands. This is the reason for her confusion.

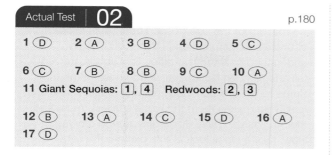

1 Ⓓ   2 Ⓐ   3 Ⓑ   4 Ⓓ   5 Ⓒ

6 Ⓒ   7 Ⓑ   8 Ⓑ   9 Ⓒ   10 Ⓐ

11 Giant Sequoias: ①, ④   Redwoods: ②, ③

12 Ⓑ   13 Ⓐ   14 Ⓒ   15 Ⓓ   16 Ⓐ

17 Ⓓ

[Questions 1 - 5]

Script 03-12

M1 Professor: Hello there. Are you next? Please come in and have a seat.

M2 Student: Thank you very much, Professor Christoph.

M1: So . . . What can I do for you today?

M2: Well, um . . . I got this note from the teaching assistant that you wanted to see me, sir. My name is Daniel Chapman.

M1: Ah, yes, Mr. Chapman. You're the student who had the big, uh, accident in the science lab last week.

M2: Er . . . Yes, sir. That was me. I don't know what exactly happened. I was carrying a bunch of test tubes, and then . . . Uh, I guess I slipped on something and fell down. The next thing that I knew, I was lying on the ground while surrounded by lots of broken glass.

M1: ⁴Yes, I heard all about it from my lab assistant. First of all, are you all right? You don't have any injuries, do you?

M2: No, I'm fine. **Well, uh . . . I guess you could say that my ego was a little bruised though.** That was pretty embarrassing after all, especially since it happened in front of some of my friends. But other than that, I'm totally fine.

M1: That's good to hear. I have a perfect safety record in the seventeen years that I've been a teacher at this school, and I don't intend to see any of my students get hurt in my lab.

M2: Yes, sir.

M1: But . . . This is rather uncomfortable for me to say this . . . But, uh, you're going to have to pay for all of the broken equipment.

M2: Oh, that's fine. I had expected you to say that.

M1: You don't mind?

M2: No, sir. Not at all. I don't know how much money all of those test tubes cost, but, well . . . I broke the

equipment. It makes sense that I pay for it.

M1: I must say that I like your attitude Mr. Chapman. Most students who break equipment complain and moan about having to pay for it. It's nice to see you taking some responsibility.

M2: Thank you, sir. So, uh, do I pay you or the Chemistry Department?

M1: Oh, don't pay me. You need to go down the hall and talk to the secretary in the Chemistry Department. She'll handle everything. And, uh, don't worry . . . It won't be that expensive. Test tubes are fairly cheap.

M2: ⁵That's a relief. Oh, I have a question, sir.

M1: Shoot.

M2: Well, I was obviously unable to finish my lab. So, um, can I make it up?

M1: Ah, yes. You'd better do that. It's worth ten percent of your final grade. If you don't do it, you'll lose an entire letter grade.

M2: Yeah, I definitely don't want that to happen. When can I do it?

M1: Hmm . . . Tomorrow afternoon is the best time. One of my assistants will be in the lab all day long. I can tell him to expect you if you think that you have enough time then. So . . . do you?

M2: Yes, sir, I do. I think I'll go there at one right after lunch. I've got a math class at two thirty though. Will I be able to finish the experiment by then?

M1: Totally. It should only take about forty-five to fifty minutes to complete.

1 [Gist-Purpose Question]

The professor sent the student a note indicating that he wanted to speak with the student. The reason was to talk about an accident that the student had in one of the laboratories.

2 [Detail Question]

The professor tells that student, "You're going to have to pay for all of the broken equipment."

3 [Making Inferences Question]

The student asks if he should pay the money to the professor. The professor responds that the student needs to go to the Chemistry Department office to pay. Since their conversation is finished, it is likely that the student will go to the office next.

4 [Understanding Attitude Question]

When the student says that his "ego was a little

bruised," he means that his feelings were hurt and that he was embarrassed by the accident.

5 [Understanding Function Question]

When a person says, "Shoot," it means that the other person in the conversation should speak. So the professor is telling the student to go ahead and ask his question.

[Questions 6-11]

Script 03-13

W Professor: Good morning, everybody. If you haven't turned in your midterm papers yet, please do so by the end of the day. I won't accept late papers without a really good excuse.

Okay, we need to get started . . . Today, I thought I would talk about some of the largest and tallest trees in the world. I'm speaking, of course, about sequoias and redwoods. Now, I know what most of you are thinking right now. I imagine that most of you are under the impression that sequoias and redwoods are the same. But that's not correct. The two trees are closely related to each other. However, they have some clear differences. Let me tell you about them. By the time I'm done, you'll be experts on how to differentiate the two.

First, let's look at their scientific names. For the sequoia, it's *Sequoiadendron giganteum*. That literally translates as giant sequoia. For the redwood, it's *Sequoia sempervirens*. As you can see, each tree has a different genus and species, so they are clearly not the same.

Both trees are found growing in the western part of the United States, yet they grow in distinctly different places. Take a look at this map . . . These are the Sierra Nevada Mountains, which are found in central California. The giant sequoia grows along the western slopes of these mountains at elevations between 4,000 and 8,000 feet. On the other hand, redwoods grow along the coastlines of the states of California, Oregon, and Washington. They grow in a region that's roughly 450 miles long and fifteen miles wide. Sequoias need full sun and well-drained soil to grow well. On the other hand, redwoods require cooler temperatures and lots of water. They grow well in the temperate rainforests that exist along the Pacific coast.

As you can see in the pictures up on the screen, there are some differences in the color of the bark of each tree. Sequoias have bark which is a bright reddish-brown color. But redwoods are a dull chocolate-brown color. If you remember those two facts, you will be able to instantly identify them even if you don't know anything else about the trees you're looking at.

What about the size of each tree? Take a look at these two pictures, and I think you'll easily understand how the two differ. Redwoods are very tall and slender. Notice the slenderness of the trunk. Some redwoods can reach heights of more than 380 feet. That makes them the world's tallest trees. And their trunks can have diameters around fifty feet. Now, take a close look at this picture of a sequoia. What really stands out is the trunk. See how thick it is. Sequoias can have trunks with diameters of more than 100 feet and grow to be around 275 feet high. As sequoias get taller and taller, their trunks don't really taper off and lose their thickness either. That helps account for their enormous sizes. These are the trees that you've probably seen pictures of cars driving through holes in their trunks. It's impressive how gargantuan these trees really are. Ah, sequoias are the world's largest trees in terms of overall size.

M Student: I heard that Douglas firs are really big, too. Is that correct?

W: Those trees can reach very impressive heights and sizes. But overall, sequoias are larger, and redwoods are taller.

All right. Those are the obvious major differences between the trees. There are some other ones though. For example, while they are both conifers, their needles are different in appearance. The needles of redwoods are similar to those of hemlock whereas those of sequoias are similar to juniper needles. Both trees produce cones that have seeds inside them. The cones are, uh, like most cones, fairly similar in appearance. But sequoia cones are roughly three times larger than redwood cones. Redwood cones typically have between three and seven seeds in them. Sequoia cones, on the other hand, can contain up to 230 seeds. Interestingly, there are forest fires in the region where sequoias live. When sequoias are exposed to extreme heat, they tend to produce more seeds in their cones. This is an effective method of assuring that if any sequoias are killed by a fire, new trees will be able to grow in their place. And here's an interesting fact about redwoods. They can grow from tree cuttings, not just from planting seeds.

Oh, I nearly forgot one last thing. Both of these trees can live for incredibly long periods of time. That makes sense considering how big they get. Redwoods are capable of living between 500 and 1,000 years. Think about that. Some redwoods are older than the United States itself. Sequoias can live even longer. Some of the ones alive now are between 2,000 and 3,000 years old. So those trees were alive during the times of the Egyptian pharaohs and the Roman Republic. It's mindboggling if you stop to

6 [Gist-Purpose Question]

The professor spends most of the lecture describing the features of giant sequoias and redwoods.

7 [Understanding Organization Question]

The professor organizes her lecture by contrasting various aspects of giant sequoias and redwoods.

8 [Connecting Content Question]

The professor remarks, "Now, I know what most of you are thinking right now. I imagine that most of you are under the impression that sequoias and redwoods are the same. But that's not correct. The two trees are closely related to each other. However, they have some clear differences." In saying that, she implies that most of the students cannot differentiate between giant sequoias and redwoods.

9 [Understanding Organization Question]

The professor states, "Take a look at this map . . . These are the Sierra Nevada Mountains, which are found in central California. The giant sequoia grows along the western slopes of these mountains at elevations between 4,000 and 8,000 feet."

10 [Detail Question]

The professor comments, "Now, take a close look at this picture of a sequoia. What really stands out is the trunk."

11 [Connecting Content Question]

According to the lecture, giant sequoia cones may have 230 seeds, and their thick trunks do not taper off much as the trees get taller. As for redwoods, their bark is dull chocolate brown in color, and they require cool temperatures and lots of water to grow.

[Questions 12-17]

Script 03-14

> **W Professor:** After the Aztecs and the Mayas, the third great civilization in pre-Columbian America was the Inca Empire. The Incas lived in the highlands of modern-day Peru. Like the Aztecs and the Mayas, they each had a monarchy and their own religion. They built cities and monuments as well. Most Incans were farmers. In this way, they were similar to the Aztecs and the Mayas. In addition, like the Mayas, the Incas developed their own communication system. Well, actually, the system existed in some forms in the Peru area even before the Inca Empire arose. And it wasn't really writing as we think of it. Instead, it was a system of knotted cords that were used to record information. Today, we call that system quipu. Spell that Q-U-I-P-U.
>
> Quipu is actually a word from the Inca's language. It means "knot." I find that appropriate since, after all, the quipu was a recording device based on a system of knots. A quipu itself consisted of many strings attached to a longer string. It was, uh, sort of like beads on a necklace. There's a picture in your books of one. It's on page . . . hold on . . . um, page 154. Take a look at it. The picture should help you visualize what I'm talking about . . . Anyway, these strings were made from either animal hair or cotton. The Incas dyed them in a variety of colors, too. The strings had knots tied in them. These knots, uh, represented information. Wait just a bit, and I'll explain how the knot system worked. But first, let me discuss the kind of information they recorded. Mostly, it was economic in nature. It was concerned with tax collecting and with payments made to and debts owed by the Incas. The Incas also used the quipu anytime they conducted a census of their people and to record important historical information.
>
> Recording information on and reading a quipu wasn't simple. Specialists trained for years to learn how to do these things. All of these specialists, by the way, were middle-aged men. Quipu recorders and readers actually formed a special class among the Incas. They settled disputes concerning, uh, taxes and debts owed. They also recited Incan history. Quipu recorders and readers specialized either in accounting or history. Oh, and many members of the upper class learned to use the quipu as well.
>
> **M Student:** What about the people in the lower class? Were they banned from learning how to use it or something?
>
> **W:** Well, they didn't use it. That's true. I suppose you could say that they were prevented from doing so by the restrictions of their society. They weren't specifically banned though. Basically, the members of the lower class had no time or opportunity to learn it. Try to recall that in almost every society on the Earth until modern times, education was restricted to the upper classes. This was true for the Incas. So, yeah, the members of the lower class never learned to use the quipu since they didn't attend the formal schools where it was taught.
>
> Now, how did the Incas record information on and read the quipu? As I already said, the key to the quipu is its knot system. It's generally agreed by scholars who study the quipu that the knot system is based on groups of ten. There were four basic types of knots. Each style represented numbers. Information could be given based on the position of the knots, by the absence of a knot, and by the number of turns in a knot. [17] In addition,

some scholars believe that the color of the strings conveyed information and that the space between the knots on the main string also meant something. Other scholars think that, somehow, the knots, the colors, and the spacing represented a code that is, in fact, a form of Inca writing . . . **Is everyone confused now?** No wonder it took years to learn. Truthfully, we could spend an entire week just discussing this information. And do you know what? There's still a lot about the quipu that we simply don't understand.

Why is that? We can blame the Spanish for this. When the Spanish first arrived in the New World, they found the quipu useful. Why? Well, it helped them conduct business with the Incas. But after they conquered the Incas, this changed. The quipu itself was a symbol of the Incas, and those who could read it and make records on it were members of the upper class. The Spanish wanted to get rid of this, uh, vestige from the past. So they started destroying quipus wherever they found them. Today, only about 600 are known to exist. Fortunately, some were translated into Spanish in the sixteenth century. Sadly, of these few translations, none matches any existing quipus. Thus, there's no key to help us translate the remaining quipus. Scholars such as myself have spent years trying, but none of us has been entirely successful.

12 [Gist-Content Question]

The professor's lecture is about how information was recorded on the quipu and how people tried to understand that information.

13 [Detail Question]

While describing the quipu, the professor states, "A quipu itself consisted of many strings attached to a longer string."

14 [Understanding Function Question]

After mentioning the page number, the professor tells the class, "Take a look at it. The picture should help you visualize what I'm talking about." She wants them to see a picture of a quipu.

15 [Understanding Organization Question]

The professor discusses the Spanish to note that they destroyed most of the quipus in existence, so there are very few of them today.

16 [Making Inferences Question]

The professor mentions, "Thus, there's no key to help us translate the remaining quipus. Scholars such as myself have spent years trying, but none of us has been entirely successful." She is telling the class that she has tried to translate some quipus, but she has so far been unsuccessful.

17 [Understanding Attitude Question]

Before asking, "Is everyone confused now?" the professor gives a lot of information on what a quipu looked like. Because she gave so much information and it was fairly complicated, she believes that it may have been difficult for the students to understand. That is why she asks the question.

MEMO

MEMO

MEMO

MEMO

MEMO

MEMO

TOEFL®
MAP
New TOEFL® Edition

Listening

Intermediate